THIRD WORLD ECONOMIC HANDBOOK

EUROMONITOR
87-88 Turnmill Street, London EC1M 5QU

THIRD WORLD ECONOMIC HANDBOOK

First Edition 1982
Second Edition 1989

Published by
EUROMONITOR
87-88 Turnmill Street
London EC1M 5QU

Telephone: 01-251 8024
Telex:21120 MONREF G
Fax: 01-608 3149

British Library Cataloguing in Publication Data
Third World Economic Handbook. - 2nd edition
    1   Developing countries. Economic conditions
    I   Sinclair, Stuart W (Stuart William) 1953-
Third World Economic Handbook.
330.9172'4

ISBN: 0 86338 163 4

Printed in Great Britain by St.Edmundsbury Press, Bury St.Edmunds, Suffolk

CONTENTS

Continued...

Continued...

Continued...

LIST OF STATISTICAL TABLES IN THE TEXT

Continued...

Continued...

Continued...

STATISTICAL APPENDIX

Continued...

CHARTS AND DIAGRAMS

ABBREVIATIONS

ASEAN	Association of South East Asian Nations
b/d	barrels per day
CBI	Caribbean Basin Initiative
CFA	French African Community
FAO	UN Food and Agriculture Organisation
GATT	General Agreement on Tariffs and Trade
GCC	Gulf Co-operation Council
GCF	gross capital formation
GDP	gross domestic product
GNP	gross national product
GSP	Generalised System of Preference
ICOR	incremental capital:output ratio
IEA	International Energy Agency
IMF	International Monetary Fund
KDI	Korean Development Institute
KIO	Kuwait Investment Office
MFA	Multifibre Arrangement
NEP	New Economic Policy (Bolivia)
NTB	non-tariff barrier
OECD	Organisation for Economic Co-operation and Development
OPEC	Organisation of Petroleum Exporting Countries
PDV	Petroleos de Venezuela
PLO	Palestine Liberation Organisation
Posco	Pohang Iron and Steel Company (South Korea)
SKC	Sunkyong
UAE	United Arab Emirates
UNCTAD	UN Conference on Trade and Development
UNIDO	UN Industrial Development Organisation
VAT	value added tax(es)

FOREWORD

The Third World represents a collection of extremely heterogeneous countries. Though they differ in terms of economics, politics and social characteristics, many of these countries are gradually becoming more active participants in the world economy as the degree of interdependence grows. The internationalisation of markets for manufactures, commodities, capital and technologies has repercussions for firms and investors in the Third World which extend far beyond any particular country's borders. Given the rapidity of change in today's world, it is important to have a clear picture of economic conditions in this group of countries which, together, account for the bulk of the world's population, a large portion of its natural resources and a growing share of world income.

Despite the heterogeneity which characterises the Third World, some generalisations may be made about the countries in this group. Many of the shared characteristics are negative in the sense that they reflect the poverty that is so widespread in the developing world. Incomes are not only low but are inequitably distributed in most countries. Other shared characteristics include the rapid growth of population, a shortage of scientific skills and research capabilities and a vulnerability to those external forces often associated with large amounts of foreign debt or excessive dependence on production of one or only a few commodities.

Not all the characteristics that apply to a majority of Third World countries are to be expressed in terms of handicaps. Labour forces in many of these countries have proven to be adaptable and capable of rapidly mastering industrial skills. The export success of several Third World countries has been founded primarily on cost advantages which an abundant and willing workforce can provide. And as the flow of technology and foreign investment to the Third World has accelerated, workers and managers in countries as diverse as India and Venezuela have demonstrated the ability to use these inputs wisely to create efficient, profitable enterprises.

The organisation of this Handbook reflects both the shared characteristics and heterogeneity of countries. The first three chapters are devoted to a discussion of broad trends which apply to most, if not all, Third World countries. Chapter 1 focuses on patterns of economic growth and structural change with particular attention to trends in the three major economic sectors - manufacturing, agriculture and services. The evolution of world markets for manufactures, agricultural commodities, oil and financial capital is considered in Chapter 2 and the involvement of Third World countries is highlighted. Chapter 3 takes up the major issues distinguishing Third World countries from their richer counterparts: these include population, investment and macroeconomic policies such as fiscal and monetary policies and inflation.

The analysis in the first three chapters provides a framework for a more detailed discussion of regional issues in subsequent chapters. The Third World is pictured as consisting of four regional groups: Latin America, Africa, West Asia and South and East Asia. Every region has advantages and problems that are somewhat distinct from others. The discussion of each of the four regions begins with an assessment of general economic conditions, trade performance and developments in major sectors, and is followed by an analysis of specific regional issues and characteristics. Altogether, eight of the Handbook's 12 chapters are concerned with regional topics and bring together and combine empirical evidence with economic assessment to yield a clear and up-to-date picture of the Third World.

Finally, Chapter 12 concludes by considering the future outlook for the regions of the Third World.

CHAPTER 1

ECONOMIC GROWTH AND STRUCTURAL CHANGE IN THE THIRD WORLD

This chapter looks at the economic performance of the Third World from several different perspectives. The chapter begins by examining the economic record in terms of the rates of growth of income in each developing region and the key factors which have influenced performance. Growth in total economic activity will alter the composition, or structure, of gross domestic product (GDP). But GDP depends also on the relative performance of major economic sectors or parts of the economy. The second section considers the pattern of structural change and the composition of GDP in each region of the Third World. Industry, services and agriculture make the largest contributions to income or GDP; developments in each of these sectors are surveyed in the remaining sections of the chapter.

I Economic Growth

World output grew at a rate of more than 3% in 1987. However, Table 1.1 shows that the pace of growth varied widely among different parts of the world. During the 1980s China led the Third World with annual rates of growth in income between 7 and 10%; estimates for 1988 suggest that growth will be even more rapid. Progress has not been so fast in other Asian countries but is nevertheless exceptional by world standards. Elsewhere in the Third World, growth in GDP either decelerated in 1987 or merely recovered from disappointingly low levels in previous years. The average rate of growth in Latin America declined to 2.5% in 1987 as many countries in the region faced continued difficulties associated with the large external debts accumulated in previous years. Performance in the two remaining developing regions has been even more disappointing: levels of GDP in both West Asia and Africa declined absolutely between 1981 and 1985 and showed little signs of recovery in 1986 and 1987.

In general, the erratic economic record that characterised the Third World during the first half of the 1980s has continued in later years. Growth in two of the largest countries, Brazil and India, slipped in 1987. Though both economies appeared to recover in 1988, these trends mean that more than half the Third World's population (excluding China) now resides in countries where GDP is growing by less than 2.5% a year. Altogether, one-fifth of the Third World's population experienced a fall in per capita output in 1987. In several countries the poor performance was merely a continuation of a trend which has prevailed since the beginning of this decade.

Climatic conditions frequently hamper economic growth in the Third World but the lacklustre performance in 1987 cannot generally be attributed to this factor. Apart from some countries in South Asia and Africa, adverse climatic conditions were not an important contributor to the poor performance. The agricultural sector in some countries did suffer from inadequate rainfall but drought was not a regional phenomenon. Wars and other forms of internal and external disturbances have limited economic growth in several countries and, where coupled with poor harvests, led to a serious deterioration in living standards.

Table 1.1   GROWTH OF POPULATION AND GDP BY REGION 1971-1987

% annually

	Forecast growth of population 1985-1990	GDP 1985 (1980 ($ billion)	Growth of GDP			
			1971-80	1981-85	1986	1987[1]
World	1.6	na	3.9	2.7	3.3	3.3
Developed market economies	0.6	7,640	3.1	2.2	2.7	3.0
Developing countries	2.3	2,217	5.6	1.5	2.9	2.7
Latin America	2.2	822	5.5	1.0	3.6	2.5
West Asia	3.2	343	6.5	-0.9	0.1	-1.0
China[2]	1.2	na	5.7	9.4	7.4	9.3
South-East Asia	1.9	606	5.6	4.8	5.5	5.6
Africa	3.1	305	4.9	-0.9	-2.1	1.0

Source: UN
Notes: [1] *Preliminary*
   [2] *Output refers to net material product*

A brief comparison of developments in various parts of the Third World illustrates the diverse growth experiences of these countries. In Latin America significant increases in per capita income in 1987 were recorded for only four countries: Chile, Colombia, Peru and Uruguay. Poor performance in other countries significantly depressed the region's average rate of growth, despite the structural improvements several undertook in response to the problems of international debt that have emerged since 1982. The most apparent of these structural changes has been the region's efforts to diversify its export base. Achievements in this area have resulted in a fall in the share of primary commodities in all non-oil exports from 25% in 1980 to 20% in 1987. Even energy-exporting countries such as Mexico and Venezuela have adopted the strategy in order to boost the share of manufactures in total export receipts.

Africa's growth performance in 1987 was heavily influenced by developments in Nigeria, which suffered another year of declining GDP due to low oil prices and external debt difficulties. A general lack of foreign exchange and budgetary crises mainly attributable to the loss of trade-related revenues have also had debilitating effects on other countries in the region. Unlike other Third World suppliers of raw materials, African producers did not benefit from the recovery in commodity prices which began in 1987. Much of sub-Saharan Africa is heavily dependent on exports of tropical beverages and markets for these products remained weak throughout 1987-8. Nor were Africa's exporters of copper able to exploit the upturn fully owing to production bottlenecks arising from the industry's previous retrenchment.

A majority of the countries in South and East Asia have maintained a relatively stable pace of growth throughout most of the 1980s. Several economies in the region reported growth rates of GDP in 1987 exceeding 10% while still others managed increases in per capita income in excess of 5%. Drought in the Indian sub-continent disrupted growth in some years during this decade although India itself was able to withstand the effects of adverse climate without resorting to large-scale imports of food. An increasing number of eastern Asian nations have gradually turned to exports as a way to stimulate economic growth. Beginning from a comparatively low base, exports grew so rapidly in the 1980s that the trade surpluses of some countries have become a matter of international concern. Many Asian countries have benefited in recent years from expanded exports to Japan. Indonesia was one of the few countries in the region where growth was disappointing, owing mainly to continued weaknesses in the international oil market.

In West Asia attention to economic progress has been overshadowed by regional conflicts and the volatility of oil prices. In 1986-7 the region's oil exporters realised their first significant increase in export volumes (nearly 10%) since the 1970s. Most of the rise was attributable to countries that had earlier experienced the largest losses in market share. However, the weakness of oil prices has continued to be the main handicap to growth. Because so few countries have made any headway in programmes to diversify their economies or to move into downstream oil-related activities, West Asia's heavy dependence on the resource will continue.

A comparison between previous rates of growth in GDP and population forecasts up to 1990 highlights the need for an accelerated pace of economic expansion. Both West Asia and Africa can expect their populations to grow by more than 3% a year in the near future though neither region has achieved equivalent rates of growth in GDP since the 1970s. The performance in sub-Saharan Africa was somewhat more encouraging as most countries managed rates of growth in 1987 which at least equalled population increases. In Latin America recent rates of growth in GDP roughly match population forecasts for the rest of this decade and that pace, if maintained, would mean no further deterioration in living standards. The outlook is far better in South-East Asia and China where higher rates of economic growth in the recent past are coupled with forecasts of only moderate population expansion.

II Economic Structure and Structural Change

Movements of labour and capital between major economic sectors are a leading determinant of economic growth. The migration of labour from low-productivity occupations in the agricultural sector to higher productivity jobs in manufacturing was a major reason for the rapid growth achieved by many Western countries in the first half of this century. Today, the pool of agricultural workers in western countries is small and affords rich countries little opportunity to achieve higher rates of productivity growth by continued transfers from agriculture to manufacturing.

The relatively large size of the agricultural sectors in most developing countries would seem to offer similar opportunities to those enjoyed by developed countries in the nineteenth and early twentieth centuries. However, one feature of the earlier pattern should be noted: the movement of workers from agriculture to manufacturing was accompanied by rapid growth of productivity among the workers remaining in agriculture. The same is not necessarily true today. Productivity in agriculture has not been rising in many of the developing countries that have experienced the most rapid rural-to-urban migration, meaning that in some cases farm output has declined. Moreover, a large proportion of today's agricultural workers find new jobs not in the manufacturing sector but in the service sector where levels of productivity are often low.

Table 1.2 gives the composition of GDP in 1970 and 1985. In the developed market economies, only services show an appreciable increase. The share of agriculture continued its long-term decline although the sector's shrinkage has slowed in recent years. Contrary to some expectations, the average share of manufacturing in developed market economies rose slightly between 1970 and 1985. Such a trend runs counter to the often expressed fear that the future of many western countries is threatened by "de-industrialisation" (ie a relative or absolute decline in the manufacturing sector).

Table 1.2   COMPOSITION OF GDP IN DEVELOPED AND DEVELOPING
             COUNTRIES 1970-1985[1]

% Country group	Year	Agric- culture	Manufac- turing	Services	Other[2]
Developed market economies	1970	4.3	25.0	54.5	16.2
	1985	3.6	25.4	58.8	12.2
Developing countries	1970	20.3	15.6	37.8	26.3
	1985	15.8	17.9	43.9	22.4
of which					
Africa	1970	33.5	7.3	32.4	26.8
	1985	23.2	8.9	37.6	30.3
South and East Asia	1970	30.3	12.0	33.4	24.3
	1985	22.2	17.0	42.3	18.5
Latin America	1970	11.6	24.1	50.7	13.6
	1985	10.5	23.9	52.8	12.8
West Asia	1970	8.2	8.2	21.8	61.8
	1985	7.3	11.6	36.3	44.8

Source: UN
Notes: [1] *Figures are calculated from data at constant prices*
       [2] *Category includes oil and mining, transport, construction and energy*

The extent of structural change has been proportionately greater in
developing countries than in developed market economies. The
average share of agriculture declined by almost 5% between 1970
and 1985. This was matched by modest increases in the shares of
both manufacturing and services. The averages for all developing
countries conceal even more dramatic shifts in several regions. In
Africa the share of agriculture has declined precipitously from
33.5% in 1970 to 23.2% in 1985. Services was the major beneficiary
of the agricultural decline although manufacturing, too, recorded a

slight gain. These structural changes result not only from widespread movement of labour out of agriculture but a virtual stagnation in farming output in many African countries. The bulk of labourers moving from rural to urban locations have found jobs in low-productivity occupations in the service sector. The net result has been that many African countries can no longer feed their populations. Nor have non-agricultural output, productivity or wages grown, leaving those countries with little income to purchase food from abroad.

The agricultural sector in South and East Asia has also contracted although the manufacturing sector has recorded corresponding gains, increasing its share from 12 to 17%. The large number of resource-poor economies in Asia means that activities such as mining, energy production and related activities (all included in the residual category) are relatively unimportant and have declined over time. Services have expanded most rapidly and accounted for over 42% of GDP in 1985. In contrast to the situation in other developing regions, the growth of services is more closely linked to overall progress in many Asian countries. The Asian service sector is based on activities such as finance, shipping, insurance, etc, rather than the types of "subsistence services" which are common in other parts of the Third World.

The countries of West Asia are widely different in terms of market size, wealth and levels of per capita income. This diversity has implications for the region's economic structure. Vastly rich countries such as Kuwait or Qatar boast a sizeable service sector though poorer ones like Jordan or Syria have a service sector of only moderate proportions. The economies of West Asia also depend much more on natural resources than do other Third World countries. This dependence means that the relative size of the manufacturing and agricultural sectors is reduced in comparison with other developing regions.

In Latin America the size of the agricultural sector is proportionately smaller than in either Africa or Asia. Latin America is the most industrialised of the developing regions and its manufacturing base is much larger than in other parts of the Third World. In relation to GDP, the share of the region's manufacturing sector is nearly equivalent to the proportions reported in developed market economies. Yet this is the only developing region where the relative size of manufacturing actually declined between 1970 and 1985; this suggests evidence of what some would call de-industrialisation, a phenomenon which has drawn much greater attention in developed countries such as the USA.

The shift to manufacturing

Historically, one of the highest development priorities of most developing countries has been to shift the composition of GDP away from agriculture and services to manufacturing. The belief that commodity prices were doomed to slide endlessly downward, and that service activities tended to concentrate rather than spread wealth, was part of the reason that many developing countries began to favour manufacturing as soon as they gained independence. In choosing this path, the leaders of many Third World governments took their inspiration from countries as diverse as Chile, Russia and the USA. They saw in these countries a pattern of economic growth which seemed to depend on heavy industry, trade protection and massive industrial investment.

Views such as these led many Third World planners to adopt policies favouring manufacturers at the expense of their counterparts in other economic sectors. Because agriculture was typically the largest of the non-manufacturing sectors, policies intended to accelerate growth of the manufacturing sector most frequently discriminated against farmers. The drive to industrialise absorbed vast amounts of resources as Third World countries

9

sought to develop the infrastructure and basic industries necessary to attain the status of an "industrialised" country. Many developing countries clung to these views for more than two decades. In doing so, they created a manufacturing sector that was often dominated by government-owned enterprises. Manufacturing enterprises were established with little regard to costs of production or ability to compete in international markets.

In many of today's poorer countries, the record of the manufacturing sector has been lacklustre. Though the Third World as a whole has seen the manufacturing share of GDP grow faster than that in rich countries, the averages hide a more complex picture. Much of the sector's growth can be attributed to a very few countries (mainly Asian). The seemingly impressive growth rates for manufacturing in many countries in Africa and the Caribbean reflect little more than the tiny industrial base from which these activities began. And in another group of large countries - including Argentina, Nigeria, Pakistan, Uruguay and Zaire - manufacturing output, after making impressive gains in the 1960s and 1970s, has shrivelled in the 1980s.

Industrialisation has not brought the expected economic wealth for many reasons. The import controls necessary to protect fledgeling industries eventually made it impossible to buy the machinery and spare parts that were needed. Protection has often confined firms to a small and sluggish home market and has insulated them from technological developments in the rest of the world. A problem which is particularly true for Africa results not so much in a shortage of able and aspiring business leaders but the fact that few are prepared to sink equity into a project. Typically, their main asset is land and they may need the agreement of an extended family before they can pledge it to a business scheme. Businesses therefore tend to start out with debts that are too high. The manager is under pressure to make a quick return so he can repay the bank.

Whatever the reasons for the disappointment with industrialisation, a more balanced view of sectoral priorities is gradually emerging in many countries. The role of services is now recognised as a source of strength for poor countries. No commodity-exporting country, for example, can expect success without the necessary services to finance such operations, to provide packaging, distribution, insurance, marketing expertise and other aspects. Other parts of the service sector - in particular, tourism - are an important earner of foreign exchange in their own right. Along with renewed interest in the development of a dynamic service sector, the need to maintain a vibrant agricultural sector has attracted the interest of many Third World planners. Accelerating growth of population, land mismanagement and a widening network of price and non-price controls have all hindered agricultural performance, forcing governments to alter their policies in many developing countries. Today, many of these hindrances are being removed as policymakers strive to meet their population's food needs and reduce the amounts of scarce foreign exchange claimed by food imports.

In conclusion, a shift in sectoral priorities is under way in the Third World. The shift does not necessarily mean a rejection of industrial ambitions. The manufacturing sector continues to offer the most dynamic growth prospects for developing countries. However, a single-minded effort to develop key industries is giving way to a new approach calling for closer integration with agriculture and/or services. Subsequent sections of this chapter examine the role of these two economic sectors more closely.

III Industry in the Third World

The industrial sector, which includes both manufacturing and mining, has experienced severe difficulties in most developing countries. Table 1.3 shows production indices for manufacturing and

11

mining, industrial employment (that is, employment in manufacturing plus mining) and labour productivity. World manufacturing output rose by 17% during the course of the present decade. Output in developing countries has grown proportionately more than in developed market economies. Virtually all the Third World's manufacturing gains, however, have been concentrated in Asian countries. Latin America's manufacturing output rose only 7% in 1980-6. Output of the mining sector (which includes petroleum) has slumped throughout the world, owing largely to the depressed level of oil and mineral prices. By the end of 1986 mining output in developing countries was only four-fifths of the level attained in 1980. Asia has been the hardest hit. However, the overall impact on Asian growth performance was not great as most of these countries are resource-poor and have relatively small mining sectors.

Table 1.3   INDICES OF PRODUCTION, EMPLOYMENT AND LABOUR
PRODUCTIVITY 1982-1986

1980 = 100

	World	Developed market economies	Developing countries[1]	Latin America	Asia[2]
Manufacturing production					
1983	102	99	106	91	126
1984	109	106	114	97	141
1985	113	109	121	102	151
1986	117	111	135	107	178
Mining production					
1983	85	98	73	98	68
1984	88	101	76	102	68
1985	86	103	72	101	63
1986	90	100	80	105	73
Industrial employment					
1982	98	93	102	93	105
1983	98	93	103	91	107
1984	99	92	105	90	111
1985	na	91	na	na	na
Labour productivity					
1982	105	103	108	101	109
1983	110	106	115	101	118
1984	117	113	125	107	128
1985	na	117	na	na	na

Source: UNCTAD
Notes: [1] *Indices include data for some African countries. Regional figures for Africa
could not be constructed, however, owing to insufficient coverage*
   [2] *Data for Asia include West Asia, South and East Asia*

13

Figures on the industrial workforce are somewhat less reliable than output data. The available evidence suggests that world employment has stagnated during the 1980s. The number of industrial workers in developed market economies has fallen, mainly due to the poor performance of labour markets in West Europe, while, in the Third World, modest increases have been recorded. Like the pattern of output, most of these gains have been confined to Asian countries. Industrial employment in Latin America is only 90% of the 1980 level. Employment patterns are related to the productivity of labour and, as the latter rises, gains in employment will be limited. All parts of the world have recorded at least modest gains in labour productivity. The increase was 17% in 1980-5 among developed market economies and 25% in the Third World during 1980-4. Asia, again, led the Third World with an increase in productivity four times greater than Latin America.

Table 1.4 focuses on the manufacturing sector in Third World countries, showing production indices by major industry. Output of the paper, printing and publishing industry has risen most rapidly, followed by chemicals, petroleum, coal and rubber, and food products. These industries, and basic metals, are the only ones with production levels greater in 1986 than in 1980. Growth of the paper, printing and publishing industries reflects a rise in literacy and the fact that several developing countries (eg Indonesia) have selected wood and paper as part of a concerted drive to diversify their economies away from other commodities. However, paper and wood-related industries account for a relatively small proportion of total manufacturing output in the Third World and even rapid expansion still brings only modest gains in terms of employment or export earnings.

Table 1.4   INDICES OF MANUFACTURING PRODUCTION IN
DEVELOPING COUNTRIES BY MAJOR
INDUSTRY 1983-1986

1980 = 100

	1983	1984	1985	1986
Paper printing, and publishing	98	105	130	148
Chemicals, petroleum, coal and rubber	102	108	115	126
Food, beverages and tobacco	105	109	114	116
Basic metals	89	99	99	105
Textiles	89	92	95	100
Wood products, furniture	92	94	95	97
Wearing apparel, leather and footwear	88	91	93	94
Non-metallic mineral products	84	85	87	88
Metal products	71	77	82	85

Source: UN

Production of chemicals and related industries has risen by 26% in the current decade, mainly due to a boom in Latin America. The need to conserve foreign exchange has received a high priority owing to the debt crisis in Latin America. This has been a driving force in the expansion of chemicals and petrochemicals, particularly for export-oriented projects. New tactics among West Asian oil producers have also boosted the growth of petrochemicals output. These countries - all members of the Organisation of Petroleum Exporting Countries (OPEC) - have begun to purchase or erect their own downstream facilities as a way to add value to the crude oil production and to avoid OPEC quotas on output of crude oil.

More significant are the gains of the Third World's food processing industries. The long-term slowdown in growth of agricultural output has depressed food processing operations throughout the Third World but signs of recovery began to appear during the 1980s. Basic metals is the only other major industry to show marked improvement in recent years. Output in 1985 was still below the 1980 level but producers recovered rapidly in 1986 and production was 5% greater than in the base year. The surge in prices of metallic minerals and related resources aided the industry's recovery.

Though output of wearing apparel, leather and footwear has fallen by only 6% and production in the textiles industry has now recovered to 1980 levels, the poor performance of these two industries has had serious consequences for Third World manufacturers. Not only do the two industries account for a substantial share of the Third World's manufacturing output but they also provide a disproportionately large share of employment opportunities. Growth patterns in the clothing and textile industries are closely linked and are determined by a complex set of forces, including fashion trends in the USA and Europe, the constantly shifting supply of quotas available to producers in Third World countries and volatile political conditions in some of the producing countries.

Both industries have been dominated by Asian producers but a combination of protectionism, currency shifts and rising competition is changing production patterns. Among the major producers - Hong Kong, South Korea and Taiwan - the outline of a new industrial trend can be seen. The main features include programmes to increase efficiency and productivity along with steady efforts to raise the fashion content and thus value added content of domestic production. Ironically, the quota system erected by the USA and EC works to the advantage of these big producers. Designed as means to limit imports, quotas have proven to be the best guarantee of continued market share for traditional suppliers of textiles and clothing. Second- and third-tier producers in the Third World, though allowed growth rates of up to 6%, are locked into the quota system which frustrates their hopes of challenging the majors. Nor can producers such as Bangladesh, Egypt, the Caribbean basin or Sri Lanka match the infrastructure offered by major Third World suppliers. The latter producers offer large buyers in Western countries hundreds of factories with proven ability to produce quality goods on time. Their communications facilities are generally well managed while fabric and yarn are readily available locally. In contrast, a decision to produce in some of the newer competitors means accepting greater risk, lower productivity and higher costs.

IV The Service Sector in the Third World

The development of the service sector in the Third World was originally in response to a different set of forces from those influencing the sector's growth in industrialised countries. In the Third World, railways, roads, ports, wholesale and retail facilities, banks and insurance companies as well as many utilities were established and expanded in response to needs arising from trade flows between the colonies and metropolitan powers. Service sector development has also been affected by the heavy reliance of Third World countries on the production and export of one, or a few, primary commodities. In such situations services have expanded in response to the need to recycle resources generated by exporting into the rest of the economy.

Table 1.5 gives a breakdown of the shares of service categories in GDP for a large number of developing countries. In general, the service sector ranges between one-third and two-thirds of GDP. Countries with relatively high per capita incomes tend to have a proportionately larger services sector. Of all socio-economic variables related to the size of the service sector, urbanisation appears to be the most important. Countries with a high degree of urbanisation have more production and employment in services. The speed of the urbanisation process also affects the composition of services, and distinguishes between the service sector in developing and developed countries.

Table 1.5   SHARE OF SERVICES IN GDP IN DEVELOPING COUNTRIES, LATEST YEAR

%

Region/ Country	Wholesale and retail trade	Transport and communi- cations	Financial and business services	Community, social and personal services	Govern- ment services
Africa					
Algeria	13.4	5.3	5.1	1.5	na
Benin	19.4	10.1	8.5	6.2	0.7
Egypt	14.1	8.4	8.3	15.0	na
Ghana	10.3	4.4	9.1	1.5	12.7
Ivory Coast	16.1	9.4	8.2	1.1	10.0
Kenya	9.6	5.6	12.6	2.1	13.5
Liberia	4.8	6.9	9.6	4.3	12.9
Mauritiana	11.4	8.5	na	na	19.1
Mauritius	11.4	9.5	14.7	5.0	10.2
Morocco	18.6	5.5	2.7	na	na
Nigeria	21.9	4.7	3.9	3.8	7.7
Swaziland	7.1	4.3	8.5	1.3	14.5
Tanzania	10.1	6.8	11.5	na	na
Tunisia	18.0	4.8	4.6	3.4	11.1
Zambia	10.8	5.8	11.6	0.9	16.7
Latin America					
Argentina	12.8	11.7	7.8	6.5	11.3
Bolivia	12.4	7.6	15.8	4.1	12.8
Brazil	13.3	4.7	19.8	12.1	5.5
Colombia	12.4	9.5	14.7	4.9	7.8

Continued...

Table 1.5 cont'd

Region/ Country	Wholesale and retail trade	Transport and communi- cations	Financial and business services	Community, social and personal services	Govern- ment services
Costa Rica	16.5	7.2	13.1	4.2	9.7
Dominican Republic	15.8	7.9	9.6	9.8	10.6
Ecuador	15.5	6.7	11.0	5.8	9.4
Jamaica	17.1	7.4	18.4	3.1	17.7
Mexico	23.4	7.5	10.6	7.5	7.2
Panama	12.1	16.4	14.0	8.9	12.9
Peru	13.4	6.9	12.9	7.1	12.4
Venezuela	8.5	12.2	21.0	5.6	13.4
West Asia					
Bahrain	9.0	6.7	8.9	7.9	5.0
Jordan	18.9	12.1	11.0	2.8	17.8
Saudi Arabia	16.9	8.2	11.2	1.5	8.7
South and East Asia					
India	3.1	13.5	14.4	1.9	6.8
Indonesia	15.4	5.8	5.8	4.1	8.1
Malaysia	12.0	6.4	9.0	2.1	12.3
Nepal	3.8	6.4	8.0	7.8	na
Pakistan	15.0	7.1	5.7	6.7	10.2
Philippines	17.2	5.5	6.5	3.3	6.5
Singapore	20.0	18.8	22.7	4.1	6.2
South Korea	13.2	7.7	11.4	3.1	5.9
Sri Lanka	25.6	10.3	3.8	2.9	5.2
Thailand	19.5	6.9	8.9	8.0	4.0

Source: UNCTAD

Note: [1] *The latest available year is generally 1985. Percentages are derived from data in constant prices of a given year, except for Brazil, Jordan and Nepal, where data in current prices have been used*

Transport, communications and financial networks, as well as health, education and housing, have all been recognised as essential elements in the national development process. The available information shows that at low levels of per capita income the shares of transport and communication are correspondingly modest. For example, in many of the poorest countries these particular types of services account for less than 6% of GDP; in other, richer countries the same services provide over 8-10% of GDP.

Wholesale and retail services are typically the largest, though not necessarily the most dynamic, category within services. The relative importance of this cluster of service activities tends to decrease as per capita income rises. In contrast to the situation in developed countries, these activities are predominantly low-skilled and have low levels of efficiency. Often, the size of the wholesale and retail sector is seriously under-reported because of the prominent role played by informal producers which is not recorded.

The relative size of banking, insurance and business services provides an indication of the broader range of producer services supplied by this sector. It is apparent from Table 1.5 that these particular services are under-represented in all but the most rapidly growing developing countries. Producer services may account for up to 20% of GDP in developed countries but in low-income developing countries are closer to 5% of GDP and even in the richer developing countries may be no more than 10-12%. The low share indicates a potential vulnerability to international competitiveness because this category has the greatest potential for being traded internationally.

Personal and community services are generally less than 15% of GDP. The category is mainly a mixture of low value-added, labour-intensive personal services, leisure activities and high-skill social services such as health and education.

The second largest category in the service sector of Third World countries is government services (mainly public information and defence). Although the importance of these activities appears to decline as per capita income rises, individual country ratios are quite disparate. Variations reflect differences in socio-economic factors and defence policies. In general, more rapidly expanding public administration activities are related to slower economic growth as a growing public sector is often intended to compensate for a lack of alternative employment opportunities.

V The Agricultural Sector in the Third World

Agriculture plays a pivotal role in the process of structural change in most Third World countries. In the poorest countries agriculture accounts for the bulk of employment and an equally large portion of GDP. The sector's importance is further magnified by the fact that it is typically the largest earner of foreign exchange. Given the high rates of population growth in many countries, a poorly performing agricultural sector will result in increased food imports as well as diminished exports. Finally, the sector represents a large pool of surplus labour which can be siphoned off as the industrial and service sectors expand. Rural-to-urban migration can prevent labour shortages as a country's structure shifts in favour of non-agricultural activities.

Table 1.6 shows the agricultural sector's share in GDP and per capita growth of agricultural production in both developed market economies and developing countries. Agriculture presently accounts for only 3% of GDP in rich countries and its share has diminished slightly since 1970. The sector's relative size has also declined in developing countries though, today, it is still much more important than in developed countries. Of the four developing regions, West Asia has the smallest agricultural sector. The region has only modest amounts of arable land but the major reason for the large fall in the

21

sector's share in the 1970s was the dramatic increase in the oil-producing sector when oil prices rose. With large increases in the price of oil, the energy sector's contribution to GDP ballooned, depressing the percentage share of agriculture. Latin America has the next smallest share of agriculture in GDP (only 11% in 1985). Latin American countries, however, are rich in farmland and several are major exporters of agricultural products. The relatively small contribution of agriculture to GDP is due to the region's large and sophisticated industrial base rather than any significant change in price levels or a marked deterioration in agricultural performance.

Table 1.6   PER CAPITA GROWTH AND AGRICULTURAL SHARE IN GDP
1970-1986

%

	Share of agriculture in GDP				Growth of per capita agricultural production[1]		
	1970	1975	1980	1985	1970-80	1980-5	1985-6
Developed market economies	4.4	4.5	3.6	3.0	1.2	0.7	-1.4
Developing countries	23.9	19.1	15.9	15.8	0.4	0.5	-0.9
of which:							
Latin America	12.8	11.9	11.1	11.1	0.7	-0.1	-3.5
Africa	31.2	26.6	20.9	22.8	-1.5	-1.0	0.4
West Asia	19.0	10.6	9.8	10.7	0.8	-0.3	2.2
South and East Asia	38.6	32.2	25.4	23.7	0.8	1.8	-0.7

Source: UN/FAO
Note: [1] *Growth rates are annual averages*

The two regions with relatively large agricultural sectors are Africa and South and East Asia. Agricultural conditions and prospects in these regions are quite different, however. The sector's share of GDP in South and East Asia has declined dramatically from 38.6% in 1970 to 23.7% in 1985, due mainly to the exceptionally rapid growth of agriculture relative to manufacturing and services. The situation is quite different in the case of Africa. Farming dominates the region's economy though production of food staples and exports have steadily declined throughout the 1970s and 1980s. The food crisis was most severe in 1982-4 when numerous African countries experienced especially poor harvests. The sector's declining share in GDP is then partly the result of its dismal performance in comparison with other parts of the region's economy. In 1970 agriculture accounted for over 31% of total income but by 1985 had fallen to less than 23%. Not until 1985 did African agriculturalists reverse this downward trend. Recent improvements, however, are largely due to exceptionally good harvests and do not necessarily indicate the results of any dramatic gains in productivity.

There are several reasons for the decline in the agricultural sector's share of regional GDP. A great proportion of African farmland is communally owned and traditional practice has been to farm small plots without regard to restoration. Land productivity has gradually declined, bringing down the level of farm production. African farmers have also been plagued by generally unfavourable prices in relation to prices of non-agricultural goods. Industry and services are represented by powerful classes located in the cities and, as a result, public policies have generally favoured them. Finally, exports of agricultural goods have been handicapped by excessively high exchange rates. Such a policy makes it cheap to import consumer items and capital goods but means that it is harder to export agricultural items. All these factors have contributed to the sector's relative decline though many African governments are now attempting to improve farmers' prospects (see Chapter 7).

Turning to the growth of per capita agricultural production, Table 1.6 shows that the developed market economies experienced a decline in the 1980s. The failure of agriculture to keep pace with population growth can be attributed mainly to policy changes: food surpluses in Europe and North America had reached unprecedented levels by 1986 and several countries introduced new policies in an effort to encourage the withdrawal of land from cultivation. This situation is in stark contrast to the Third World, where food stocks are sometimes perilously low. Every adverse shift in climate or rainfall can reduce food supplies below subsistence level for sections of the Third World's population.

Agricultural output in the Third World grew slightly more than population during 1980-5 but failed to meet this target in 1986. The downturn was due mainly to poor performance in Latin America though no developing region can claim a steady rate of growth in per capita agricultural output during the 1980s. The best record, perhaps, is in South and East Asia where per capita production rose 1.8% in 1980-5 per year but then contracted in 1986. West Asia's annual output per capita fell slightly in the first half of the decade while the African agricultural situation deteriorated seriously, declining 1% in 1980-5.

Programmes for economic reform of the agricultural sector have gained acceptance in recent years. Drought at home and debts abroad have forced many poor countries to seek financial help from the International Monetary Fund (IMF) and the World Bank. In return, governments have been urged to introduce reforms that usually required them to free agricultural prices and to cut food subsidies. Although the pressure to reform agriculture is sometimes great, governments have moved cautiously since the dangers are also great. Abolishing subsidies on food hurts the urban poor. And if town dwellers riot or plot they can bring a fragile government down. Some of these reform efforts are considered in later chapters dealing with individual regions.

CHAPTER 2

THE THIRD WORLD IN THE GLOBAL ECONOMY

The developing countries' economic links with the rest of the world are varied and extensive. Some observers see these relationships as a form of dependence which ties the economic performance and prospects of Third World countries to conditions in more advanced economies. These analysts favour steps to establish a greater degree of self-reliance and self-sufficiency so that economic circumstances in developing countries will not be unnecessarily constrained by events or decisions in other parts of the world. Others, however, argue that interdependence (though not dependence) is a by-product of economic progress. The opportunity to specialise in production and export of those manufactures and commodities in which a country has a competitive advantage is essential for development.

The ability to earn foreign exchange and to acquire the capital goods and technologies embodied in these products is obviously one of the major benefits of participation in the international trading system. This chapter begins by looking at the involvement of developing countries in the world trading system. Trade success depends partly on the types of products being produced and the policies adopted by the countries that are major suppliers and buyers. Although the share of manufactures in developing countries' exports has risen, many countries still depend heavily on the export of raw materials and semi-processed goods and their foreign exchange earnings are determined by conditions in world commodity markets. Section II examines this aspect, focusing on long-term trends in commodity markets. Because so many developing countries either rely heavily on energy exports or depend on foreign supplies of energy, trends in this market are of special importance and are examined in section III. Finally, Third World countries have begun to make increasing use of international capital markets, borrowing heavily from both commercial banks and international lending institutions. As these countries' debt has mounted, their economic prospects have become inextricably tied to events in international capital markets and this aspect is examined in the final section of the chapter.

I International Trade and Trade Policy

After growing at spectacular rates in the 1970s, the pace of world trade slowed. It recovered in 1985-6 but this was due mainly to improved trade performance of developed market economies. Recent rates of growth in world trade are nevertheless considerably below those recorded in the 1960s and 1970s.

Table 2.1 shows trade performance among major country groups and developing regions. Led by Asian exporters, in the 1970s the developing countries recorded substantially greater rates of export growth than those of the developed market economies. That situation was reversed after 1983. Exports of developed market economies rose briskly (15.9% in 1986) although, with the exception of South and East Asia, the value of Third World exports was declining. The pattern for imports is very similar. Africa and West Asia have seen their imports decline in each year since 1983. Although Latin America and South and East Asia both reported an increase in imports in 1986, the gains were substantially less than those enjoyed by developed market economies.

Table 2.1   VALUE AND GROWTH[1] OF WORLD TRADE BY REGION 1970-1986

% growth rate

	Exports					Imports				
	Value in 1986 ($billion fob)	1970-80	1983-4	1984-5	1985-6	Value in 1986 ($billion cif)	1970-80	1983-4	1984-5	1985-6
Developed market economies	1,486.3	18.8	6.3	3.7	15.9	1,553.6	19.5	8.6	3.6	12.1
Developing countries	420.0	25.9	4.3	-5.3	-7.4	421.0	23.8	-0.5	-7.0	0.0
of which:										
Africa	50.4	21.7	2.6	-3.1	-17.6	60.5	22.2	-7.8	-3.4	-0.2
South and East Asia	194.0	25.8	15.4	-2.9	9.0	181.9	23.5	6.6	-5.5	5.2
Latin America	90.1	20.8	6.5	-6.4	-13.3	83.9	20.6	2.0	-2.4	3.3
West Asia	75.9	34.4	-10.7	-10.6	-22.6	82.4	33.6	-8.0	-16.6	-8.5

Source: UN/IMF/UNCTAD
Note: [1] Growth rates are annual averages

Table 2.2 suggests some underlying reasons for the divergent experiences of developed and developing countries. The volume of world trade has risen steadily during the 1980s. In 1986 and 1987 Third World export volumes grew significantly faster than those of developed market economies. Because of severe foreign exchange constraints, the imports of developing countries have contracted slightly (0.3% per year) during 1981-7. The key factor shown in Table 2.2 is the terms of trade. On average, the developing countries' terms of trade deteriorated by 3.0% per year in 1981-7. Although they improved modestly in 1987 (mainly owing to favourable trends in energy markets) the terms of trade had fallen drastically in 1986. Trends in developed market economies have been in the opposite direction. Terms of trade have improved throughout the 1980s and rose significantly in 1986.

Table 2.2   ANNUAL RATES OF CHANGE IN VOLUMES AND PRICES OF TRADED GOODS 1976-1987

%	1976-80	1981-7	1985	1986	1987[1]
Volume of exports					
World	5.1	2.6	2.8	4.5	4.1
Developed market economies	6.6	3.2	4.5	2.6	4.0
Developing countries	1.9	1.0	-0.8	10.3	5.7
China	na	14.2	8.8	18.4	27.0
Volume of imports					
World	5.5	3.2	3.1	4.2	4.0
Developed market economies	5.6	4.3	5.3	8.0	5.1
Developing countries	5.5	-0.3	-4.7	-6.3	2.0
China	na	9.3	58.2	-14.5	-8.4

Continued...

Table 2.2 cont'd

	1976-80	1981-7	1985	1986	1987[1]
Terms of trade[2]					
Developed market economies	-2.1	1.9	1.0	8.0	2.1
Developing countries	5.8	-3.0	-2.5	-19.5	1.2
China	na	-3.6	-2.1	-19.7	-8.5

Source: UN

Notes: [1] *Preliminary*

[2] *Defined as the unit value of exports relative to the unit value of imports*

In addition to unfavourable price movements, the developing countries' export performance has been hindered by the proliferation of trade restrictions. Though tariffs were once widely used, non-tariff barriers (NTBs) are now more usual, ranging from bans on imports to surveillance and monitoring of prices and volumes of imports. Some are violations of the rules of the General Agreement on Tariffs and Trade (GATT). Others, such as the Multifibre Arrangement (MFA), are partly outside the purview of GATT rules. Altogether, GATT was notified or knew of 135 major restraints arrangements in 1987 (see Table 2.3). Of these, 64 were directed against developing countries, 51 against developed market economies and 20 against socialist countries. Most of the restrictions against Third World countries were aimed at major exporters. South Korea was the target for the largest number (23).

Table 2.3   TRADE RESTRAINTS IN OPERATION 1986-1987

number

April-September 1986	93
October 1986-March 1987	118
April-September 1987	135

Source: GATT
Note: Excluding restrictions under the Multifibre Arrangement

The use of NTBs is more pervasive than these figures actually suggest. A large proportion of commodities traded internationally - over 30% - were subject to quantitative restrictions in the 1980s. There are various reasons for the widespread use of NTBs: developing countries are permitted by GATT (article XVIII) to make use of them to protect their balance of payments; developed countries may impose trade restrictions in special cases, most often as a form of emergency measure to protect a domestic industry from import surges. In other instances, however, trade restrictions imposed by developed market economies circumvent GATT rules and are used to protect some of their largest industries including textiles, steel, transport equipment and electronics.

II The Composition and Direction of Trade

An important change in the Third World's trade pattern has taken place with regard to the destination of exports. Those exports to Latin America, Western Europe and Japan fell sharply in the 1980s. A decline in fuel exports was one prominent reason for this shift.

The sharp decline in exports to Latin America was mainly due to the region's debt problem which has limited its ability to purchase products from all parts of the world. By contrast, the Third World's exports to countries of South and East Asia have been extremely dynamic in the 1980s. Exports to North America and to other developing areas decreased only slightly in value terms. The better performance in these markets was mainly due to demand for manufactures and industrial inputs. The value of US imports of engineering products from the Third World, for example, nearly tripled in 1980-6.

Along with changes in the destination of the Third World's exports, there has been a major shift in the composition of trade. Table 2.4 documents the latter trend, showing exports by major classes and product categories for 1980 and 1986. In 1980, exports of primary products were four times as large as manufactures, but by 1986 the ratio had fallen to 1:4. A major reason for the shift was the fall in the value of petroleum exports. The share of food products in Third World exports increased, mainly as a result of the recovery in coffee prices in 1986. In fact, food exports are the second most important category of exports after fuels, with a share even greater than engineering products or textiles and clothing.

31

Table 2.4   PRODUCT COMPOSITION OF MERCHANDISE EXPORTS FROM
DEVELOPING COUNTRIES 1980/1986

%	1980	1986
All products	100	100
Primary products	80	59
of which:		
Food	12	17
Fuels	61	34
Manufactures	19	41
of which:		
Iron and steel	1	2
Chemicals	2	3
Engineering products	7	16
Textiles and clothing	5	10

Source: GATT

Although important exporters, the developing countries are by no means the world's major suppliers of food products. Brazil is the only developing country among the world's ten largest food exporters. Table 2.5 shows the ten largest food exporters among Third World countries. In five of these countries - Argentina, Cuba, Thailand, Colombia and Ivory Coast - food amounted to more than half of total exports. Ten years ago, the same was true of Brazil but food now accounts for a significantly lower share owing to the rapid growth of manufactured exports. Relative to their ranking in 1975, Singapore and Malaysia have made substantial improvements in their position. In Singapore, however, much of the food trade involves re-exports. For example, the ratio of imports to exports for major items such as coffee, cocoa and spices ranged between 90 and 95% in 1985.

Table 2.5   THE TEN MAJOR DEVELOPING COUNTRY EXPORTERS
OF FOOD 1985

Rank in 1975	1985	Country	Items accounting for half of food exports[1]
1	1	Brazil	Coffee (22.5); Feeding stuffs for animals (19.5); Fruit preserves and preparations (14)
3	2	Argentina	Wheat and meslin, unmilled (20.4); Fixed vegetable oil, "soft" (15.8); Maize, unmilled (13.8); Oilseeds and oleaginous fruits for "soft" oils (13.2)
2	3	Cuba[2]	Sugar and honey (79)
5	4	Thailand	Rice (25.5); Vegetables, fresh, etc (18); Fish, crustaceans and molluscs, prepared or preserved (8.7)
9	5	Malaysia	Other fixed vegetable oils (69.6)
4	6	India[2]	Tea (26.9); Crustaceans and molluscs (13.1); Fruits and nuts (8); Feeding stuffs for animals (7.6)
7	7	Colombia	Coffee (85)
8	8	Mexico[2]	Coffee (33); Vegetables, fresh, etc (31.8)
17	9	Singapore	Other fixed vegetable oils (26.4); Animal and vegetable oils and fats (9.9); Coffee (7.7); Spices (7.6)
11	10	Ivory Coast	Cocoa (46.8); Coffee (36)

Source: GATT
Notes: [1] *Figures within brackets show the estimated share of the item in the country's total food exports*
[2] *1984 estimates*

Among manufactures, engineering products and textiles and clothing are the two largest export categories. Table 2.6 shows world exports of textiles and clothing to developed countries (the only countries for which current data are relatively complete) along with exports of major Third World suppliers. A strong recovery in the textile industry in Hong Kong, South Korea and Taiwan in 1986 has contributed to a big surge in textile trade during this decade. Exchange rate developments also affected the pattern of exports. The fastest-growing exporters have been those countries whose currencies appreciated against the US dollar. When expressed in national currencies, however, many of these same countries' exports actually declined. Like textiles, exports of clothing also recovered strongly in 1986 after a poor performance in 1985. Led by Asian suppliers, the developing countries' share of the North American clothing market reached 23.5% of total imports in 1986. The corresponding figure for Western Europe was 11.5%.

Table 2.6   EXPORTS OF TEXTILES AND CLOTHING TO DEVELOPED
COUNTRIES 1986

$ billion

Export origin	Textiles	Clothing
World	42.7	52.1
Selected developing countries:		
China	4.3	3.0
Hong Kong[1]	3.9	8.4
South Korea	3.2	5.5
Taiwan	3.1	4.2
Total	14.5	21.1

Source: GATT
Note: [1] *Includes re-exports*

Data on world trade in engineering products are given in Table 2.7. For the developing countries, exports of office and telecommunications equipment is the largest product group in this category, accounting for nearly $16 billion or 34% of the group's total exports of engineering products. Asian exporters - Japan along with Asian developing countries - became the world's major suppliers of computers in 1986, replacing the USA. Exports of computers from Singapore, South Korea and Taiwan all expanded by more than 50% in 1986. South Korea also emerged as a world supplier of other electronic products and consumer appliances such as videotape recorders. Owing to exchange rate movements, Korea's competitiveness improved greatly vis-à-vis Japan. The country's exports of videotapes more than doubled in 1986, reaching $550 million.

Table 2.7   EXPORTS OF ENGINEERING PRODUCTS TO DEVELOPED COUNTRIES 1986

$ billion

Category	Exports from world	Exports from developing countries
Machinery for specialised industries	100.25	3.10
Office and telecommunications equipment	87.65	15.70
Road motor vehicles	169.30	2.95
Other machinery and transport equipment	162.95	14.45
Household appliances	52.40	10.20
TOTAL	572.55	46.40

Source: GATT

In conclusion, Asian exporters clearly dominate among Third World suppliers of manufactures. Latin America is a moderately important source of supply for ores, some minerals, non-ferrous metals and certain agricultural commodities. West Asia's main export is crude oil while tropical products are Africa's major earner of foreign exchange. Given these diverse patterns of specialisation, the movement of commodity prices affects each region differently. Resource-poor areas such as South and East Asia suffer when commodity prices rise though other parts of the Third World may benefit. When commodity prices fall, the competitiveness of Asian exports improves as they acquire their industrial imports at better prices. The next section examines movements of world commodity prices and considers their impact on Third World producers of raw materials.

III Trends in Commodity Prices

In the mid-1970s neo-Malthusians forecast that commodity prices would soar because farmers would soon be unable to feed the world's growing population. Other forecasters simultaneously warned that resource depletion would lead to global shortages of most natural resources by the beginning of the 1990s. These expectations were so widespread that they prompted many governments to begin to search for new strategies to cope in a world of commodity shortages. Countries in Latin America and Africa hoped to copy the OPEC model, using "commodity power" in an era of shortages to bolster foreign exchange earnings. Developed countries, too, were caught up in this atmosphere. Resource-poor countries such as Japan foresaw a threat to national security and began investing in overseas sources of supply for minerals and oil.

The neo-Malthusians were proven to be wrong. The world began to produce large food surpluses while most metals markets experienced prolonged periods of oversupply. The long-term effect of these imbalances was to depress commodity prices. By 1987 real prices of agricultural products and metals had reached their lowest levels in 30 years. Commodity markets then recovered dramatically in the next year, so much so that, by mid-1988, the average price of raw materials was at its highest point in 15 years. The long-term decline of commodity prices and their recent recovery stem from different sources. The same is true of the consequences for Third World producers. The discussion begins by considering the forces leading to the long-term decline in commodity prices. Reasons for the latest upswing in commodity prices are then examined in more detail.

The long-term decline in commodity prices

Commodity prices, like all other prices, represent the outcome of an interaction between supply, demand and government policy. All three moved in a way that undermined the expectations of a world rise in prices. Supply expanded at unanticipated rates as a result of technological changes and because the expectation of higher prices led to increased investment and overcapacity. Technology also altered demand patterns, leading to the creation of cheaper substitutes for many primary commodities, especially metals. Meanwhile, government intervention in the form of agricultural price support policies (particularly in OECD countries) contributed to oversupply and depressed the free market prices paid to farmers in developing countries.

Technological change, because it alters both demand and supply, has been the most important single reason for the slide in depressed commodity prices. High-yielding, disease-resistant varieties of plants, coupled with better fertilisers and pesticides, have turned India, China and even Saudi Arabia into surplus producers of wheat or grain. The effects of technological change on raw material usage have been equally great. Producers of everything from motor vehicles to household utensils began to use new composite materials in place of metals. The consumption of major minerals such as aluminium and nickel has grown much more slowly than overall levels of manufacturing output. An even more ominous prospect for metals exporters in developing countries is that composite materials have only just begun to make inroads in the traditional uses of metallic substances.

The net effect of all these forces on agriculture is summarised in Table 2.8. Growth of world agricultural output soared in the early 1980s and in 1983-4 was more than twice the average for 1970-80. Rapid growth was mainly attributable to improvements in North American and, to a lesser extent, Western European agriculture. World food production followed roughly the same pattern. The pattern of growth in developing countries was quite different. Rates of increase in the early 1980s were lower than historical trends. By 1984, however, the production of food and agricultural products in developing countries began to pick up slightly. The upward trend is most apparent in Africa and West Asia. This improvement must be weighed against the fact that the agricultural sector of most countries in these two regions remains small and unlikely to achieve self-sufficiency given the high rates of population growth.

Table 2.8   GROWTH OF AGRICULTURAL AND FOOD PRODUCTION
1970-1986

%

Country grouping	Total agricultural output 1970-				Total food output 1970-			
	80	1983-4	1984-5	1985-6	80	1983-4	1984-6	1985-6
World	2.4	5.1	2.2	1.4	2.5	4.8	2.1	2.1
North America	2.3	13.4	5.4	-2.5	2.4	12.4	5.6	-1.8
Western Europe	1.8	5.4	-1.6	0.4	1.8	5.4	-1.7	0.5
Developing countries of which:	2.8	2.7	4.3	1.3	3.0	2.5	3.9	2.1
Africa	1.4	0.4	9.1	3.5	1.6	0.0	9.4	3.6
West Asia	3.8	0.8	5.0	5.0	4.0	1.1	5.6	5.4
South and East Asia	3.1	3.1	3.5	1.2	3.2	2.6	2.9	1.8
Latin America	3.2	3.7	3.8	-1.3	3.4	4.1	3.2	0.5

Source: FAO

Table 2.9 shows the effects of these production gains on free market prices. Of the four broad categories included in the table, prices of food and tropical beverages have deteriorated least since 1980. Prices of vegetable oils and oilseeds have been especially volatile, declining abruptly in 1986 after a steep rise in 1984. Producers of ores and metals also suffered greatly. The index for this category has declined steadily in the 1980s until prices reached levels only two-thirds of those at the beginning of the decade.

Table 2.9   INDICES OF FREE MARKET PRICES FOR SELECTED
COMMODITY GROUPS 1970-1986

Product category (no. of commodities)	1970	1975	1981	1982	1983	1984	1985	1986
Food and tropical beverges (19)	29.2	57.5	81.4	67.3	70.8	71.9	64.9	77.1
Vegetable oils and oilseeds (12)	45.8	76.0	95.8	75.0	91.7	124.3	85.3	53.3
Agricultural raw materials (15)	29.4	50.5	87.2	75.2	80.7	78.5	70.6	70.8
Ores and metals (17)	38.2	53.6	83.6	74.5	77.3	71.2	68.5	64.4

Source: UN/IMF/World Bank

Together, these trends present a rather gloomy picture for commodity producers throughout the world. However, they also offer some hope of better times for producers in developing countries. Plant closures are gradually reducing excess capacity. The low returns earned by metal producers have also persuaded some firms to switch to higher valued products. Those reducing capacity or making the switch are mainly producers in developed countries which have the capital and/or technology to take these steps. US producers of aluminium, for example, accounted for only 40% of the non-communist world's output in 1987, compared to 60% in 1961. Rather than producing a surplus of ingots they make what they need for fabrication and buy the rest from low-cost suppliers elsewhere in the world. When all these marginal adjustments have finally taken effect, longer term trends in mineral prices are unlikely to be as soft as they have proved to be in the 1980s.

The recent recovery in commodity prices

Commodity prices began to rise in 1988 reversing the long-term downward trend. According to Figure 2.1 food prices in mid-1988 were more than 30% higher than January 1987. The increase in prices of metals was even greater, peaking at more than 160% in the same period. The turnaround can be attributed partly to the fact that supplies of both food crops and metals have been temporarily disrupted after a long period in which stocks fell. In the case of metals, strikes in some of the bigger mines have recently accentuated the effects of the slow reduction in world capacity which followed the uneconomic build-up of the early 1980s. Government policy has been the main reason for the rise in food prices. In both Western Europe and the USA the cost of farm support soared between 1984 and 1986. Europeans responded by introducing quotas on output and the USA initiated a programme to take agricultural land out of farm production. Once both programmes began to take effect, the prospect for sales out of American and European stockpiles have grown. This has sent buyers rushing to commodity markets before supplies tighten even further.

The recent recovery of commodity prices does not necessarily mean that Third World producers can expect many short-term benefits. Improvements in prices of copper and aluminium will be welcome in developing countries such as Chile, Jamaica, Zaire and Zambia. But only half the world's primary commodities come from the Third World and the four developing countries noted here are not typical. Other commodities such as nickel and zinc have contributed greatly to the overall rise in the index though the bulk of the world's supplies of both metals comes from OECD countries. The situation is much the same for many agricultural goods: the prices of temperate crops - wheat, maize and soyabeans - have risen most; the prices of tropical products, so important in the exports of many Third World countries, have changed very little.

Figure 2.1 World price indices[1] of food and metals 1987–1988
January 1987 = 100

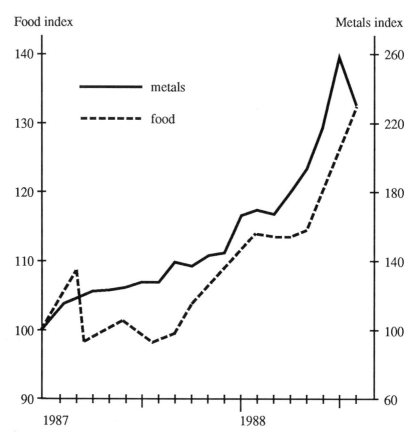

Source: The Economist Intelligence Unit

Note: [1] Price indices are calculated in US dollars

In conclusion, a few developing countries will reap some gains from the recent market recovery. However, the list of beneficiaries is a select one consisting of producers lucky enough to have obtained large market shares of particular commodities. The general increase in prices of minerals and metals will not result in any broadly based transfer of wealth from industrialised to developing countries. At least in this particular upswing the redistribution is more likely to be from resource-poor countries in OECD to resource-rich ones (eg Canada and Australia) in the same group. In the Third World the significance of developments in international markets for agricultural produce, minerals and metals is overshadowed by energy. Developments in this vital market are considered in the next section.

IV Energy Markets

Like international commodity markets, the global trends in energy markets (including oil, hydroelectric and other energy forms) have undergone significant changes since the 1970s. Table 2.10 shows that the increase in world production and consumption of energy slowed in 1975-85 relative to 1970-75. Production of primary energy rose only moderately in developed market economies and negligibly in developing countries. The reason for the latter group's poor performance is clear: output of primary energy in West Asia declined between 1975 and 1985 by more than 600 million tonnes of coal equivalent. Changes in the pattern of world consumption are somewhat different. Although consumption of primary energy has continued to rise in developing countries, this group accounted for only 14% of the world total in 1985. Developed market economies used over half the world's primary energy and the growth of consumption in this group has slowed considerably since the first round of oil price hikes by OPEC in 1973.

Table 2.10   PRODUCTION AND CONSUMPTION OF PRIMARY ENERGY
BY REGION 1970, 1975 AND 1985

million tonne of coal equivalent

	Production			Consumption		
	1970	1975	1985	1970	1975	1985
World[1]	6,982.1	8,013.0	9,465.4	6,381.6	7,400.6	8,739.5
Developed market economies	2,971.2	3,007.9	3,588.2	4,089.3	4,381.8	4,554.5
Developing countries of which:	2,091.1	2,501.4	2,640.6	543.3	760.4	1,228.0
Latin America	451.0	408.4	633.0	233.2	315.4	429.5
Africa	429.3	372.6	432.1	43.1	64.1	123.9
West Asia	1,021.0	1,452.0	834.0	63.6	107.4	213.4
South and East Asia	168.3	243.0	444.8	171.7	232.0	399.2

Source: UN
Note: [1] *Includes socialist countries*

For developing countries the issue of energy is dominated by events in the world's oil markets. OPEC's pricing committee has struggled for several years to find a way to bolster oil prices. Weak demand in Western countries is part of the oil producers' problem; the slowdown in their oil consumption, which began in the 1970s, has continued in this decade. Negligible increases in real oil prices in most countries should have encouraged greater demand. However, the general trend towards more efficient automobile engines and the gradual shift away from oil-using industries - which began in Western countries more than ten years ago - seem to be little affected by cheaper oil. With slow economic growth everywhere, world consumption has risen by only 1-2% in each year since 1983. Estimates for 1988 show a continued deceleration: world oil consumption should grow by just 1%. This is equivalent to an additional 400,000 barrels per day (b/d) but nevertheless represents a further slowdown in demand.

Meanwhile, most OPEC countries have been raising their output, and in doing so have pushed down oil prices even further. During 1987 OPEC members routinely broke the cartel's output rules. In the second half of the year they overshot the cartel's output target of 16.6 million b/d by 15%. That surplus has swollen world stocks. The International Energy Agency (IEA) estimated that at the beginning of 1988 OECD oil stocks were 454 million tonnes, or 6.6% higher than in January 1986 - just before oil prices collapsed.

The cartel's difficulties are complicated by the fact that non-OPEC production has risen by a quarter since 1980 while OPEC's own output has shrunk by 30%. Though the growth of non-members' output has now slowed, it still rose by almost 1% in both 1987 and 1988. These increases would have been even greater had several countries - Egypt, Malaysia, Mexico and Oman - not co-operated with the cartel and restricted output. These four countries, with other non-OPEC producers (Angola, China and Colombia), have also considered how they might co-operate more closely with the cartel. Together, the seven countries produce around 8 million b/d, and have discussed a proposal to cut their exports if OPEC should make corresponding reductions in its own output. Such an arrangement would raise world oil prices but it would further erode OPEC's market share. The danger to the cartel is that non-OPEC countries' co-operation will evaporate with any strong price rise.

The fall in the value of the dollar between mid-1985 and the end of 1987 has posed even more difficulties for OPEC. Its efforts to raise prices began in mid-1986 in the midst of this process of currency

45

realignments. Oil revenues in 1987 were slightly higher than in 1986, but after allowing for exchange rate movements these petrodollars actually purchased 11% less. Exchange rate movements have also had important repercussions for non-OPEC countries in the Third World. Oil-poor countries whose currencies have moved with the dollar saw the price of imported oil decline since 1985. Other countries whose currencies depreciated even faster than the dollar have experienced an increase in the cost of oil imports.

V Foreign Debt in the Third World

Third World producers of oil, minerals and agricultural commodities have seen their foreign debts rise at a time when they have found it more difficult to earn foreign exchange by exporting. Western governments have yet to agree any overall strategy for managing the high international debt of developing countries. The debt problem has not evolved into a full-blown crisis but so long as no practical strategy is in place, the potential for crisis remains.

In 1987 the total outstanding debt of developing countries reached $1.2 trillion - a 10% increase over the 1986 US dollar value. However, after taking account of movements in exchange rates the underlying rise in debt was only 3%. The cost of servicing debt also rose, from $143.9 billion in 1986 to $146.6 billion in 1987. Total financial flows to the Third World are estimated to have fallen 10% in 1987, due partly to accelerated repayments of commercial bank loans by South Korea. Excluding South Korea and speculative inflows to Taiwan, total financial flows to developing countries fell by 5% in 1987.

One reason the overall situation did not worsen in 1987 was a sharp improvement in the current account deficit of developing countries. Table 2.11 shows that the developing countries' balance of payments deficit on current account was $9.3 billion in 1987 after soaring to

$45.6 billion in 1986. The deficits in both these years were greatly influenced by sharp fluctuations in the price of oil. The accounts of energy importers have improved considerably since 1985, registering a deficit of under $9 billion in 1986 and less than $5 billion in 1987. These gains were very much the result of strong performance in three Asian economies - Hong Kong, South Korea and Taiwan - whose combined surpluses on current account exceeded $20 billion in both 1986 and 1987. Other energy importers have not fared so well: they faced a combined deficit of about $30 billion in each of the last two years. Though importing countries have benefited when the price of oil declined, they have been hurt by a similar fall in prices of their own commodity exports.

Table 2.11   BALANCE OF PAYMENTS ON CURRENT ACCOUNT[1] BY COUNTRY GROUP 1980-1987

$ billion	1980	1982	1984	1985	1986	1987[2]
Developed market economies	-36.9	-6.7	-39.0	-21.7	14.1	-12.7
Developing countries	36.7	-77.5	-29.9	-29.5	-45.6	-9.3
Capital-surplus countries	105.8	16.2	-2.2	8.0	-8.6	5.6
Capital-importing countries	-66.7	-99.6	-30.1	-26.0	-29.8	-14.5
Energy exporters	2.1	-34.9	-0.2	-3.5	-20.9	-10.0
Energy importers	-68.8	-64.7	-29.9	-22.5	-8.9	-4.5

Continued...

47

Table 2.11 cont'd

	1980	1982	1984	1985	1986	1987[2]
Recent surplus economies[3]	-7.4	-1.6	7.1	10.4	22.5	27.0
Other	-61.5	-63.1	-37.0	-32.9	-31.4	-31.5
China	-2.4	5.9	2.4	-11.5	-7.2	-0.4

Source: UN/IMF
Notes: [1] *Balance of payments on goods, services and private transfers*
[2] *Preliminary estimates*
[3] *Hong Kong, Republic of Korea and Taiwan*

The world debt crisis, of course, affects each developing country quite differently. However, debt problems have now reached such a magnitude as to be reflected dramatically in the financial indications for the aggregate of all developing countries. Table 2.12 gives some impression of the seriousness of the debt problem. The net transfer of financial resources (defined as net capital flows less net payments of interest and dividends) became negative in 1984 and exceeded $20 billion in each of the following three years. Although total capital inflows (ie the sum of credit, direct investment and grants in aid) are still positive, they are exceeded by net payments of interest and dividends. This situation is mainly due to the steady shrinkage of credit since 1984 coupled with continually high levels of net interest paid.

Table 2.12   NET TRANSFER OF FINANCIAL RESOURCES OF THE
CAPITAL-IMPORTING DEVELOPING COUNTRIES 1980-1987

$ billion

	1980	1982	1984	1985	1986	1987[1]
Transfer on account of direct investment[2]						
Net investment flow	6.4	7.9	6.2	7.5	5.7	7.5
Net investment income	-10.9	-10.0	-8.8	-8.1	-7.0	-8.5
NET TRANSFER	-4.5	-2.1	-2.6	-0.6	-1.3	-1.0
Net transfer on account for private credit flows[3]						
Net credit flow	34.0	24.2	8.8	2.0	1.6	-1.0
Net interest paid	-18.5	-42.4	-41.4	-39.3	-33.6	-31.5
NET TRANSFER	15.6	-18.2	-32.5	-37.2	-32.0	-32.5
Net transfer on account of official flows[4]						
Official transfer (grants)	13.5	11.3	12.5	14.4	14.4	15.0
Net credit flow	22.0	29.5	25.0	14.2	15.0	13.5
Net interest paid	-6.2	-8.8	-11.8	-13.5	-16.2	-17.5
NET TRANSFER	29.2	32.0	25.7	15.1	13.2	11.0
TOTAL TRANSFER	40.3	11.8	-9.5	-22.7	-20.1	-22.5

Source: UN/IMF/World Bank/other national and multilateral sources
Notes: *Data are for a sample of 98 countries for which adequate information was available*
   [1] *Preliminary estimate, rounded to the nearest $0.5 billion*
   [2] *Direct investment income excludes retained earnings and investment flow is shown net of reinvested earnings*
   [3] *Including long-term and short-term flows of foreign private liabilities and assets of the developing countries*
   [4] *Net disbursements by official government agencies including use of IMF credit and other international monetary arrangements*

49

Once the net transfer for all capital-importing countries became negative, large amounts of domestically earned income had to be set aside to purchase the foreign exchange to be transferred abroad. This reversal in capital flows is dramatic when seen in relation to the situation in 1980. The Third World was the recipient of an annual transfer of roughly $40 billion in that year but in every year since 1985 there has been a net transfer of over $20 billion out of these countries. Economic recovery would require an acceleration of investment, which is not practical given the current pattern of resource transfer.

The main reason for the net negative transfer involves private credits: primarily bank loans but also including private suppliers' credit, bond finance and short-term commercial and bank credits. In the early part of the 1980s, developing countries took up to 40% of total international medium-term bank credit. Since 1985, that figure has declined to 15-20%, much of which is "forced lending" arranged as part of debt-rescheduling operations.

Net transfers provided through official channels are the one major category of capital flows which is still positive, though these funds are some 60% below levels attained at the beginning of this decade. Official assistance in the form of grants has not significantly exceeded amounts provided at the beginning of the 1980s but it has recovered slowly from the trough experienced in 1982. Indeed, by 1987 the net transfer through official sources would also have been negative if not for grants. Official development assistance (ODA) of OECD countries increased by 21% in nominal dollars in 1986 and is expected to rise even further in the coming two years.

Many countries, together accounting for well over half the Third World's population, do not have serious debt problems. They may struggle with development problems but their debt-service obligations are not large relative to export earnings and are therefore met without disruption. In some cases, policymakers were reluctant to accumulate large debts that entailed heavy debt-servicing payments. Other countries were never accorded significant access to credit because of the fragility of their economies. In still others, large debts were accumulated but export growth was rapid and terms of trade did not deteriorate.

The reasons certain countries now find themselves with excessive debt burdens are not as varied. Today's debtors had access to a rapidly expanding - and highly elastic - supply of credit. More important, there was a shared expectation that the capacity to repay would not deteriorate in the future. Finally, today's debtors usually lack official national accounting systems and have been unable to control the run-up in foreign obligations. When the debt crisis emerged in many of these countries, there was no readily available record of how much debt was outstanding.

When the issue of foreign indebtedness is considered in geographical terms, the problem affects developing regions in significantly different ways. Though Latin America has the greatest debt burden, several of the region's larger countries can still hope that sufficient economic growth will provide a remedy given the right mixture of economic policies. That solution is not readily available to African countries. Growth rates are already depressed, while African imports and investments are being severely limited. Given these conditions, African countries cannot realistically expect that they will ever be able to service their debts in full.

The severity of the African problem cannot be judged from the region's total outstanding debt. Sub-Saharan Africa owed about $90 billion at the end of 1987, equivalent to only 8% of all Third World debt. However, the region's ratio of debt to export earnings has risen from 148% in 1980 to 325% in 1987. In contrast, the corresponding ratio for all developing countries rose from 82% to 157% in the same period. Other indicators are equally ominous. Black Africa was the only part of the Third World where the debt ratio rose in 1987. In 1988 the proportion of export earnings needed to make debt payments is put at 30% in Africa compared with an average for all developing countries of 19%.

The distinction between Africa and Latin America extends beyond relative differences in region's abilities to service foreign debt: three-quarters of Africa's debt is owed to official creditors; in Latin America's case, three-quarters is due to banks and other private creditors. Debt forgiveness for Latin America could edge those countries out of commercial capital markets as they depend mainly on private lenders. The same is not a danger for African countries which rely on official (government) lenders.

The World Bank has identified 17 individual developing countries as being "highly indebted". Table 2.13 shows several key trends in this group. Between 1985 and 1987 their total foreign debt rose by $39 billion. Only two, Argentina and Chile, managed a reduction in their foreign obligations during this period. Interest payments as a proportion of export earnings represent the most important measure of the strain debt puts on a country's ability to pay. Most of the larger debtors spend 30% or more of their export earnings on interest. For the group as a whole, the share of earnings claimed by interest payments rose; slightly during the period, reaching 23.8% in 1987.

The most encouraging trend in Table 2.12 is that economic growth in the highly indebted countries accelerated after 1985. Between 1980 and 1984 average GDP shrank by 0.3% per year with significant declines in Argentina, Bolivia, Ivory Coast, Nigeria, Uruguay and Venezuela. Thereafter growth resumed, averaging 2.8% in 1984-7. But faster growth did little to halt the decline in consumption: per capita consumption dropped by 1.8% per year in 1980-4 and continued to fall thereafter. Altogether, per capita consumption declined by an average of 11% between 1980 and 1987.

Table 2.13   FOREIGN DEBT AND ECONOMIC GROWTH IN HIGHLY INDEBTED COUNTRIES 1980-1987

Developing country	Total outstanding debt $ billion		Interest as % of exports		Annual average growth of GDP (%)		Average annual growth in per capita consumption (%)	
	1985	1987	1985[1]	1987	1980-4	1984-7	1980-4	1984-7
Argentina	50.8	49.4	25.4	33.1	-1.6	2.2	-2.7	0.7
Bolivia	4.0	4.6 [2]	43.0	31.5	-4.7	-1.9	-7.8	-1.4
Brazil	107.3	114.5	38.2	30.2	0.1	8.0	-1.2	4.2
Chile	21.0	20.5	42.9	29.5	-1.4	4.0	-2.1	-2.3
Colombia	11.3	15.1	16.4	16.6	1.8	4.1	-0.1	0.6
Costa Rica	4.2	4.5 [2]	24.0	18.9	-0.4	4.1	-4.8	3.3
Ecuador	8.5	9.0 [2]	24.8	24.4	1.1	1.8	-2.3	-2.1
Ivory Coast	8.0	9.1	18.4	17.1	-2.3	1.7	-6.6	-1.1
Jamaica	3.4	3.8	12.5	17.4	1.3	-1.3	-1.4	-1.4
Mexico	99.0	105.0	34.1	32.7	1.3	-1.0	-1.4	-4.4
Morocco	14.0	17.3	12.7	25.4 [1]	2.5	4.6	-0.2	2.2
Nigeria	19.3	27.0	12.1	11.6	-4.7	-1.6	-4.3	-9.4

Continued...

Table 2.13 cont'd

Developing country	Total outstanding debt $ billion		Interest as % of exports		Annual average growth of GDP (%)		Average annual growth in per capita consumption (%)	
	1985	1987	1985[1]	1987	1980-4	1984-7	1980-4	1984-7
Peru	13.4	16.7	7.9	29.0	-0.7	2.6	-3.7	4.7
Philippines	24.8	29.0	12.3	19.0	0.8	-2.2	0.0	-2.3
Uruguay	3.6	3.8 [2]	21.8	15.3	-3.7	1.8	-4.7	0.8
Venezuela	33.6	33.9	10.4	22.5	-1.8	0.8	-6.4	-2.1
Yugoslavia	19.6	21.8	12.4	7.7	0.6	1.8	-0.5	-0.5
TOTAL	445.9	485.0	23.5	23.8	-0.3	2.8	-1.8	-1.3

Source: World Bank
Notes: [1] Excludes private debt
[2] 1986

In some countries the drop in consumption was severe. Mexico's declined by 17%, Bolivia's by nearly a third.

The export performance of the heavily indebted countries adds to the disappointing picture. In 1987 the exports of this group were the same in nominal terms as in 1982. Yet during those years industrialised countries increased their imports by $740 billion, a rise of 44%. Despite their failure to capture any of these growing export markets, heavily indebted countries still managed to cut their current account deficit by more than $40 billion a year. Part of that fall reflects a reduction in interest rates but about $24 billion represents a fall in imports.

There are some grounds for optimism in the fact that commercial banks have recently become more flexible in the debt instruments they are willing to use. They have tried to speed up talks on rescheduling and new credit and are participating in debt-equity swaps. All these efforts can be neutralised, however, if industrialised countries fail to maintain low and stable rates of interest. Such a shift could be enormously disruptive, coming at a time when Latin America and other heavily indebted countries have made great sacrifices to redress their financial plight.

The efforts of commercial banks are constructive but piecemeal. And they are being undertaken against a larger background of uncertainty as Japan now seems poised to challenge the USA for "leadership" on the international debt issue. Japan's new debt initiative is the Miyazawa Plan, named after its Finance Minister, Kiichi Miyazawa. Unveiled in late 1988, the plan aims to improve the middle-income debtors' ability to pay what they owe. The Japanese argue that only by restricting the flow of new capital can debtors' economies grow. Since private banks are reluctant to oblige, multilateral and bilateral agencies must step in. In return, debtor nations would have to accept a variety of economic reforms.

The Japanese plan seems flexible enough to accommodate most of the US-imposed criteria for solutions to the debt problem. It fits a case-by-case approach and it avoids the possibility that debtor nations would be forgiven their debts. Finally, it does not advocate bailing out private banks. Despite this agreement between the American and Japanese positions, rivalry between the two countries has slowed progress. The Japanese dismiss the notion that they are trying to challenge the USA for leadership on the issue. However, they stress the leading role which the IMF and their own export-import bank would play. The Americans see a threat in the fact that the Japanese are concurrently trying to increase their influence in the IMF. The danger here goes beyond possible rivalries between the West's two economic superpowers. Procrastination and uncertainty about the West's ability to construct an effective programme to deal with Third World debt can only add to the burdens placed on an already fragile financial system.

CHAPTER 3

GROWTH IMPEDIMENTS AND POLICY ISSUES IN THE THIRD WORLD

Economic progress in the Third World obviously must overcome a variety of economic, political and social problems. The developing countries, however, are markedly different in terms of their resource endowments, market size, labour skills, political systems and other features. This heterogeneity makes it difficult to generalise about the cause of problems or their possible remedies. A few features are nevertheless shared by virtually all Third World countries, or are at least common to a majority, and are examined in this chapter. The chapter begins by looking at population trends in developing countries in relation to rates of economic growth. The depressed level of investment spending is another characteristic shared by many developing countries and is treated in section II. Subsequent sections deal with inflation, systems of taxation and the tax revenue base and fiscal and monetary policies.

I The Population Problem

The world's population is simply growing too quickly: global population surpassed 5 billion in mid-1988, twice the 1950 total and one billion more than in 1974. The uneven distribution of population growth, however, is enlarging the gap between living standards in slow growing parts of the world and those in faster growing parts. The world's total population rises by about 250,000 each day. Of these new inhabitants, roughly 90% are in developing countries. In many of the poorest countries the pace of population growth swamps the capacity to cope. As a result, governments of developing countries are finding it increasingly difficult to provide their growing populations with rising standards of education and living.

Not all developing countries are experiencing excessively rapid population growth. A few have very slow rates of increase. Developing countries in East Asia (principally China but more recently South Korea and Taiwan) have rates of population growth significantly below the world average. Africa, however, has the highest population growth rates in the world. For example, if present rates of growth in Nigeria were to prevail for the coming 50 years, the country would have as many people as the whole of Africa today. Growth in Kenya is higher still - increasing at a rate of 4.2% each year, a level matched only by Zimbabwe and Mozambique. The consequences of these trends for levels of per capita income are ominous. If countries like Kenya or Mozambique are to raise their presently modest living standards, they would have to achieve sustained rates of GDP growth of 6% or better over several decades: an achievement no African country (or few other developing countries) has managed in the post-war era.

High rates of population growth avoid one problem more common to industrialised countries: when the population is declining or growing only slowly the number of elderly that must be supported by a shrinking workforce surges. In developing countries the proportion of elderly is unlikely to change greatly over the next 50 years. As the population expands, the number of potentially productive workers will increase much more rapidly than the elderly. The old, however, are not the only dependants on society; the young are too. The proportionate burden of the young also tends to rise as development continues. While the dependence of the old is potentially reduced (because they are healthier and better able to remain in the workforce), the young become more dependent by staying at school longer.

In developing countries with rapid population growth the proportion of inhabitants under 15 years is large. Nigeria presently has 1,170 children for every 1,000 workers while in Mexico the figure is even higher, 1,250 children per 1,000 workers. These proportions are likely to remain stable or decline only moderately over the next 50 years. Compared with industrialised countries, the figures strongly suggest a deterioration in the living standards of the young in most developing countries. The number of young to be supported by each 1,000 workers will be significantly greater in most Third World countries than in Britain or the USA, while the productivity of these workers will be very low compared with their Western counterparts.

Some of these demographic features are illustrated by the data in Table 3.1. The median age of the population in developed countries ranges from a high of 37.6 years in an ageing West Germany to a low of 30.1 years in Canada. But even Canada's comparatively young population (mainly due to immigration) has a median age which exceeds the highest in a developing country (29.0 years in Argentina). The same contrasts apply to the percentage of the population that is of working age: in developed countries it typically ranges between 60% and 70% but in developing countries it is much lower, sometimes even below 50%. Indeed, in many developing countries population growth is so fast that more than half the inhabitants are under 20 years.

Table 3.1   MEDIAN AGE AND WORKING POPULATION IN SELECTED
COUNTRIES 1985

	Median age	Population of working age[1] (% of total)
Developed countries		
Austria	35.5	67.7
Belgium	35.3	67.9
Canada	30.1	68.3
France	33.7	66.6
Germany, West	37.6	70.6
Italy	35.7	66.8
Japan	35.0	68.7
Spain	31.1	64.3
United Kingdom	35.5	66.4
United States	31.0	66.1
Developing countries		
Argentina	29.0	63.1
Brazil	20.9	58.2
Egypt	20.5	57.4
India	20.5	58.8
Indonesia	21.1	59.9
Kenya	14.3	45.5
Liberia	15.8	49.0
Mexico	18.2	53.6
Nigeria	16.1	49.7
Pakistan	17.7	53.2
Zimbabwe	16.1	49.6

Source: UN
Note: [1] *Working age is defined as between 15 and 64 years*

The possibility that the economies of developing countries can grow fast enough to keep up with their population is remote. Most face the double constraints of commodity dependence and external debt. But this is only part of their problem. Countries in Africa and Latin America are still in a phase of demographic development where birth rates remain high although death rates are falling as improved health care brings longer life expectancy and fewer deaths at birth. Under such conditions the population of these countries will obviously grow rapidly. Developed countries such as the UK or USA took decades to pass through the same phase before their populations began to stabilise or decline. Many developing countries may require another 60 years before they, too, are able to stabilise their populations. A long period is needed even if women maintain only "replacement-level fertility" (that is, slightly more than two children per family). The large proportion of children approaching the age of procreation is a major reason for the lengthy transitional period to population stability.

What can developing countries do to reduce their population growth rates to those prevailing in developed countries? China's policies represent an extreme approach that is unlikely to serve as a model for other Third World countries. In 1979 China introduced a programme of incentives for late marriages reinforced by penalities for couples having more than one child. Parents often preferred their only child to be a boy; as many as 250,000 unwanted girls are thought to have been killed before their births were registered. China's policy may also lead to unexpected hardships for its elderly: they cannot depend on the government for support but must rely entirely on their families. The Chinese experience suggests that effective population control does not, by itself, ensure a successful transition to a stage where the population is stable or grows very little. India's experience with its sterilisation programme in the 1970s reveals the danger of such methods in less authoritarian societies. Not only did India's methods have little effect on the birth rate but they created serious social and political problems.

It was once thought that an extensive network of family planning facilities throughout a country could be as effective as more authoritarian policies. Implicitly, this premise attributed the spread of new forms of contraception to the fall in the European birth rate in the 1970s. Although the timing of the two trends coincided, it now appears that European methods of contraception had no appreciable effect on the decline in birth rates. Some developing countries where family-planning programmes have been widely praised are still experiencing exponential rates of population growth. In Mexico one million young Mexicans will enter the job market each year for the remainder of this century. Not surprisingly, the country's unemployment rate has doubled since 1982. Mexico's population explosion has dissipated much of the benefit of its "Green Revolution" in agriculture and its emergence as a major oil exporter.

The emphasis on family planning has now given way to a more complex but credible strategy intended to change the values of a society. Essentially, the new strategy maintains that population control will be successful only if people - male and female - believe that family planning will help them to achieve a richer life. This attitude is not so widespread as many might expect: fertility surveys carried out in 1984 found that only 5% of Nigerian women wanted no more children while in the Ivory Coast the figure was 4%. Other evidence suggests that even these estimates may be low. But whatever the actual percentage, a much lower proportion of males than females seem to be willing to accept smaller families. In male-dominated societies the husbands usually determine the number of children. Successful family planning requires men to recognise the benefits of having fewer children.

II Investment and Foreign Savings

If the economies of developing countries are to expand at rates that will at least match the growth of population, levels of investment will have to rise. However, in recent years investment spending has been depressed and is a major reason for the slow growth of output in the Third World. Several factors contribute to the lack of investment spending: domestic economic circumstances, the cessation of bank financing and the cumulative effects of past indebtedness.

Through efficient use of the investment share in GDP the developing countries can themselves do much to improve their growth performance. Table 3.2 shows average rates of saving, investment and trends in the incremental capital:output ratio (ICOR). Investment rates in capital-importing developing countries have slipped after rising in the 1970s. As external sources of financing began to dry up, investment bore a disproportionate share of the burden. Among commercial borrowers with debt-servicing problems, investment suffered even more. In these countries much of the additional financing of the late 1970s was already being used to offset a fall in savings rates while investment was allowed to decline. Once external financing became difficult in the 1980s, investment fell drastically as savings rates continued to decline. Such trends suggest a tendency for consumption to be safeguarded at the expense of investment. The relative importance placed on consumption over investment was pronounced as a result of cutbacks in external financing in the early 1980s. Although per capita consumption was maintained in countries with debt-servicing problems, per capita investment fell dramatically.

Table 3.2   AVERAGE RATES OF SAVING, INVESTMENT AND ICORs[1] IN
CAPITAL-IMPORTING DEVELOPING COUNTRIES 1973-1986

% of GDP				
	1973-7	1978-80	1981-2	1983-6
All developing countries				
Savings	24.0	24.0	20.9	20.9
Investment	26.2	27.0	25.2	22.2
Inverse of ICOR	2.2	1.8	0.9	1.6
Countries with recent debt-servicing problems				
Commercial borrowers[2]				
Savings	23.7	22.9	18.9	17.5
Investment	26.4	26.6	24.6	18.4
Inverse of ICOR	2.3	2.3	0.3	1.6
Official borrowers[3]				
Savings	8.1	8.4	4.1	6.0
Investment	13.0	14.4	13.1	12.6
Inverse of ICOR	2.7	0.7	0.7	1.5

Source: IMF

Notes: [1] *Inverse ICOR, calculated as the ratio of the average growth of GDP to the
share of GDP devoted to gross investment, multiplied by ten*
[2] *Countries classified by the IMF as either market or diversified borrowers*
[3] *Countries that obtained two-thirds or more of their external borrowings from
official creditors between 1978 and 1982*

The effects of declining rates of growth in investment have been
magnified by a fall in investment efficiency. The measure of
efficiency used here is the inverse of the ICOR, which represents
the additional output associated with incremental additions to
capital stock. The inverse ICORs for capital-importing countries
showed little change from the early 1970s until the 1980s.

Afterwards they declined reflecting the adjustment problems in countries with debt-servicing problems. All countries had similar ICORs in the early 1970s but the differences which began to emerge in later years reflect varying degrees of investment efficiency.

Trends in investment have been strongly influenced by the availability of foreign savings. During 1970-81, gross inflows of foreign savings were on average about 4% of the GDP of developing countries. The supply of foreign savings originates from two sources. One group, official creditors and private direct investors, tends to focus on long-term developments. The flow of funds from this group reflects the long-term nature of their lending commitments and has remained relatively stable. The other group consists of private lenders who have a much shorter-term perspective governed largely by capital market considerations. Table 3.3 shows that gross inflows of foreign savings fell away sharply following the emergence of the debt crisis - especially for commercial borrowers.

Table 3.3   GROSS AND NET INFLOWS OF FOREIGN SAVINGS[1] 1970-1986

period averages as % of GDP

	Gross inflows			Net inflows		
	1970-9	1980-1	1982-6	1970-9	1980-1	1982-6
Developing countries	3.8	5.0	3.0	0.4	0.3	1.9
Countries with recent debt-servicing problems[2]	4.9	7.0	3.1	3.4	4.9	2.3
Commercial borrowers	4.9	6.9	2.7	3.4	4.6	1.9
Official borrowers	5.2	9.5	7.5	4.1	8.3	6.9

Continued...

65

Table 3.3 cont'd

	Gross inflows			Net inflows		
	1970-9	1980-1	1982-6	1970-9	1980-1	1982-6
Countries without recent debt-servicing problems[2]	3.7	4.5	3.0	1.4	2.4	1.6
Commercial borrowers	3.5	4.5	2.9	1.2	2.3	1.4
Official borrowers	6.0	4.4	3.6	4.1	2.8	2.7

Source: IMF
Notes: [1] *Gross inflows of foreign savings less residents' purchases of foreign assets equals net inflows of foreign savings*
[2] *Country sub-groups are defined as in Table 3.2*

Countries that borrowed mainly from commercial sources did well in the 1970s; the impressive rates of growth in the borrowers' economies were taken to indicate that the investments were efficient. Moreover, because debts were not large and interest rates were low, debt-servicing obligations were modest and credit-worthiness was not a concern. Official borrowers, by contrast, were generally too poor to borrow large sums at market terms. Investment in the latter countries was limited to levels that could be financed from domestic savings. These circumstances changed drastically by the 1980s. Debts had grown and concerns about credit worthiness were heightened by sharp increases in rates of interest. Spontaneous private lending fell abruptly. Many official borrowers also incurred problems in adjusting to the unfavourable global climate.

Reversing the recent decline in investment rates and the deterioration in investment efficiency is now a major task facing policymakers. Both macroeconomic and structural policies have a role to play in governments' efforts to boost investment rates and improve the efficiency of investment. In the first instance, policies will have to raise domestic savings rates and ensure that funds are channelled to the most promising investment opportunities. Domestic investors, too, must be rewarded. Finally, policies ensuring that investment reflects economic rather than non-economic considerations are necessary if projects are not to be a drain on the economy. In the second instance, market-determined interest rates and exchange rates are likely to be important structural signals. Both types of policy moves must be reinforced by close attention to the level and range of government spending.

III Inflation

Along with the slow growth of output and deteriorating living standards, the failure to contain inflation has been a lasting problem for many Third World countries. This failure is in marked contrast to the success of industrial countries, which have steadily reduced the rate of price increases in the 1980s.

Table 3.4 shows that in 1982 inflation exceeded 20% a year in 20 of 76 developing countries. The experience of individual countries has in fact been quite varied. Several (28 in 1986) managed to hold their inflation to rates of 5% or less, but at the same time a growing number have experienced runaway rates greater than 20%. By 1987 a total of 25 developing countries were facing price increases of 20% or more. Surging inflation occurred even in countries with records of greater price stability in earlier years. The inability to control inflation appears to reflect large slippages in implementing policies for demand restraint. The future pattern of price movements in some of these countries is uncertain as it has become difficult to sustain the shock effect that contributed to the initial success of the programmes.

Table 3.4   INFLATION IN DEVELOPING COUNTRIES 1971-1986

number of countries

	1971-80	1981-6	1982	1983	1984	1985	1986	1987 [2]
Inflation rates[1]								
5% and lower	0	12	6	14	18	22	28	24
5 to 10%	26	22	24	19	15	13	13	15
10 to 20%	41	20	26	22	16	16	11	12
20 to 50%	7	13	13	12	15	14	13	14
50 to 100%	2	4	4	2	7	4	8	4
over 100%	0	5	3	7	5	7	3	7

Source: UN
Notes: [1] *Measured by consumer price indices of 76 countries*
[2] *Preliminary*

The resumption of inflation was most evident in Latin America. After a slowdown in 1986, several countries faced rates of price escalation sometimes exceeding 100%. High rates of inflation in Argentina and Brazil reflect the collapse in 1987 of these two countries' recovery strategies - the "austral" and "cruzado" plans (see Chapter 5). Inflationary pressures in other countries were exacerbated because price and exchange rate adjustments were not adequately buttressed by measures of demand restraint.

Third World countries' efforts to control inflation fall into two broad groups: a heterodox approach, and a more conventional programme relying on fiscal and monetary controls. The heterodox approach begins from the idea that inflation has its own inertia: without controls, prices would continue to rise at the current rate indefinitely. Advocates of this version maintain that inflation feeds on itself through widespread indexation and the effects of price increases on expectations. They argue that temporary price and wage controls are useful because these remove the inertia, allowing the economy to shift from high to low inflation.

In contrast to the heterodox approach, the orthodox cure for inflation control calls for a fiscal and monetary squeeze. Tight money policies force up interest rates and cut back on consumer and investment spending from borrowed funds. These steps may be combined with higher taxes and reduced government spending to cut budget deficits and further restrict consumer and investment demand. Such anti-inflation programmes have sometimes worked well but are found to entail heavy costs in terms of lost output and higher unemployment.

Though no one approach has proved to be singularly effective, the varied experiences of developing countries suggest that efforts to curb inflation cannot be successful without reducing budget deficits. Wage and price controls can be a relatively painless way to curb inflation, but only if underpinned by budget cuts. Trade union support for a wage freeze also appears to be essential. Finally, it seems easier to implement inflation-control programmes in small economies than in large, diversified ones like Brazil or Argentina.

IV Taxes and Government Revenues

Problems such as hyperinflation and mounting budget deficits are usually accompanied by meagre government revenues. In 1985 the tax revenues raised by low-income developing countries were equivalent to only 15% of GNP. Figure 3.1 shows that this percentage has been roughly constant since 1975. A higher proportion of income is allocated to taxes in middle-income developing countries: about 17% in 1975, rising ten years later to 20%. Neither of these two groups of developing countries can match the share of GNP collected through taxes by Western industrialised countries, where government revenues rose from 27% of GNP in 1975 to over 32% in 1985.

Figure 3.1   TAXES AS A PERCENTAGE OF GNP 1975-1985

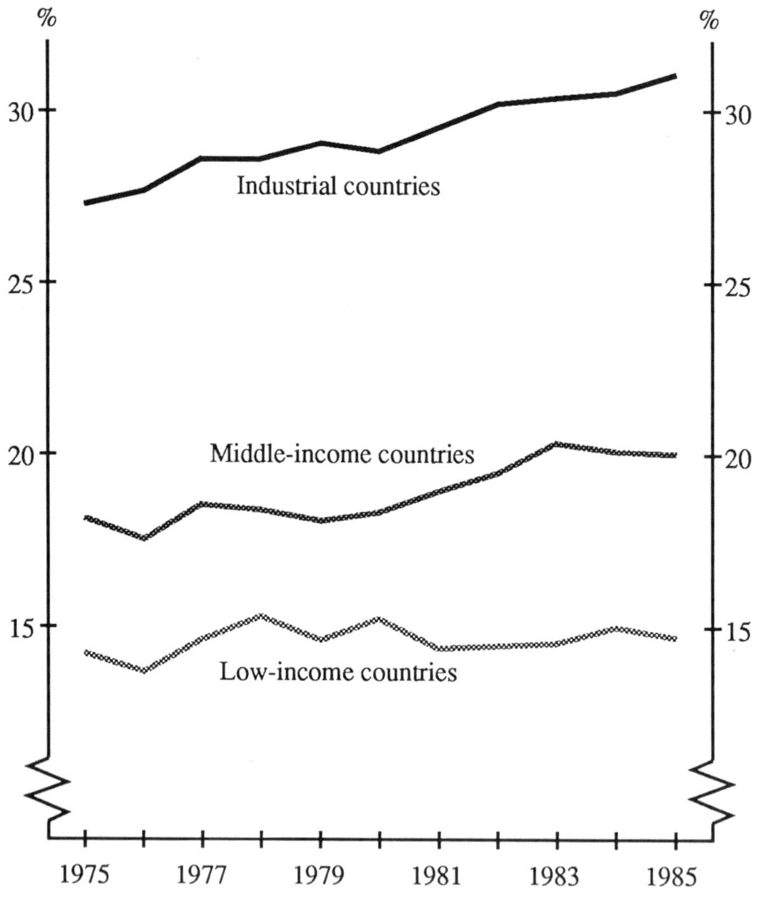

Source: World Bank

70

Although the tax burdens of developing countries are light, their systems of revenue collection create problems which businesses and consumers in developed countries do not encounter. One of these undesirable effects results from the narrow base on which taxes are applied. When a relatively few firms and/or consumers are required to pay taxes, the tax rate tends to be higher. This in turn means that the distorting effects of the tax are accentuated.

The fact that the high tax rate is levied on a very few also leads to avoidance and evasion. Recent studies have shown that in developing countries with a narrow personal income tax base as little as a third of the families eligible to pay taxes actually did so. The problem is illustrated by the experience of India where avoidance has persisted despite the government's recent liberalisation of the tax structure. It is estimated that illegal funds held by Indians totalled 370 billion rupees in 1983-4, or about 20% of gross national product (GNP). Huge amounts of illegal funds are held abroad. Indian deposits in Swiss bank accounts stood at 13.22 billion rupees at the end of 1985. The problem is a general one: an estimated 80% of taxable income actually remains unreported in many Third World countries.

A third problem is that the most common types of taxes used in developing countries are precisely those forms that penalise important activities such as exporting. Developed countries raise more than half their revenue from personal income taxes and social security taxes. Developing countries, however, rely more heavily on company taxes and taxes on trade (with the poorest countries depending mainly on the latter). A related weakness is that company taxes are sensitive to the effects of inflation. This sensitivity means that the tax on income earned from incremental investment varies widely from one industry to another. For those paying the highest marginal rate, investment is discouraged. Trade taxes (eg import duties) can create even more serious distortions. These are relatively easy to collect but they raise prices in the domestic market, both for final goods and industrial inputs. The increase in prices of final goods will mean that firms often prefer to sell in their home market and forgo exports. The increase in costs due to tariffs on imported inputs means that firms are less competitive and makes exporting more difficult.

These undesirable side effects can be avoided once developing countries turn to broadly based commodity taxes or value added taxes (VAT). Roughly 20 countries (mainly in Latin America) now have VAT down to the retail level. Where primitive distribution networks make taxes difficult to collect at the retail level, countries have introduced VAT at the manufacturer/importer stage. India greatly simplified its tax system by introducing a manufacturing-stage VAT as part of a tax reform in 1986. Some African countries, too, have turned to VAT at the manufacturing stage.

V International Constraints on Macroeconomic Policies

In recent years monetary and credit policies in most Third World countries have been geared to reducing inflation. Table 3.5 shows a sharp deceleration in growth of broad money aggregates in 1986, which largely reflects anti-inflationary measures taken in high-inflation economies. This was especially true for Latin American countries (eg Argentina, Bolivia and Brazil) where the growth of broad money supplies was nearly halved in 1986. Rates of monetary expansion also declined in other regions (especially in West Asia and Africa) though much more moderately than in Latin America. Because many developing countries face severe constraints on sources of external borrowing, they have increased their reliance on domestic sources of finance. This shift has accelerated the slowdown in growth of domestic credit supplied to the private sector.

Table 3.5   GROWTH OF BROAD MONEY AGGREGATES 1979-1986

% annual change

	1979	1980	1981	1982	1983	1984	1985	1986
Africa	15.4	26.2	19.4	17.5	16.4	18.9	17.7	12.3
South and East Asia	25.3	27.3	20.2	18.6	19.5	24.7	18.2	16.4
West Asia	27.0	32.7	31.4	20.5	16.6	20.4	13.7	7.9
Latin America	61.0	59.1	74.6	82.6	102.4	141.4	150.0	85.1
TOTAL	33.9	37.5	37.5	35.9	37.8	49.4	46.2	31.5

Source: IMF

Though external constraints have had only a moderate influence on monetary policy in developing countries, they have played a much greater role in the case of fiscal policy. The need to adjust to terms of trade losses has been a major factor forcing countries to tighten their financial policies. The terms of trade effects on fiscal balances can be best illustrated when countries are distinguished according to whether their major exports are fuels or non-fuels. Table 3.6 indicates central government fiscal balances as a percentage of GDP. Efforts to tighten fiscal policy are not readily apparent since cutbacks in government spending occurred at a time of pronounced weakness in export prices. Many countries depend heavily on revenues from trade taxes (eg tariffs). Therefore, cuts in expenditures were often sufficient to offset only part of the losses from these receipts. The combined central government deficits of developing countries had been declining throughout the first half of this decade and by 1985 were 4.6% of GDP. In 1986, however, deficits rose to 6% of total income. This reversal is attributable mainly to the significant deterioration of the fiscal situation of fuel-exporting countries although increases in the fiscal deficits of some exporters of manufactures or primary products also contributed to the overall rise.

Table 3.6   CENTRAL GOVERNMENT FISCAL BALANCES 1985-1986

% of GDP	1985	1986
All developing countries		
Revenues	22.9	21.3
Expenditures	27.5	27.3
Balance	-4.6	-6.0
Fuel-exporting countries		
Revenues	27.7	23.4
Expenditures	33.7	33.5
Balance	-6.0	-10.1
Non-fuel-exporting countries		
Revenues	20.6	20.3
Expenditures	24.6	24.4
Balance	-4.0	-4.1

Source: IMF

Differences in the fiscal situation of various groups of Third World countries can largely be explained by the external factors affecting them. In fuel exporting countries, for instance, oil income accounts for roughly 60% of government revenues. Declines in oil prices have led to correspondingly large falls in government receipts. Despite their previous efforts at fiscal retrenchment and import restraint,

74

further cuts in expenditure were forced on these countries as a result of the fall in oil prices.

The impact of external developments on the fiscal position of non-fuel exporters has been mixed. Lower export prices exerted a depressing effect on government revenues but this was at least partly offset by lower international interest rates. Countries that depreciated their currencies in order to promote greater competitiveness benefited through an increase in the domestic currency value of taxes levied on international trade but, for the same reason, had to raise more domestic revenue to cover foreign interest payments. The most heavily indebted countries reaped the greatest benefit from the decline in international interest rates as they held the largest amounts of floating rate debt.

For exporters of manufactures, this relaxation of financial pressure coincided with a healthy revival of foreign demand which enabled them to adopt a more broadly neutral fiscal stance. The experience of primary exporters has been far less favourable. The stagnation of export earnings and fiscal revenues in many of the poorer African and Asian countries has forced an increase in budget deficits despite attempts to curb spending. Some primary exporters fared better, however. For example, a number of coffee producing countries improved their fiscal position because of the strong gains in export earnings and associated revenues.

VI Privatisation

The issue of privatisation has been a recurrent feature of the industrial debate in both industrialised countries and the Third World. Although the approach to privatisation varies with the country and the industries involved, there are certain common themes, methods and weaknesses. After discussing these, the recent experiences of several developing countries are examined.

The post-World War II period witnessed an enormous expansion of government ownership as developing countries rushed to create the sort of economic base they hoped would lead them to economic prosperity. By the 1970s the weaknesses of public sector institutions had become apparent. The widespread influence of governments came to be questioned as the inability of economies to adjust to external price shocks led to a deterioration of macroeconomic performance. This reassessment brought about a reversal of policy positions in many countries. Privatisation - the transfer of public sector activities to the private sector - has been frequently discussed in this context.

Surprisingly, perhaps, privatisation is essentially an industrialised country phenomenon; the extent is much less in developing countries. Public ownership in the Third World is still regarded as essential because of the underdeveloped nature of resources and markets. The consequences in terms of efficiency, however, are sometimes adverse. Developing countries are gradually turning to privatisation as a means of achieving some retrenchment of the public sector.

Though up to 15 developing countries have now embarked on privatisation programmes, enterprise sales have been few. Even when these programmes are defined to include leasing, contracting out and other activities in addition to the sale of assets, the results are modest. Part of the reason is that few enterprises are suitable candidates for privatisation. The most inefficient loss-makers are seldom attractive to the private sector; resources may not be available to finance the sales; or interested buyers are unacceptable because they belong to particular ethnic or religious groups, or because they are foreigners.

The process can be helped by innovations such as debt-to-equity conversions (see eg Chapter 4, section III). But governments cannot simply turn firms over to the domestic or external private sector; it is also necessary to create an environment where resource allocation can be guided by greater reliance on market signals. Another complicating factor is that the case for privatisation is not as clear as it is often made out to be, and the instances where it is the appropriate policy option are frequently limited.

Privatisation can be part of a broader effort to enhance market forces, decentralise decision-making responsibilities and improve the allocation of resources. Paradoxically, a critical part of a successful programme is to improve public sector management. Government must be capable of managing divestiture, regulating monopolies and delivering efficient services. Given all the complications of the process and the variety of circumstances required, it is not surprising that efforts to privatise parts of the public sector in developing countries have progressed very slowly.

Latin America

Latin American countries have gone furthest in their efforts to privatise industries. The region has a long history of import substitution. Many firms started out as state enterprises and continued to be publicly owned operations long afterward. Latin America also has the most sophisticated and diverse industrial base in the Third World and the number of state-owned firms is large. Finally, many Latin American governments have in the past strongly opposed multinationals and, in doing so, have often nationalised firms or created state-run competitors. For all those reasons, Latin America came to have a relatively large public sector. As the growth of world income slowed and the effects of the debt crisis mounted, the strategy placed a great strain on federal budgets and forced authorities to seek ways to reduce the government's involvement in industry.

The Mexican government has long been saying that it wants to sell off public sector enterprises, but with few exceptions progress has been slow. The government boasted that in early 1982 it inherited over 1,100 public enterprises but cut the number to 400 over the next five years. Most of the reduction, however, came from the dissolution or merger of small firms, or the transfer of companies from federal to state government or to government-affiliated unions. Such sales had little impact on the federal budget or public employment.

Like other countries, the Mexican government has wanted to sell its money-losers first, though businessmen wanted to buy only the profitable ones. Other problems are unique to Mexico: a shortage of capital means that the most frequent bidders for companies are foreigners; another handicap is the close ties between Mexico's ruling party and the trade unions. Feather-bedding and inefficiency are widespread in many state-owned companies and breaking labour contracts is politically difficult.

Mexico renewed its efforts to privatise the public sector in 1987. Foreign firms such as Chrysler and Kobe Steel received permission to purchase government firms, a state-owned airline was declared bankrupt and sold off and debt-equity swaps were used to dispose of other companies. The dissolution of still more state-owned operations is likely to follow. Candidates include the country's largest steel company, firms producing newsprint, fertiliser manufactures and the country's telephone company.

The share of state-owned enterprises in Brazil is much larger than in most Latin American countries, roughly 60% in 1986. Furthermore, the role of the state as an operator of businesses is well established and support for privatisation is not great. In 1987 the government had a list of some 65 enterprises earmarked for sale to the private sector. Significantly, these firms represented only 5% of total assets in the state-owned public sector.

78

Chile has embraced the strategy of privatisation more vigorously than most Latin American countries. It had already reduced the share of value added by state enterprises from 39% in 1972 to about 24% by 1981. In the 1980s the privatisation programme has received a boost from the country's efforts to reduce its foreign debts. When Chile sold off its telephone system, national electricity grid and even its state-owned insurance company, it allowed foreigners to buy portions of the companies with the foreign debt they had previously accumulated.

Similar success cannot be found in Argentina although public sector firms operate at a substantial loss. The borrowing requirements of government-owned firms amounted to 3.9% of GDP in 1987. One problem is the high rate of worker absenteeism in the public sector, running at 20-25%. Several state industries were swept into a holding company in 1988 and told to expect nothing from the central government except external debt payments. Argentina's authorities are trying to privatise two of the largest of these firms - the sale of a stake in Aerolines Argentinas to Scandinavia's SAS and the purchase of Entel by Spain's Telefonica.

South and East Asia

Privatisation programmes in South and East Asia differ somewhat from those in Latin America. The fact that many countries in the region rely heavily on exports for growth has put a premium on efficiency. Economies that choose to compete vigorously in international markets can ill afford to have inefficient state-run industries. In Asian countries which have relied on strategies of import substitution, the size of the public sector is relatively large and the opportunities for privatisation are greater. There are numerous privatisation deals though very few involve firms as big as those in Mexico, Chile or Brazil.

Asian countries with a relatively large public sector which have considered or even experimented with privatisation include India, Indonesia and the Philippines. Talk of privatisation in India has met fierce ideological opposition, however. Soon after independence in 1947, it was decided that the public sector should control the "commanding heights" of the economy, including most of heavy industry and defence. India's public sector became large, accounting for 66% of all fixed capital investment in 1986 and 27% of industrial output. The fact that India's state-owned industries were recording net annual losses of 2 billion rupees ($160 million) forced the government to reconsider its traditional strategy. India quietly began to use the private sector in several ways to remedy the worst deficiences of its state-owned industries.

The government has sought to recruit private sector businessmen to run its publicly owned firms. Though public sector pay is a problem, some progress has been made in this area. The private sector is being allowed to invest in areas formerly reserved for state-owned firms, including power, communications and mainframe computers. Finally, profitable public sector companies are now being allowed to borrow from the markets. Despite these efforts, India's public sector is still immense and powerful interest groups support it for reasons of ideology or profit. Private industrialists enjoy profitable deals or public sector construction, maintenance and supply contracts. And the public sector's trade unions are strong, providing the votes and support infrastructure for political campaigns. Faced with such resistance, India's approach to privatisation will continue to be cautious and, at most, piecemeal.

Indonesia's efforts at privatisation arise from the government's desire to reduce the power of some of the big state monopolies which grew up during the era of high oil prices. The government wants to dismantle many of the monopolies in steel, construction, fertilisers, pesticides and other important industries. These state-run enterprises often enjoy exclusive rights to import, produce or distribute essential goods and raw materials. Policymakers also see privatisation as a way to deal with the recurrent charges of corruption in state industry, a practice which is also widespread in India but has received less publicity.

However, the issue of privatisation in Indonesia is only a peripheral one in a wide-ranging debate. As in India, the government's state-run industries have created a web of business privilege and power. Attempts to break up these monopolies and sell parts to the private sector would face great opposition. Instead, long-running arguments between government technocrats and monopoly representatives have usually been limited to proposals to liberalise parts of the monopoly system, for example deregulating imports and opening up distribution systems.

China's reform programmes also include privatisation although such steps represent a much more dramatic departure from customary policies than is true for either India or Indonesia. Chinese economists argue that to revitalise the economy, the government must withdraw completely from direct enterprise management, allow bankruptcies and layoffs to enforce stricter financial discipline. Policies such as these would have a great impact on a country where 60% of the value of industrial output is supplied by state enterprises. Moreover, these firms employ more than half the urban workforce, account for 85% of urban industrial investment in fixed assets and contribute 85% of industrial profits and taxes.

China's programme of industrial reform began in 1979 at the same time as its highly successful agricultural reform (discussed in Chapter 11). But the industrial reform, including privatisation, has been implemented at a much slower and more timid pace. Leasing of small state enterprises and the issue of stock to state workers are examples of some of the experiments to find a politically acceptable socialist framework for denationalisation. As semi-independent, profit-orientated economic entities, state factories scramble to

81

produce popular goods. A drawback is that factory managers and workers concentrate on short-term profits and bonuses rather than being concerned with a plant's long-term development. The attitude results from the fact that these groups have only a limited financial stake in the plant and little authority for its longer-term performance. Technical modernisation, productivity improvement and long-term investment are all part of the state's responsibility, not that of the factory.

Although semi-independent enterprises have not necessarily proved to be any less of a burden on the state's finances, their numbers are growing. In 1987 China had 98,000 state-owned enterprises (almost all of them large) along with 1.85 million collectives and 5.6 million private and mostly small firms. It is the collective industries which have been growing; their share of industrial output rose from 19.2% in 1978 to 34.6% in 1987. Collective enterprises, unlike state-owned firms, must find their own raw materials, labour and markets. This struggle for survival has built up the competitive abilities of the collectives. Though international experience has shown that privatisation (in the capitalist sense) can be one solution for ailing industries, it is not really a feasible form for communist China. Government authorities prefer forms of collective, social ownership with the government, individuals and various groups sharing ownership.

The need for privatisation is less pressing in countries such as South Korea or Taiwan. One of the few important privatisation decisions in the East Asian sub-region has been Korea's plan for the part sale of its largest state-owned steel firm, the Pohang Iron and Steel Company (Posco). The government's decision to relinquish some of its ownership in the firm, which is discussed more extensively in Chapter 10, is not an attempt to reduce state subsidies or improve efficiency. Posco, in fact, is highly profitable. Korean banks were expected to sell their shares in Posco in order to build an equity cushion. This would allow the banks to write off some of their many bad debts, which have weakened the Korean financial system.

Africa and West Asia

Attempts at privatisation in Africa are far less advanced, and such programmes are not to be found in West Asia. Many African countries are revising their entire approach to industry and privatisation is sometimes an element in the new policy structure (though not a major one). An example is found in Togo, where the government has had a programme of privatisation since 1983. Prior to that time, Togo had 72 state enterprises, but by the end of 1987 the government had sold five of these, leased four more and sold a majority share in another two. Eleven more were closed or liquidated. For the most part, however, African policy reforms have adopted means other than privatisation, such as making the structure of policies neutral, introducing more realistic exchange rates and exposing industry to more international competition (see Chapter 7, section II).

CHAPTER 4

ECONOMIC PERFORMANCE AND TRENDS IN LATIN AMERICA

When pictured as a single region, Latin America is the most developed and industrialised part of the Third World. However, the region's long-standing reliance on import substitution as the major strategy for growth, its mounting government deficits and ineffective systems of inflation control have all impinged on economic growth. In the 1980s Latin America fell behind other areas of the Third World in its economic performance. The region was plagued by dismal rates of growth, a fall in both savings and investment, high amounts of international debt and an inefficient industrial base.

Table 4.1 summarises the main economic features of countries in the region. Three countries - Argentina, Brazil and Mexico - account for the bulk of Latin America's inhabitants and have a combined population (250 million) roughly equivalent to that of the USA. Per capita GDP is highest among the larger economies and the oil exporters. Medium-sized countries and several small Central American and Caribbean countries are the region's poorest. Haiti is the poorest country shown in Table 4.1. Though its per capita GDP was only $330 in 1986, there are 20 poorer African countries and it is placed above Kenya and Sierra Leone, both of which are comfortably well off by African standards.

When debt is measured as a share of GNP, major debtors include Jamaica (189%), Guyana (169%) and Bolivia (140%). Several of the countries with the largest foreign debt obligations - Argentina, Brazil, Mexico and Colombia - have lower debt-to-GNP ratios but their ability to service these loans is very limited. Many economies

Table 4.1   ECONOMIC INDICATORS FOR LATIN AMERICA[1] 1986

	Population (million)	GDP per capita ($)	Growth of GDP 1980-6 (annual average (%)	Trade balance[2] ($ million)	Ratio of debt to GNP[3] (%)	Direct investment in country ($ million)
Argentina	31.0	2,350	-0.8	2,456.6	61.8	574.9
Belize	0.2	1,170	na	-16.5	56.8	1.1
Bolivia	6.6	540	-3.0	160.6 [3]	140.1	10.0 [3]
Brazil	138.4	1,810	2.7	12,411.5 [3]	43.9	1,361.6 [3]
Chile	12.3	1,430	0.0	1,099.3	120.0	59.8
Colombia	29.0	1,230	2.4	1,890.0	33.2	673.4
Costa Rica	2.7	1,420	1.3	41.8	110.4	66.9
Dominican Republic	6.6	710	1.1	-544.1	81.6	50.0
Ecuador	9.6	1,160	1.8	554.9	61.0	70.0
El Salvador	4.9	820	-1.0	-216.0 [3]	45.5	12.4 [3]
Guatemala	8.2	930	-1.2	173.2	30.2	67.5
Guyana	0.8	500	na	5.0 [3]	169.0	1.8

Continued...

Table 4.1 cont'd

	Population (million)	GDP per capita ($)	Growth of GDP 1980-6 (annual average (%)	Trade balance[2] ($ million)	Ratio of debt to GNP[3] (%)	Direct investment + in country ($ million)
Haiti	6.0	330	-0.7	-140.3	31.1	5.0
Honduras	4.5	740	0.6	1.2	78.2	30.0
Jamaica	2.3	880	0.0	-435.6	189.5	-9.0
Mexico	80.8	1,850	0.4	4,576.5	45.2	895.1
Nicaragua	3.4	790	0.2	-541.0	98.0	-
Panama	2.2	2,330	2.6	-542.4	18.0	-3.9
Paraguay	3.8	820	1.1	-162.4	65.0	31.6
Peru	19.0	1,130	-0.4	-3.5	74.1	19.9
Surinam	0.4	2,510	na	54.2	4.3	-33.2
Trinidad and Tobago	1.2	5,120	-6.3	153.7	21.9	-14.5
Uruguay	3.0	1,870	-2.6	296.8	58.9	-
Venezuela	17.8	2,930	-0.9	814.2	35.4	16.4

Source: World Bank

Note: [1] Countries included in this region but not shown here are: Antigua and Barbuda, Bahamas, Barbados, Bermuda, Cuba, Netherlands Antilles, Saint Lucia, St Kitts-Nevis and St Vincent-Grenadines

[2] Exports (fob) less imports (fob)

[3] 1985

with heavy debts have experienced a form of "import compression" as they struggle to earn the foreign exchange necessary to meet debts. It is this reduction in imports, just as much as an improved export performance, which explains recent improvements in the trade balances of several countries. Like levels of foreign debt, the largest favourable trade balance is claimed by Brazil, followed by Mexico, Argentina and Colombia. Finally, levels of direct investment vary greatly among the region's economies, being concentrated in the four or five larger economies.

Subsequent sections of this chapter look at the main features of the region's economy. Section I deals with the composition and direction of trade. Industry and industrial progress is the focus of section II. Investment in Latin America has been severely handicapped by levels of foreign debt and other problems, both domestic and international; this subject is surveyed in section III. Section IV deals with the unique set of countries in the Caribbean and the forms of international assistance offered to these island countries.

I Trade Performance and Trading Patterns

Latin America has experienced wide swings in growth rates for imports and exports. Year-to-year changes have been especially erratic in the 1980s. Table 4.2 shows that both exports and imports dropped significantly in several recent years. The volatile pattern of annual movements of trade flows was only part of a larger problem. After declining gradually for several years, the terms of trade plummeted in 1986, reaching a low of only 79% of the 1980 level. These trends are in sharp contrast to those of the 1970s, when the region's trade expanded at a pace which roughly matched the development of world trade while the movements of prices for traded goods posed no serious problems.

Table 4.2 GROWTH OF EXPORTS, IMPORTS AND TERMS OF
TRADE IN LATIN AMERICA 1975-1986

% change

	1975-86[1]	1982	1983	1984	1985	1986
Growth of exports	7.7	-12.8	1.5	6.5	-6.4	-13.3
Growth of imports	3.7	-18.0	-22.3	2.0	-2.4	3.3
Terms of trade[2] (1980 = 100)	-	93	92	93	90	79

Source: UNCTAD
Note: [1] *Average annual rate*
[2] *Ratio of export unit value index to import unit value index*

Overall trade performance depends, in part, on conditions in the
major markets that buy Latin America's exports and supply its
imports. Directions of Latin American trade are summarised in
Table 4.3. The bulk of the region's trade is with developed market
economies (mainly the USA). Although this share has been falling,
more than 58% of Latin America's imports came from developed
market economies in 1985 while 65% of its exports went to these
countries. Expansion of the North American market provided a
major boost to the region's exporters in the 1980s. Most of this was
due to increased sale of fuels (mainly from Mexico to the USA)
during the years before 1986. Exports of manufactures also rose
sharply as Latin American producers took advantage of the
expanding North American market. During 1980-6, manufactured
exports to the north increased by 15% per annum. Fuels account for
the largest export category in the case of West Europe but food
exports, too, have grown most rapidly, followed by manufactures.
Latin America's exports to socialist countries are relatively small.

Cuban exports of sugar and Argentine exports of meat, both to the USSR, account for more than half the region's total sales to socialist countries.

Table 4.3   LATIN AMERICA'S TRADE STRUCTURE BY ORIGIN
             AND DESTINATION 1970-1985[1]

%	Developed market economies	Socialist countries	Developing countries	of which: Intra-region
Imports				
1970	74.6	5.0	19.9	16.3
1975	64.7	4.4	30.7	16.1
1985	58.4	7.0	33.9	17.9
Exports				
1970	73.8	5.8	19.4	17.3
1975	65.9	8.1	23.8	19.5
1985	65.0	8.1	24.2	16.5

Source: UNCTAD
Note: [1] *Excludes trade with socialist developing countries*

The share of the region's imports from other developing countries has grown steadily since the mid-1970s and presently amounts to just over one-third of the aggregate. In return, Latin America sent nearly a quarter of its exports to other developing countries. Asia is the most important and rapidly growing market for Latin American exports to other Third World regions. Exports to China have more than doubled in the 1980s. By the beginning of 1986, China was purchasing about one-fifth of Latin America's exports to Asia, mainly from Argentina, Brazil, Chile and Mexico. Markets in Hong Kong and Taiwan have also grown rapidly in the 1980s.

Intra-regional trade accounts for a larger portion of the Latin American total than for other developing regions. In 1985 intra-regional imports were almost 18% of all imports, or more than a half of imports from all developing countries. Intra-regional exports were two-thirds of all goods shipped to developing countries, equivalent to 16.5% of Latin America's world exports. Because intra-regional markets account for nearly a fifth of the Latin American total, the impaired import capacity of many of these markets has limited overall export performance in the 1980s.

The composition of traded goods is another determinant of trade performance. Table 4.4 shows Latin America's trade broken down into five categories. The share of food items in the region's exports has fallen from 41% in 1970 to 29% in 1985. This decline, along with a similar drop in export shares for ores and metals, reflects the region's efforts to restructure its trade base as well as a relative deterioration in international prices for both categories since the late 1970s. These shifts were offset by a rise in the export share of manufactures, which more than doubled between 1970 and 1985. Fuels, however, continue to be the largest category, accounting for slightly more than a third of all Latin America's exports. On the import side, over half the regional total is made up of manufactures, down from two-thirds in 1970s. These goods, together with fuels, amounted to 79% of all imports in 1985. The most disconcerting shift in the region's import pattern has been a drop in the proportion of investment goods within manufactured imports. That trend, if continued, will seriously diminish Latin America's medium-term prospects.

Table 4.4   COMPOSITION OF TRADE BY MAJOR COMMODITY
GROUP IN LATIN AMERICA 1970-1985

%

	Exports			Imports		
	1970	1975	1985	1970	1975	1985
Food items	40.9	35.1	28.9	11.0	9.6	9.6
Agricultural raw materials	5.8	3.3	2.6	3.0	1.8	2.0
Ores and metals	18.7	10.4	10.4	8.3	8.4	4.9
Fuels	24.7	38.3	35.0	11.7	23.3	25.4
Manufactures	9.5	12.4	18.9	63.8	54.8	53.6
TOTAL ($ million)	17,513	47,842	107,043	18,617	57,960	98,347

Source: UNCTAD

The fact that intra-regional trade plays a relatively important role in Latin America is no accident. The encouragement of greater intra-regional trade has been a long-term objective of most countries in the region. Since the 1950s the Inter-American Development Bank and the UN Economic Commission for Latin America have laboured to promote this objective. In 1960 the 11 largest countries formed the Latin American Free Trade Association while the five small Central American countries established a common market of their own. A shortage of dollars has recently restricted growth of intra-regional trade as countries were forced to service their debts rather than buying their neighbours' goods. In response, Latin America has begun to search for ways to get around its dollar shortages while still promoting intra-regional trade. Barter deals rather than ordinary buying and selling have become popular.

Members of the Central American common market have also proposed that they pay for trade amongst themselves in units called Central American Import Rights.

In the new drive to integrate the continent, the grandiose plans of the 1960s have given way to smaller, more realistic efforts. There have been many bilateral trade agreements. One of the most important is the proposal involving Argentina and Brazil, which have always had rather complementary economies. Under the proposal, Brazil would get cheap Argentine wheat while Argentina would obtain cheap Brazilian manufactures. Both governments have also agreed to swap ideas on nuclear technology and are developing a small passenger aircraft together.

Such possibilities for Latin American integration, of course, have their limits. The major drawback to the Brazil-Argentina plan is that Brazil has a much larger and more diverse economy. Moreover, Argentina has already accumulated a deficit of $400 million in its trade with Brazil which it can ill afford. Numerous long-standing quarrels between Latin American countries have also slowed efforts to bolster intra-regional trade. Despite these difficulties, the growing spirit of co-operation may help to shape the region's economic future and lessen tensions between neighbours.

II Industry in Latin America

As the most industrialised region in the Third World, Latin America's economic performance and prospects are heavily dependent on circumstances in the manufacturing sector. Table 4.5 shows recent output trends for major industries within this sector. Growth of total industrial production has stagnated since the late 1970s and began to recover only in 1985. Manufacturing has borne the brunt of this stagnation but has recovered quicker than mining.

Table 4.5   PRODUCTION IN SELECTED LATIN AMERICAN INDUSTRIES 1977-1986

1980 = 100	1977	1978	1979	1981	1982	1983	1984	1985	1986
Total industrial production	86	88	96	98	96	94	99	103	108
Mining	86	92	99	101	99	98	102	101	105
Manufacturing	85	88	96	97	95	91	97	102	107
of which:									
Food, beverages and tobacco	91	89	98	104	106	105	109	114	116
Textiles	91	93	100	94	92	89	92	95	100
Wearing apparel, leather and footwear	91	92	98	99	95	88	91	93	94
Wood products, furniture	83	88	98	98	95	92	94	95	97
Paper, printing and publishing	88	92	95	97	98	98	105	130	148

Continued...

Table 4.5 cont'd

	1977	1978	1979	1981	1982	1983	1984	1985	1986
Chemicals, petroleum, coal and products	83	87	94	101	102	102	108	115	126
Non-metallic mineral	83	89	95	98	93	84	85	87	88
Basic metals	79	87	97	91	91	89	99	99	105
Metal products	82	84	93	88	79	71	77	82	82

Source: UNIDO/UNCTAD

Within the manufacturing sector, industries producing food, beverages, tobacco and chemicals and related products were least affected by the slowdown in the early 1980s. By 1986, production of agro-related industries was 16% above the 1980 level while production of chemicals and related products had risen by 26%. Paper, printing and publishing was the only other activity to record substantial gains by 1986: output of paper-related industries in 1986 was 48% above the 1980 level though almost all these gains were made in 1985 and 1986. Production of textiles and basic metals has been flat since 1980 and in other industrial groups current output is below 1980 levels. Hardest hit has been the metal products industry, where output is now 18% below the figure for 1980. The fall in output was less severe in non-metallic minerals, wearing apparel and related industries and wood products and furniture.

The foregoing figures illustrate patterns of growth but provide no information on the relative importance of various manufacturing industries. Though Latin America has a diversified and sophisticated industrial base, several manufacturing industries stand out in terms of their contribution to total industrial production, their capital requirements and export prospects. The prominence of these industries makes them the subject of frequent attention for Latin American planners and policymakers. Included are petrochemicals, steel, car manufacturing and electronics, each of which is discussed briefly below.

Petrochemicals

Petrochemicals is one of the largest and fastest-growing industries in Latin America. At the beginning of 1988, region-wide plans for investment in new plastics and petrochemical capacity totalled $8 billion. If realised, these investments would double Latin America's bulk chemicals capacity to 4 million tonnes by the mid-1990s. Much of this new output is intended for export. Of Brazil's additional capacity, about a third is marked for export while nearly all of Venezuela's investment in plastics and a plant for MTBE (an additive for lead-free petrol engines) would be exported. New bulk chemical plants in Argentina, Chile and Colombia would also export some 30% of the chemicals produced.

World demand for petrochemicals has recovered substantially since 1982 and is expected to continue to grow in Latin America. In line with this prospect, Latin American governments are hoping to entice some foreign companies to pay for their chemical projects, mainly for ethylene derivatives. Shell, Rhône-Poulenc and Bayer have all shown an interest in expansion in Brazil. Demand within the Latin American market should benefit from the region's expanding car and housing industries which will require lots of plastics, adding to demand for petrochemicals. The growing population of Brazil, Venezuela and other countries promises to boost demand further.

Venezuela's strategy for its petroleum industry relies not on foreign investment but represents an attempt to achieve "overseas downstream integration". The strategy, which consists of buying up refineries and petrol stations abroad, differs from that of Kuwait which has also endeavoured to establish an overseas presence (see Chapter 9). Petroleos de Venezuela (PDF) does not buy overseas assets but acquires them through joint ventures. These partnerships let the country tap the expertise of experienced foreign operators, and also tend to raise fewer political issues than Kuwait's more aggressive approach. Since 1983 PDV has invested in West Germany, Sweden, Belgium and the USA. Venezuela now has a guaranteed overseas outlet for 500,000 b/d of oil processed in domestic refineries plus a leased refinery in Curaçao. Altogether, Venezuela is able to sell three-quarters of its OPEC quota as refined products - free of OPEC's price controls. This success explains why the country's oil exports have remained stable during the recent years of turmoil in oil markets.

Iron and steel

In the iron and steel industry, Brazil boasts the world's largest iron-ore project. The Carajas complex is expected to produce 35,000 tonnes a year from reserves of 18 billion tonnes. Nearly $6 billion has been spent to develop Carajas. Brazil's iron-ore deposits are one reason for the rapid development of its steel industry. The country already produces 23 million tonnes and further expansion is planned. Mexico's efforts to reduce the extent of state ownership have changed its steel industry. The government's approval for Kobe Steel of Japan to acquire control of a joint venture is a major example of this new strategy.

Car manufacture

Car manufacture is the province of multinationals throughout Latin America. In Brazil firms like Ford, Fiat, Volkswagen and General Motors have made especially large investments. Two of them, Volkswagen and Ford, have decided to merge their operations in Argentina and Brazil. The new firm, Autolatina, is expected to produce $4 billion in goods each year and employ 77,000 workers. This would make it the world's 11th largest car producer. Autolatina would have around two-thirds of Brazil's market and a third of the Argentine market. Japanese firms have avoided Brazil's automobile industry. Honda makes motorbikes and Toyota produces rugged vehicles but neither has a car plant despite requests from the government to establish operations. In contrast, the largest and oldest Japanese investor in Mexico is Nissan. The company recently surpassed America's big three and the traditional leader, Volkswagen, in terms of domestic sales. However, US firms have invested very heavily in Mexico. Ford's new $500 million plant in Hermosillo, Sonora turns out 288 cars a day and obtains 30% of its parts from Mexican partners producing car seats, car panels and other parts. Together, local subsidiaries of five international car companies - Chrysler, Ford, GM, Nissan and Volkswagen - account for a third of all Mexico's exports.

Electronics

In the case of advanced electronics (eg computers of all sizes, components and robotics), Brazil has assumed regional leadership. Though IBM has a $75 million investment in the country, it is increasingly difficult for US firms to penetrate Brazilian markets for computerised banking and robotics. To protect this nascent information-technology industry, Brazilians have adopted several harsh laws prohibiting imports and restricting foreign investment. In 1987 Brazilian firms had around $2 billion of the country's $4 billion information-technology market.

III Investment in a Debt-Ridden Region

Domestic savings form part of the capital used for growth in Latin America. Much of the rest comes from borrowing abroad, piling up debts which may one day be redeemed when productive investment comes on stream. Foreign capital represents another source of investment funding, though Latin America's long-standing scepticism about its benefits have made it a less attractive host than Third World countries in Asia.

Table 4.6 shows the percentage of gross domestic savings and gross domestic investment in GDP along with growth of gross domestic investment. Of the 20 countries included in the table, only seven managed to increase the share of domestic savings in GDP between 1965 and 1985. In several, the savings rate is now dangerously low and in three - Bolivia, Paraguay and Argentina - the rate was halved between 1965 and 1985. Gross domestic investment expressed as a percentage of GDP has followed a similar downward trend: though generally higher than that for gross savings, it has declined precipitously in several countries. The most alarming statistics concern the growth of gross domestic investment during this decade. Only four of the 20 countries reported a positive rate of growth and in no country has gross investment grown at an annual rate greater than 1%.

Table 4.6   SAVINGS AND INVESTMENT IN LATIN AMERICA 1965-1985

% of GDP	Gross domestic savings[1]		Gross domestic investment[2]		Growth of gross domestic investment (% annual change)
	1965	1985	1965	1985	1980-6
Haiti	2	6	7	12	-1.8
Bolivia	22	8	17	5	-17.3
Honduras	15	13	15	17	-2.6
Nicaragua	18	-2	21	19	0.2
El Salvador	12	7	15	13	-0.8
Jamaica	23	19	27	19	0.8
Guatemala	10	9	13	11	-9.8
Paraguay	14	7	15	24	-6.0
Peru	31	18	34	20	-13.9
Ecuador	11	20	14	20	-5.6
Colombia	17	20	16	18	0.1
Chile	16	18	15	15	-7.4
Costa Rica	9	24	20	23	0.7
Brazil	22	24	20	21	-2.7
Mexico	21	27	22	21	-7.6
Uruguay	18	13	11	8	-16.3
Panama	16	21	18	17	-5.2

Continued...

100

Table 4.6 cont'd

	Gross domestic savings[1]		Gross domestic investment[2]		Growth of gross domestic investment (% annual change)
	1965	1985	1965	1985	1980-6
Argentina	22	11	19	9	-12.6
Venezuela	34	21	24	20	-8.4
Trinidad and Tobago	21	18	26	22	-15.8

Source: World Bank
Notes: Countries are listed in ascending order by per capita GDP in 1986
    [1] Gross domestic savings in GDP less consumption
    [2] Gross domestic investment includes all outlays for additions to fixed assets

In the case of foreign direct investment, Latin American countries are among the few whose currencies have fallen against the dollar in recent years. Hence, if investors can overcome local disadvantages, large countries like Brazil and Mexico would be good locations from which to export to the USA. Foreign direct investment in Mexico reached $21 billion in 1987 of which about two-thirds came from the USA. In Brazil America invests less ($8 billion), followed by West Germany ($4.3 billion) and Japan ($2.6 billion). These figures are comparatively modest in relation to the size of these two countries. The major reason is the widespread restrictions on foreign investment, a practice common throughout Latin America.

Japanese investment in Mexico and Brazil is small in comparison with American and European involvement but is growing. Japan's investment in Mexico is on the Pacific coast and is largely geared for exporting while in Brazil it is aimed at the domestic market. In Mexico some of the biggest "maquilidera" assembly plants are now

101

owned by Japanese electronic companies though the largest and oldest Japanese investor is Nissan.

Venezuela's recent efforts to attract foreign investment have understandably centred on its petrochemicals industry. The government liberalised foreign investment controls in 1987, resulting in a substantial rise in the inflow of foreign direct investment. Italy's ENI, Japan's Mutsui Petrochemical Industries and Norway's Norsk Hydro all responded. However, the law nationalising Venezuela's oil industry in 1987 still prevents equity participation by foreigners in its domestic oil and gas businesses.

Much of the Latin American investment by foreign firms represents expansion by companies that have been serving the domestic market for decades. Latin American attitudes toward quality control and punctuality have discouraged some firms from investing for export to other parts of the world. Nevertheless, the region has other attractions which should boost foreign investment. Mexico and Venezuela have oil, fast-growing domestic markets and offer a low-cost base for exporting to the USA. Brazil and Argentina have fertile agricultural sectors, abundant resources (as does Chile) and medium-to-large domestic markets.

Sources of domestic capital in several Latin American countries have dried up at times as potential investors used their funds to speculate in dollars. Private companies in several Latin American countries began 1988 flush with cash though they had little intention of investing it. In part their motives have nothing to do with investment conditions in the region; alterations in US tax laws in 1986 encouraged the repatriation of profits to the parent country. In Brazil, for example, remissions of profits even outweighed investments in 1986 - that is, there was net business disinvestment.

Peru is one of the countries which has tried to persuade companies to channel their cash into investment. It has developed tax incentives for investment and hopes that new savings certificates carrying returns linked to the US dollar will help to repatriate capital that was previously moved abroad. Recent policy shifts in Brazil have been prompted by an unexpected drop in savings rates. Surprisingly, the rate of savings fell in 1987 to well under 20% of GDP from 24% in 1985. Mini-devaluations and price freezes were part of the response but these resulted in renewed inflation (see Chapter 5, section II) while saving's share of income did not stabilise.

The Brazilian approach to the macroeconomic issues of savings and investment represents a rather special case owing to the country's large size and the fact that its ample resource endowments offer ready investment opportunities. Nevertheless, Brazil's strategy has influenced much of the region's thinking on these issues. Significantly, the economy is one of the most state-dominated outside the Soviet bloc. The state takes 70% of the country's domestic savings. Many of the government's investments have turned out to be productive but the drawback with a centralised economy is that appalling mistakes can also be made. The biggest recent mistake has been the failure of Petrobas, Brazil's giant state oil company, to embark on a programme of oil exploration in the 1970s in order to reduce the country's import bill. Another obvious white elephant has been the country's nuclear programme, which cost $2.5 billion and ended with only two of eight power stations being started. Other countries have sometimes followed Brazil's lead in establishing state-run industries to ensure an economic structure that matches with their planners' goals. In some cases the results have been successful though investment patterns have become subject to the state's priorities. This fact, coupled with a regional reluctance to welcome foreign investment, has greatly influenced movements in gross investment.

Figure 4.1 summarises the net effect of all these circumstances, showing gross capital formation (GCF) as a percentage of GDP during the 1980s. At the beginning of the decade GCF was over 23% of GDP but fell sharply in the next two and a half years. Afterwards, the percentage recovered slightly but then fell again in 1987. Though forecasts for 1988 suggest a small improvement, the region's investment has probably not met replacement needs in several recent years, making it even more difficult to boost production and export capability.

Figure 4.1   GROSS CAPITAL FORMATION IN LATIN AMERICA
1980-1987

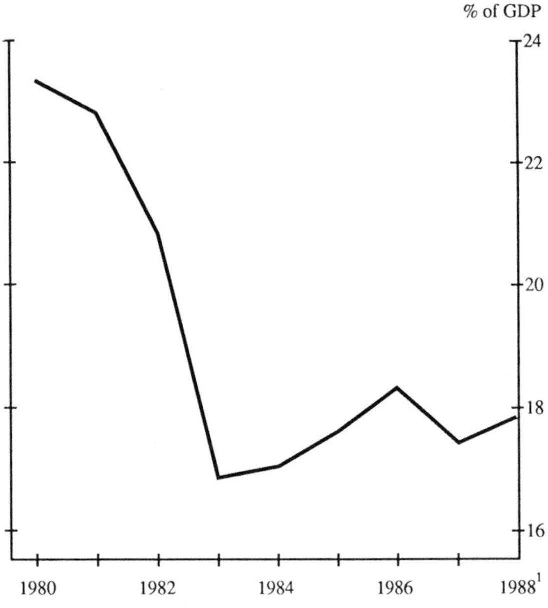

% of GDP

Source: IMF
Note: [1] Forecast

IV The Caribbean Basin

The economies of the Caribbean are unique within Latin America. Though several are rich, most are miniscule in population (see Table 4.7). Unlike much of Latin America, farming has always been the mainstay of Caribbean economies.

104

Table 4.7   CARIBBEAN POPULATION AND GROWTH OF GDP
1973-1986

	Population 1986 (000s)	Growth of real GDP 1973-86 (% annual change)
Antigua and Barbuda	61	4.3
Aruba	68	na
Bahamas	236	4.1
Barbados	254	1.8
British Virgin Islands	12	na
Cayman Islands	20	na
Cuba	10,185	5.6
Dominica	79	2.3
Dominican Republic	6,564	3.2
Grenada	96	3.9
Guadeloupe	335	2.9 [1]
Haiti	6,039	2.2
Jamaica	2,261	2.4
Martinique	329	3.0 [1]
Montserrat	12	na
Netherland Antilles	191	na
Puerto Rico	3,312	1.9
St. Christopher-Nevis	43	3.3
St. Lucia	140	5.0
St. Vincent	119	4.4
Trinidad and Tobago	1,205	2.5
Turks and Caicos Islands	8	na
US Virgin Islands	107	2.1

Source: Caribbean Development Bank
Note: [1] 1973-85

For over 150 years sugar was pre-eminent. But ever since it was discovered that sugar beet could be grown in temperate climates and that sugar cane would thrive in the USA, Caribbean producers have had to compete with the domestic sugar lobbies of developed countries. In 1981 the USA imported about 5 million tonnes of sugar from the Caribbean but by 1987 imports were only a fifth of that amount. Sugar exports to the EC declined by 1% each year in the period 1980-6. The decline in sugar markets was followed by other export failures. Trinidad saw its oil exports halved in this decade while the refineries on Aruba and Curaçao became insolvent. Jamaica's earnings from bauxite plunged from $234 million in 1978 to $77.5 million in 1985. Of the traditional Caribbean exports, only bananas have proved to be major export earners in the 1980s.

The Caribbean's economic problems have been exacerbated by a severe drop in capital flows. Net foreign finance declined by about 45% in nominal terms between 1981 and 1986. Jamaica and Antigua have especially troubling levels of debt while the Dominican Republic is seeking IMF support. The financial gap has restricted public investment and, therefore, employment. During 1987-8 islands as diverse as Trinidad, Jamaica, Martinique, Curaçao and the Dominican Republic have experienced unemployment rates above 20%.

In the face of these problems the USA launched the Caribbean Basin Initiative (CBI). Conceived in 1980 and taking effect in 1985, it has three parts: tariff-free entry to the USA for all Caribbean exports except oil, textiles, shoes and leather goods; tax advantages for US business conferences in CBI countries; and an increase in economic aid. It follows the model of the Lomé Convention which gives access to the EC for many goods from developing countries.

Despite these policies, America's imports from the 22 countries in the CBI fell by 30% between 1983 and 1986 while its exports rose by

)% (see figure 4.2). These trends continued in 1987, leading to a US trade surplus with the Caribbean for the first time. The sharp fall in American oil imports from the Netherlands Antilles after the closure of some US refineries has been an important reason for this turnaround in regional trade. Most of the 22 Caribbean countries have managed to increase their exports to the USA since 1984. However, these gains have been small and are outweighed by large declines in the exports of a few (eg Jamaica and the Bahamas).

Figure 4.2   US TRADE WITH CARIBBEAN BASIN INITIATIVE
COUNTRIES 1983-1987

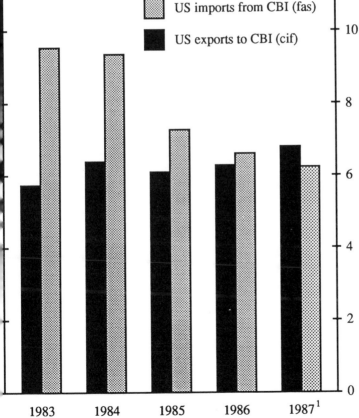

$ billion

☐ US imports from CBI (fas)

■ US exports to CBI (cif)

Source: US Department of Commerce

Note: [1] *Preliminary*

CBI countries have made a determined effort to send new exports to the USA - and with some success. Most countries, however, are finding it difficult to switch from single-crop economies to diversified economies with an export bent. They are also handicapped by high transport costs and a shortage of marketing expertise. Some countries have assembled attractive investment packages, hoping to lure foreign companies with the prospect of tariff-free entry into the USA. Free-trade zones have been established and industrial parks built. Airfreight services have been created and telephone systems have been improved. It is also easier to register a company in these countries than before.

These efforts have certainly brought foreign investment but some of the larger projects have later proved to be disappointing. An example of the problems which can arise is Tropicana International, a firm which invested $10 million in an ethanol plant in Jamaica. Its exports were supposed to enter the USA duty free. The project was expected to bring $1.5 million of foreign exchange every month and to give a needed boost to the island's sugar industry which would provide the necessary feedstock. Since then, Congress voted to put import restrictions on ethanol by 1989, partly in response to pressures from the industry. Under these conditions the plant will obviously be less attractive and its continued operation is in doubt.

The CBI pledged an increase in US aid to the 22 countries. Recipients argue, however, that aid increases are far short of meeting the costs of the infrastructure development needed before business investment can reach the levels required to take advantage of the trade concessions. The effects of meagre financial assistance are worsened by the fact that creation of export enclaves of American firms are especially costly. Many governments are particularly resentful about the limited aid programme because they have gone through the painful process of an IMF structural adjustment programme.

CHAPTER 5

LATIN AMERICAN ISSUES AND POLICIES

Latin America's economic performance in the 1980s has been a disappointment, both to its citizens and its creditors. Abroad, major exporters have lost markets either to more efficient suppliers in other parts of the Third World or to competitors in industrialised countries. At home, workers have lost jobs or seen their real wages fall as their governments fail to find remedies to regional problems such as inefficiency and hyperinflation. Chapter 5 begins by looking at two of the fundamental causes of these problems: mounting foreign debt and accelerating inflation. Poverty, or even a substantial decline in relative standards of living, has many causes and creates numerous problems, both socio-economic and political. One of the threatening developments in the region - the emergence of cocaine economies - can be attributed, in part, to the severe poverty in certain areas. At the beginning of the 1980s few would have imagined that some Latin American countries would soon emerge as the centre of an international drugs cartel. Today, however, three countries are major producers of cocaine and operate an international distribution network that spans the region and stretches to North America and Europe. This subject is examined in the concluding section of the chapter.

The Politics and Policies of Foreign Debt

The impasse over Latin America debt has now continued for more than seven years. Optimists maintain that the region's debt problem is abating while others contend that only the outright default of a major debtor could make the situation any worse. The former group sees reasons for hope in the fact that Brazil is now trying to catch up on its payments after refusing to pay any interest for most of 1987. Argentina was saved from the effects of falling commodity prices in 1987 by a bridging loan from the American Treasury and received further assistance from the World Bank in 1988. Subsequently, the US Treasury and Federal Reserve Board offered £3.5 billion to Mexico to help it recover from the recent effects of falling oil prices and surging imports. Pessimists see these moves as nothing more than desperate attempts to patch over an increasingly serious problem. Whatever their outlook, all agree that progress on the Latin America debt problem has been too slow and that there is an urgent need for new types of remedies.

Table 5.1 shows the evolution of long-term debt and debt service in Latin America in the 1970s and 1980s. The absolute value of outstanding debt rose nearly five fold between 1975 and 1985. The largest debt in 1987 was owed by Brazil ($117 billion) and represents a more than five fold increase over 1975. Mexico and Argentina are the region's other large foreign debtors. However, the greatest proportionate increases in debt occurred among the smallest and poorest countries in the region. In several countries debt in 1985 was eight to ten times greater than the 1975 level. The growth in foreign obligations has made major debtors increasingly vulnerable to any change in international economic circumstances. For example, each percentage point increase in dollar interest rates would presently add about $1 billion to Brazil's annual interest bill and $500 million to Argentina's. Similarly, a slump in the price of oil severely reduces the debt-servicing ability of Mexico and Venezuela.

Table 5.1   LONG-TERM DEBT AND DEBT SERVICE IN LATIN
AMERICA 1975-1985

$ million

	Value of debt outstanding		Debt service Total		% of exports of goods and services	
	1975	1985	1975	1985	1975	1985
Argentina	4,313	37,445	992	6,582	27.7	63.6
Barbados	30	363	3	49	1.4	6.2
Belize	11	100	0	11	1.0	9.3
Bolivia	839	3,659	93	205	18.8	27.8
Brazil	22,754	88,687	3,986	10,274	40.1	35.2
Chile	3,746	17,065	635	2,181	34.5	46.7
Colombia	2,668	10,945	284	1,577	13.0	34.2
Ecuador	538	7,128	86	768	7.7	23.1
El Salvador	232	1,546	62	230	10.4	24.2
Guatemala	174	2,969	22	586	2.8	49.1
Haiti	56	620	7	29	7.2	8.3
Honduras	334	2,051	20	219	5.9	23.5
Jamaica	670	3,270	99	415	8.9	32.8
Mexico	16,561	75,510	2,484	11,372	39.0	38.2
Nicaragua	614	4,925	62	169	13.7	46.7
Panama	773	4,282	72	544	5.9	8.7
Paraguay	217	1,774	28	177	12.0	15.0
Peru	3,251	11,499	500	640	29.0	16.3
Surinam	186	43	5	4	1.5	1.3
Uruguay	654	2,769	226	478	40.9	36.1
Venezuela	2,257	17,202	499	2,605	5.0	15.4
LATIN AMERICA[1]	65,265	315,011	10,803	41,065	18.6	30.0

Source: OECD/World Bank/national sources
Note: [1] *Includes countries other than those shown here*

Table 5.1 also indicates levels of debt service in 1975 and 1985. The region's total payments for debt service rose fourfold during these ten years, only slightly less than the corresponding rise in debt. Mexico alone accounted for over 27% of Latin America's debt service payments in 1985. Together, Argentina, Brazil and Mexico paid nearly 69% of all Latin America's debt service payments in that year. The burden these payments place on a country can best be determined by considering them in relation to foreign exchange earnings obtained through the export of goods and services. Measured by this standard, the burden is greatest for Argentina, which must allocate 64% of its export earnings to debt servicing. Not far behind are Guatemala (49%), Chile and Nicaragua (47%) and Mexico (38%). Altogether, 30% of Latin America's export earnings were siphoned off for debt servicing in 1985, up from 19% in 1975.

Not all debt-related problems pit Latin America against Western banks and governments. A sizeable portion of the region's trade is not with industrialised countries but with other developing countries in Latin America or elsewhere. Latin America's most publicised internal financial problem involves Argentina and Bolivia: Argentina imports natural gas from Bolivia (about $250 million in 1986) but has stopped paying for it. Most trade between Latin American countries is settled three times a year when the Central Bank of Peru works out which countries have surpluses and deficits with one another. The net deficits and surpluses are then reconciled if the country has the foreign exchange. Peru itself defaulted on its last payment under the scheme.

The trade in oil and gas between Bolivia and Argentina is excluded from this system. In an agreement worked out in 1987, Argentina said it would pay $130 million of the $500 million it owed, and would pay the balance over 25 years at an annual fixed interest rate of 8% with principal repayments not starting for 15 years. Argentina also agreed to pay for future Bolivian gas imports partly with food and some manufactured exports. But by 1988 Argentina was behind on the rescheduling. Venezuela and Mexico have encountered similar repayment problems over their plan to sell cheap oil to the non-oil economies in Central America.

As the debt problem has worsened, relations between Latin American countries and the international community have become more acrimonious. Both sides embarked on a search for new ways to resolve their dilemma. The development of secondary markets for debt offers one means of settling international obligations. Debt reductions, mainly in the form of swaps, have become the latest fashion in Latin American finance. Rather than paying the interest due on debt, countries reduce the stock of outstanding debt. They repay their debt at a discount with either assets or cash. The method is particularly attractive to small banks as their Latin American loans are few and they have not bothered too much about the prices they get for their debt. Such a cheap supply of paper has made it easy for the buyers - usually big banks acting on behalf of multinational companies - to make money in the form of fees. At Brazilian debt-for-equity auctions banks have accepted discounts of 20 to 30% when they sold dollar debt for cruzedos at Brazil's central bank.

The Latin American secondary market grew rapidly in its early years, expanding from $100 million in 1983 to at least $10 billion in 1987. The biggest sellers of debt have been American regional banks and continental European banks. Bank of Boston, for example, has reduced its $1 billion of loans to Brazil, Mexico, Argentina and Venezuela to $620 million. The larger banks, such as Citicorp, Bankers Trust, Chase Manhattan and JP Morgan, have all followed suit. Citicorp's efforts have been the most spectacular. Its loans to rescheduling countries fell from $15 billion at the end of 1986 to $13 billion in March 1988. Spanish and Swedish banks have also been especially heavy sellers. They were instructed by their regulators to make provisions on their loans to Latin America a year before Citicorp made the use of secondary markets fashionable.

113

Figure 5.1 shows the movement in market prices for external debt expressed as a percentage of face value for Latin America's four largest debtors. Since mid-1986 the price of Argentina's debt has declined from 58% of face value to about 27%. Chile is the favourite of international banks and its debt has depreciated the least: in mid-1988 its external debt was selling on secondary markets at 58% of face value. The discounted prices of Mexican and Brazilian debts have moved between these two extremes. Both, like Chile, have sometimes been actively engaged in secondary debt markets but have been less fortuitous in export markets and less successful in controlling domestic prices and public spending.

Figure 5.1   MARKET PRICE OF EXTERNAL DEBT OF MAJOR LATIN
AMERICAN DEBTORS 1986-1988

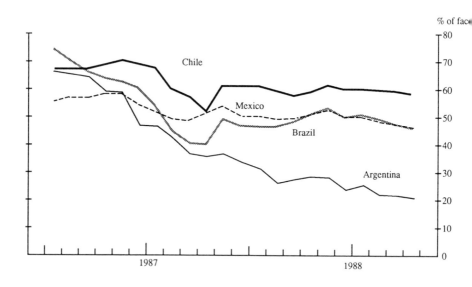

Source: Salomon Brothers

Brazil

Secondary markets are only one means of dealing with foreign debt and must be combined with other strategies. Brazil's debt is being rescheduled. Around 200 of the 350 foreign banks that still have Brazilian loans have agreed to the plan and will supply almost all the additional $5.2 billion Brazil needs. Another 50 (mostly small) banks have chosen to take "exit-bonds" thereby swapping their Brazilian loans for fixed-interest Brazilian bonds. These types of swap have reduced Brazil's debt by about $7 billion and concentrated it among banks that want to go on lending to the country.

Argentina

Setting up rescheduling arrangements has proved to be much more difficult in Argentina than in Brazil. Between 1982 and mid-1988 Argentina rescheduled its debt three times and has taken $7.75 billion in new cash from foreign banks. By mid-1988 the country owed between $700 million and $900 million in overdue interest. Argentina's trade surplus in 1988 is expected to be nearly $2 billion less than its annual interest bill, an amount that will have to be covered by money from abroad. Argentina's economy minister has accepted that the country should meet about half its $5 billion annual interest bill from its own resources (though it is unclear where these funds will come from). The country wants the banks to finance the remainder. That is unlikely as the banks have wearied of rescheduling and refinancing the debt. The most which might be offered is interest capitalisation. Argentina would convert its interest payments into principal to be repaid at a future date. The country could then avoid transferring cash to the banks. Argentina's prospects are not helped by the fact that it has been particularly slow to make use of any debt-swapping arrangements. By late 1988 it had shed only $700 million of its $55 billion in debt through swaps.

Against this background, the World Bank announced a $1.25 billion package of loans for Argentina in October 1988. In return, Argentina agreed to reduce its fiscal deficit from 4.6% of GDP in 1988 to 2.4% in 1992. The Argentines regard the loan as an extension of their own Primavera Plan to control inflation (see section II). The money will be used for investment loans for low-cost housing, power generation and restructuring the Argentine banking system.

Mexico

Mexico has until recently made extensive use of swapping arrangements to reduce its debt to Western banks. But in countries where inflation is rampant, debt reduction in the form of equity swaps can enlarge the money supply and add to the rate of price increase. Inflationary fears have stopped such conversions in Mexico. Since Mexico stopped taking new applications for its debt-to-equity programme, private sector companies have contributed most to the reduction in national debt, by buying back their debt at discount. Companies usually have fewer bank creditors, so find it easier to arrange such deals. The debt buy-back deal organised by Citicorp for Cylsa, a Mexican petrochemicals firm, is typical. The firm offered its creditors 60 cents in the dollar for its $422 million debt. Helped by a combination of buy-backs by the private sector and the occasional privatisation partly paid for in foreign debt, Mexico managed to reduce its overseas obligations by $6 billion in 1987.

Another variation on the debt-swapping arrangement is that tried out by Mexico and Costa Rica. Each country buys the other's debts and then uses them to settle their bilateral trade debts. In other words, when Mexico purchases Costa Rican goods it would pay for them not with cash but with cheap Costa Rican debt. This sort of arrangement avoids laws that prevent borrowers from using their reserves to repurchase their own debt at a discount and has attracted the interest of other Latin American countries. Advocates of such financial bartering predict that debt will be used increasingly as a means of exchange.

In October 1988 the US government stepped in with a fresh $3.5 billion loan to the Mexicans. Because the bulk of the country's foreign debts do not fall due until next century, any rescheduling of loans can provide little relief, and the fall in oil prices in 1988 cost Mexico about £2.5 billion. The repercussions are several: Mexico's ability to service its debts was jeopardised, its prospects for growth were undercut and the government's ability to control inflation was weakened. All these facts gave an urgency to the need for debt relief in some form. The loan may indicate a change in the US government's approach to Third World debt, at least for some preferred countries. Heretofore the USA had relied on international institutions and commercial banks to put together emergency packages. Other hard-pressed borrowers may now want to appeal directly to the USA for similar cash infusions.

Chile

Chile's programme for dealing with its debt problem is regarded by many as one of the region's most successful. Certainly, it has restored international confidence in the country's economy although the cost to workers (in terms of the decline in real wages) has been great. One indication of Chile's success is that foreign direct investment through the debt-equity programme totalled more than $1.1 billion between 1984 and mid-1988. In 1985-7 Chile's debt swaps amounted to $4.8 billion, equivalent to 25% of GNP in 1987. The results are less impressive, however, when considered in relation to Chile's total debt. After four years in operation the country has managed to reduce its debt only to roughly its 1984 level ($18.4 billion).

Chile continues to operate its debt-to-equity programme although the number of buyers has declined. The Central Bank's target is to reduce debt from 109% of GDP (at the end of 1987) to 70-80% by 1992. Foreign banks have also agreed to make the terms of restructuring agreements more flexible. They will allow peso repayments for creditors who want them and will permit Chile to look for ways to re-enter international financial markets; this is important since Chile will face a big hurdle in 1991 when $1 billion of capital repayments fall due. Chile's other debt-conversion scheme - which allows Chileans to buy foreign-bank debt with money from their own foreign bank accounts - has been shelved.

To achieve all this domestic demand and imports have been squeezed into a recession-like condition while export industries have been boosted to obtain more foreign exchange. A much higher price for copper has also helped to alleviate foreign exchange constraints and boost foreign investors' confidence. Copper prices average more than $1 per pound in 1988, compared with the 75 cents the government had budgeted for. Chile has announced plans to use part of its reserves, as well as $80 million of its windfall from the surge in copper prices, to purchase even more of its debt.

Peru

Peru's debt problem has attracted great attention outside Latin America due to the populist policies adopted by President Alan Garcia. In 1985 the President stated his intention to limit interest payments on Peru's debt to 10% of export earnings, and reaffirmed this intention in 1987. More recently, the President has had to retreat from this policy as well as others. Pressure has mounted as the country's foreign exchange reserves have steadily declined. The business community, too, has always been sceptical about the country's decision to cut itself off from external finances. As a result, business investment in 1987 was flat though demand was growing at an impressive pace.

Venezuela

Like Mexico, Venezuela's debt concerns are closely linked to the price of oil. The fall in oil prices in 1988 is expected to cut the country's exports by around 25%. In other ways Venezuela is more fortunate than some of its neighbours because it still has some foreign exchange reserves. However, at the end of June 1988 these were down to $3.7 billion, 16% lower than at the end of 1987. The country's last debt-rescheduling agreement stipulated a minimum of $2 billion in reserves and Venezuela is having difficulty obtaining new credit. All it managed to borrow in 1988 was a $3.5 billion increase in short-term credit lines and a $100 million bond issue.

II Inflation in Latin America

Latin America has long been plagued with rates of inflation far exceeding the average for other parts of the Third World. Table 5.2 shows the seriousness of the problem. Annual rates of price increase in the 1970s were nearly double the Third World average and the gap widened in the 1980s. In the period 1983-5 inflation was three to four times greater than the average for all developing countries. Inflation fell in the second half of this decade though Latin America continues to experience annual rates approaching 100%.

Table 5.2   INFLATION[1] IN LATIN AMERICA AND THE THIRD WORLD
1969-1988

% annual change

	Developing countries	Latin America
1969-78	16.7	31.0
1979	21.5	31.0
1980	27.2	54.6
1981	26.4	59.7
1982	25.0	68.4
1983	34.0	106.3
1984	39.4	129.3
1985	40.6	150.3
1986	28.6	86.5
1987	30.1	97.7
1988	29.5	98.8

Source: IMF
Notes: [1] *Consumer prices weighted by average US dollar value of GDPs over the preceding three years. Data prior to 1978 exclude China*
[2] *Average compound annual rate of change*

The cumulative costs of runaway inflation are great. They affect all aspects of Latin America's economy including income distribution, living standards and the ability to compete in international markets. Persistent inflation cannot be attributed to any single underlying problem, but there are several common circumstances in the countries which have suffered worst. Latin American governments, belatedly perhaps, have begun to try to redress their inflationary problems. In doing so, they have employed a variety of methods to control prices, wages, exchange rates and budget deficits.

Argentina

Argentina's decision to bring inflation under control was announced with much fanfare in 1985. The initial plan included a new currency, the austral, pegged to the US dollar. The basis for the plan depended not so much on the new currency from which it took its name but on wage and price controls combined with tight fiscal and monetary policies. Within a year inflation was cut from 1000% to 80%. Since then, Argentina's ability to control price increases has been seriously eroded. By mid-1988 inflation reached an annual rate of 320%.

Argentina's major problem was its budget deficit. The government had agreed with the IMF that it would cut the deficit to 3.9% of GDP in 1988, from 7.2% in the previous year. Instead, it continued to rise. One flaw in the Austral Plan is that there are no hard measures to cut spending. Another difficulty is that the reduction in real wages caused by the initial wage freeze prompted widespread strikes. Heavy pressure from both state corporations and trade unions has severely limited the government's ability to impose stringent spending limits.

President Alfonsin attempted to rejuvenate the programme in 1988. His new approach was known as the Primavera Plan and included a 10.5% devaluation of the austral. It also depended on voluntary restraint of private sector prices and control of public prices. Other parts of the new programme include a 30% rise in charges for energy and petrol and the government's decision to transfer half the industrial export earnings from the free market exchange rate to the commercial exchange rate in order to close the gap between the two exchange rates.

In September 1988 the government announced a 4% rise in public sector wages together with a 3% devaluation of the austral. Together, these steps will result in a large reduction in real public

121

sector wages. Such moves, however, are being sorely tested by big unions, insisting on more generous wage increases, and industrialists, who threaten to oppose price controls unless the government abandons its intention to reduce import barriers.

The Primavera Plan has received a boost from higher grain prices which improved Argentina's trade surplus for the first half of 1988. The central bank has also built up its foreign exchange reserves. Together, these two factors give Argentina's exchange rate policy some credibility though its fiscal policy is much shakier. The budget deficit still exceeds 7% of GDP and revenue collection is falling in real terms. Cuts in public spending would seem to be inevitable though, again, both trade unions and industrialists are fighting attempts to reduce funds for government-owned industries.

Brazil

Brazil's Cruzado Plan was launched in February 1986. The results have proved even more disappointing than Argentina's programme. Though modelled on the Austral Plan, the Brazilians placed more emphasis on wage and price controls. The initial impact of the Plan was to cut the annual rate of inflation to less than 100%, down from a 1985 high of nearly 300%. However, demand built up once wages were frozen. This created a situation of repressed inflation with frequent shortages and a thriving black market. Upward pressure on prices could not be contained and inflation resumed.

Despite earlier promises of financial stringency, in 1986 and 1987 the government decided to proceed with various large-scale projects. Spending on several megaprojects such as a railway and a steel mill went ahead. At the same time efforts to slow the rise in wages failed. Government-imposed wage freezes were overturned by several unions and eventually the method employed to prevent further increases was declared unconstitutional. The relationship

122

between inflation and government deficits is pictured in Figure 5.2. In 1985 and 1986 Brazil's budget deficit was declining and so too was its rate of inflation. However, public sector wages and government spending rose in the next year resulting in a budget deficit of 5.5% of GDP. Brazil's rate of inflation also soared from 120 to 400-500% per year.

Chile

In contrast to Argentina and Brazil, Chile's annual inflation rate was less than 20% in mid-1988. Domestic demand has been squeezed drastically during both recession and boom while export industries have led an economic recovery. The result is that much of Chile's growth can now be financed through export earnings, not foreign bank loans. Because of higher copper prices and tax revenue from high-value imports, Chile's budget deficit is likely to be no more than 1% in 1988. At the same time, real average wages are 16% below 1981 levels and the minimum wage is 35-40% lower.

These figures reflect some of the costs of Chile's anti-inflationary programme. Urban workers are significantly poorer today than they were at the beginning

of this decade. Figure 5.2 again shows the relationship between budget deficits and rates of inflation. Chile's deficit has steadily fallen from a high of 4.4% in 1984 and rates of inflation have followed.

Figure 5.2   INFLATION AND BUDGET DEFICITS IN BRAZIL AND CHILE
1984-1988

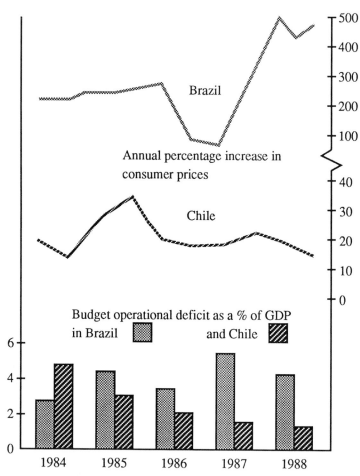

Source: IMF/Manufacturers Hanover

Bolivia

Bolivia's New Economic Policy (NEP) was introduced in September 1985 and is unique among Latin American countries. Rather than relying on price and wage controls, the Bolivians imposed stringent and unrelenting fiscal and monetary restrictions. Many lost their jobs in overmanned industries. In the tin mining industry alone more than 20,000 workers were released. Simultaneously, the budget deficit was cut brutally: it fell from 36% of GDP in 1984 to 5% in 1987. Before the NEP was imposed, inflation was estimated to be 24,000% a year but by 1988 it was reduced to 10%.

Such a draconian programme may have cost Bolivia greatly in terms of growth. After six years of decline, the country's real GDP grew by 2.2% in 1987 and results in 1988 should be slightly better. Some of the capital that fled the country is beginning to flow back as foreign investors are being made to feel welcome. Despite these and other indications of improvement, Bolivia's people remain extremely poor. Many have so far seen none of the benefits of the economic turnaround.

Mexico

The Mexican government's most recent effort at inflation control dates back to December 1987. At that time, the monthly rate of inflation was 15%. The government responded by establishing an Economic Solidarity Pact with businesses and trade unions. The pact was intended to avoid some of the weaknesses of the Austral and Cruzado Plans. Prices of 63 goods and services ranging from tortillas to petrol, all of which had fallen behind the rate of inflation, were increased by about 85%. Wages, not formally indexed, were to be raised in line with deliberately low estimates of future inflation. At the same time, private sector executives promised price restraint on some 400 goods.

Mexico's erratic pattern of inflation is shown in Figure 5.3. Afte reaching 100% in 1983, annual rates fell back to 50%. Upwar pressure on prices resumed in 1985. Even worse, Mexico's livin, standards were falling, just as they had done in 1983 at the previou inflationary peak. As the government's programme began to tak effect, inflation again declined and modest increases in GDP wer obtained.

Figure 5.3   INFLATION AND GROWTH OF GDP IN MEXICO 1982-1988

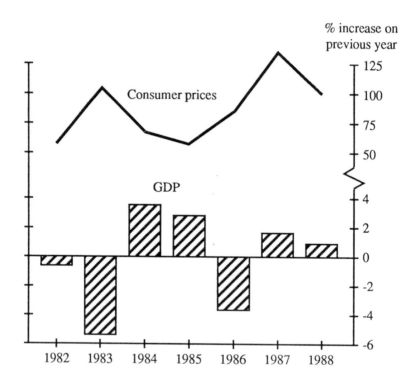

Source: IMF/Manufactures Hanover

126

Mexico's inflation had been brought down to 3.1% per month by May 1988. Nominal monthly interest rates also declined to 3%, down from 13% in January 1988. If the solidarity pact can be sustained, the government's interest bill for servicing national debt should fall and public sector borrowing should decline from the perilous 16% of GDP which prevailed in 1987. However, the recent change in government and the political problems associated with the transition have made it more difficult for the government to persist with its current inflation-control programme. In response, Mexican ministers are quick to point out the difference between their programme and those of Argentina and Brazil. Both those countries tried to grow while braking inflation, whereas Mexico has opted for a policy of tight credit and no growth. Argentina and Brazil have also tolerated inflationary budget deficits while Mexico does not. Furthermore, both countries arbitrarily imposed their wage and price freezes though Mexico did not.

Despite these disclaimers, Mexico's latest attempt at inflation control rests heavily on one especially risky policy. The country has held its exchange rate steady at around 2,300 pesos to the dollar. The attraction of this policy is that Mexico has been in the enviable position of receiving returning flight capital. The inflow pushed reserves to about $14 billion by May 1988. The drawback of this policy is that a strong peso has erased the country's trade surplus. In the first eight months of 1988 Mexico's trade surplus was only $2.5 billion compared with $6 billion over the same period in 1987. Imports of consumer goods rose by 123% in 1988 in response to the strong peso and Mexico's recent cuts in import tariffs. Capital has now started to move out again as investors anticipate a large devaluation. Mexico's foreign reserves have fallen by a third from their peak in mid-1988.

Uruguay

Of all Latin American countries, Uruguay has one of the better records in inflation control during recent years. The monthly rate of inflation, 3.4%, is only a tenth of that in some of the region's larger countries. Although this translates into an annual rate of nearly 50%, the figure is still impressive by Latin American standards. Uruguay's situation is made easier because it has a comfortable foreign exchange reserve and a healthy trade surplus. Government spending has been cut and several large loss-making firms have been closed despite union objections. The major danger is that because the economy is operating close to full capacity, future growth in income will be slow. This, in turn, will mean slow growth in government revenues at a time when the public deficit is expanding.

III Latin America's Cocaine Economies

Latin America includes three cocaine-producing economies: Bolivia, Colombia and Peru. Colombia has the most impressive overall economic performance of these countries, being untroubled by exceptionally high levels of unemployment, having only modest debt and maintaining steady rates of income growth in the 1980s. Though the country has followed an exemplary set of development policies in many ways, some of its economic achievements must necessarily be attributed to its involvement in illegal drugs. The region's other two cocaine producers, Bolivia and Peru, have compiled less successful economic records. Widespread poverty and the absence of any viable economic alternatives are pressing reasons why the rural poor in these countries have turned to cocaine production.

Produced from the coca leaf, a large portion of the world's cocaine is supplied by these three countries. In Colombia cultivation is concentrated in the Amazonas territory in the south and south-east; Peru's main cocaine-producing area is a 150-square-mile zone in the centre of the country; Bolivia has three regions which are all big coca-growing areas. Cocaine is the leading export of the two poorer countries, exceeding gas and tin in Bolivia and copper in Peru. In Colombia cocaine may be the second largest export after coffee.

Figure 5.4 documents the development of cocaine production in South America. In 1981 and 1982 production was between 110 and 150 tonnes. In the next two years, it rose substantially. By 1984 production may have been nearly 300 tonnes. Though estimates of the value of this activity are understandably incomplete, retail sales of South American cocaine in North America and Europe are put at $22 billion in 1987. Of this, the South Americans received $3 billion with the rest going to middlemen. The bulk of these supplies come from Bolivia and Peru. Colombia, however, is the centre for refining and exporting. Bolivians and Peruvians sell the paste to Colombians who convert it to cocaine before exporting it. In 1987 a Colombian refiner could purchase 2.5 kilos of paste for as little as $500, and then covert it into one kilo of cocaine with an export price of up to $6,000.

The countries producing cocaine do not necessarily receive the foreign exchange from their exports. A large portion is not repatriated but is invested abroad. Most estimates put the exporting countries' receipts at about half the export revenues earned by traffickers, or roughly $1.5 billion. Colombians, because they are most heavily involved in the overseas trafficking, receive the largest portion. Some of the money from overseas profits that is returned to the countries comes through openly and is exchanged by the central bank. In Colombia over $500 million dollars is thought to be smuggled in each year, laundered through local businesses and purchases or used to finance imports. To hide the drug money, the value of exports is overstated and credits from abroad are often faked.

Figure 5.4   ESTIMATED PRODUCTION OF SOUTH AMERICAN COCAINE
1981-1987

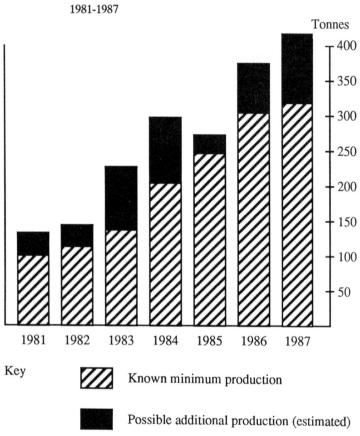

Key

Source: National Narcotics Intelligence Consumers Committee

Farming is the most labour-intensive part of the business, and most leaf-pickers are employed in Bolivia and Peru. In 1983 a Bolivian government report estimated that about 300,000 inhabitants were engaged in cultivating, processing or transporting coca and its derivates. In 1987 that estimate was updated to 500,000. Since the official workforce of Boliva is 1.7 million, the figures imply that one in every three or four jobs depends on the drug economy. Peru produces twice as much coca leaf as Bolivia and has a nationwide workforce of 7 million. Thus the proportion of Peruvians employed in coca farming is probably about half the Bolivia figure. Colombia has a much larger workforce (11 million) and is the third largest grower of coca. Because Colombia's involvement is based on relatively sophisticated services such as processing and transport, the number of people employed is less than in Bolivia and Peru.

Drug traffickers in Colombia put their money into real estate, businesses rich in cashflow, livestock and other prestigious investments. Real estate prices have soared as a result. Rents for luxury flats in Bogota, for example, rose about 75% in 1987. The gains to the economy of spending large sums of money in such ways (as well as in bribing politicians and building large personal armies) is less than if the same amount were spent building roads and other infrastructure. Nevertheless, the drug money has made Colombia's economy run more smoothly. Net capital outflow is small and more imports are available than official figures would suggest. The cocaine trade has also created some jobs and has boosted wages. The harmful economic effects of this illegal money are equally evident. Though much of the land devoted to coca is very poor and otherwise useless, farmers in some rural areas can no longer feed themselves. Drug traffickers maintain privately armed forces and their violence hampers normal economic activities.

The influx of cocaine money has been sufficient to create several macroeconomic problems. The new money encouraged banks to be less prudent about their lending and bad debts have soared. Eventually, the surge of drug money into Colombia spurred inflation. Some analysts even see a form of de-industrialisation occurring as a result of the surge in drug money. The coca boom (coupled with a rise in coffee prices) has forced up the value of the Colombian peso. This has made the country's traditional exports less competitive and has undermined its efforts to boost non-traditional exports.

131

Despite all the difficulties and dangers of attempting to control the drug cartel's power, Colombian authorities - with American assistance - estimate that they have intercepted nearly $1.5 billion in drugs, chemical stocks and arms. Altogether, up to 30% of Colombian cocaine is intercepted at some point. The government has also offered subsidies for production of other crops and some farmers have begun to switch away from coca. The Colombians are boosting their spending in the poorer rural areas where much of the coca is produced, from 6% of total public investment in 1986 to 15% in 1987 and 1988.

Programmes to deal with the drug problem will be much more difficult to develop in the poorer countries of Bolivia and Peru than in Colombia. Tentative estimates of income from cocaine exports for 1987 suggest that it amounts to 75% of Bolivia's foreign exchange earnings, though much less (14.5%) of Peru's. Thus, cocaine trade has a high impact on growth, employment and balance of payments in Bolivia. In recent years the Bolivian economy has stagnated while unemployment has been high and legal exports have brought in only modest revenues. Peru, too, is more vulnerable than Colombia. The economy is weaker and far more peasants depend on coca for their livelihood.

The problem of foreign debt is also intermingled with the drug issue. Ever since Latin America's debt saga began in 1982, bankers have paid great attention to the ability of debtor countries to boost foreign exchange earnings so that they could service their debts. Although coca dollars have had a big effect, they are nearly always ignored in economic analysis. In fact, the governments of Bolivia, Colombia and Peru have occasionally created financial mechanisms through which coca dollars could be absorbed into the official economy. One method is to open exchanges, known as "left-hand windows", at banks to convert black-market dollars into local currency. In Peru exchange controls were abolished in the late 1970s probably in an effort to attract cocaine dollars. These were exchanged for local currency or for dollar-dominated certificates of deposit with no questions asked. At the same time Peruvian banks expanded rapidly into the country's cocaine regions to attract these funds. Bolivia embarked on a similar strategy in 1985 when its NEP was launched. In an appeal for the cocaine money to return to Bolivia the new policy required that no proof need be given at national, departmental or municipal level of the origins of assets invested in the country during the first four months of the new policy. The Bolivian central bank also began marketing bearer certificates of deposit in dollars with a guaranteed rate of return of 10%.

CHAPTER 6

ECONOMIC PERFORMANCE AND TRENDS IN AFRICA

African countries offer a multitude of contrasts with regard to resource endowments, size and degree of external dependence. As shown in Table 6.1, Nigeria is the largest African country, with a population of 100 million. At the opposite end of the scale are many small countries such as Gambia, with 700,000 inhabitants, and even tinier ones like Sao Tome and Principe with populations of only 100,000. Libya is the richest African country, having a per capita GDP of nearly $7,500. Libya's riches contrast with Ethiopia, the world's poorest country, whose per capita GNP is only $109. In terms of debt, Mauritania is one of the world's most indebted countries, having foreign obligations more than twice its GNP. Other heavily indebted countries include Guinea-Bissau, Zambia and Gambia. At the opposite end of the spectrum are Libya, Angola, Chad and Uganda, all with debt ratios below 25% of GNP although several are capital-starved. Direct investment, too, varies widely. Led by Cameroon, Nigeria, Botswana and Tunisia, some countries have successfully managed to attract foreign investors. Many, however, receive very little in the way of foreign investment or have had negative outflows.

Africa's economic prospects rest heavily on the performance of its external sector and this subject is examined in section I. Section II looks at developments in the agricultural sector with special attention to the region's abilities to meet its food needs. Section III is concerned with African industry which, like agriculture, is now undergoing a period of transition.

Table 6.1 MAJOR ECONOMIC INDICATORS IN AFRICAN COUNTRIES 1985/1986

	Population 1985 (million)	GDP per capita[1] 1986 ($)	Growth of GDP[1] 1980-6 (%)	Trade balance 1986 ($ million)	Ratio of Debt/GNP 1985 (%)	Direct investment in country 1985 ($ million)
Algeria	22.6	2,648	2.4	176.0	31.7	-
Angola	8.7	1,094	-2.9	na	15.8	na
Botswana	1.1	855	7.4	272.1	59.1	90.5
Burkina-Faso	7.9	134	1.7	-196.1 [4]	47.6	20.3 [3]
Cameroon	10.2	857	3.7	490.4 [3]	41.4	316.0 [2]
Central African Republic	2.6	259	-0.4	-71.4	45.6	-
Chad	5.0	128	-2.4	-104.5 [3]	21.8	53.6 [2]
Congo	1.9	1,189	3.2	514.8 [3]	138.8	12.7 [2]
Ethiopia	42.3	109	0.7	-501.2 [3]	38.1	- [2]
Gabon	1.1	3,184	5.0	79.4	48.0	120.8
Gambia	0.7	737	1.6	-20.8	132.8	na
Ghana	12.7	469	-1.9	60.9	35.5	4.3
Guinea	6.2	349	na	na	72.6	na

Continued...

Table 6.1 cont'd

	Population 1985 (million)	GDP per capita[1] 1986 ($)	Growth of GDP[1] 1980-6 (%)	Trade balance 1986 ($ million)	Ratio of Debt/GNP 1985 (%)	Direct investment in country 1985 ($ million)
Guinea-Bissau	0.9	152	0.3	-43.1	166.3	-
Ivory Coast	10.1	712	2.2	1,372.5 [3]	95.9	29.1 [2]
Kenya	20.4	284	2.1	-290.9	57.6	43.2
Lesotho	1.5	167	2.5	-318.2	30.5	-0.2
Liberia	2.2	370	-0.9	149.0	99.6	-5.7
Libya	3.8	7,484 [3]	0.6	4,639.1 [3]	4.4	-315.8 [2]
Madagascar	10.2	234	-0.9	-19.5 [4]	104.2	- [2]
Malawi	7.0	156	2.1	28.5 [3]	75.7	- [4]
Mali	7.5	143	0.2	-115.0	118.4	4.3
Mauritania	1.7	366	0.6	17.5	220.2	-5.3
Morocco	21.9	542	1.7	-1,066.4	98.2	-
Mozambique	13.8	na	-3.5	-409.3	55.4	-
Niger	6.4	258	-0.9	-40.7	58.6	-
Nigeria	99.7	806	0.9	2,528.2	18.2	195.9
Rwanda	6.0	274 [3]	na	-75.0	20.4	17.6
Senegal	6.6	394	-1.3	-221.2 [2]	89.5	29.1 [2]
Sierra Leone	3.7	324	1.9	-9.3 [3]	33.1	-31.0 [2]

Continued...

Table 6.1 cont'd

	Population 1985 (million)	GDP per capita[1] 1986 ($)	Growth of GDP[1] 1980-6 (%)	Trade balance 1986 ($ million)	Ratio of Debt/GNP 1985 (%)	Direct investment in country 1985 ($ million)
Somalia	5.4	261	-1.9	-217.2	107.4	-0.1
Sudan	21.9	406	0.0	-306.2	63.2	-
Swaziland	5.4	590	2.9	-33.8	62.3	27.5
Togo	3.0	235	1.9	-83.4	129.9	-
Tunisia	7.1	1,168	3.5	-935.0	61.8	63.4
Uganda	15.5	220	-2.5	85.4	15.8	na
Tanzania	22.2	279	1.5	-416.5	53.9	na
Zaire	30.6	161	-0.8	560.8	113.0	-7.0
Zambia	6.7	337	0.0	171.3	150.8	-
Zimbabwe	8.4	572	0.4	313.5	33.3	4.1

Source: World Bank/UN/UNCTAD
Notes: [1] Exports (fob) less imports (fob)
[2] 1984
[3] 1985
[4] 1983

I Trade Performance in Africa

Africa's involvement in the world trading system has never been great but has deteriorated even further in the 1980s. In 1986 the region's share of world exports was only 3% while 3.5% of world imports went to Africa. Africa's heavy dependence on non-manufactured exports partly explains its poor trade performance in the 1980s.

Table 6.2 shows the growth of exports, imports and terms of trade. Although export growth averaged 3.4% per year in 1975-86, a positive rate of growth was attained only once in the years between 1982 and 1986. Imports have followed a similar downward trend: though growing moderately over the entire period 1975-86, they have contracted in every year since 1982. After remaining relatively stable for several years, Africa's terms of trade have also deteriorated. In 1986 the price ratio of exports to imports (measured in unit values) fell to only 64% of the 1980 level. The decline was mainly due to weaker community prices which hit African exporters especially hard.

Table 6.2 GROWTH OF EXPORTS, IMPORTS AND TERMS OF TRADE IN AFRICA 1975-1986

% change	1975-86[1]	1982	1983	1984	1985	1986
Growth of exports	3.4	-12.7	-6.7	2.6	-3.1	-17.6
Growth of imports	4.4	-13.0	-8.6	-7.8	-3.4	-0.2
Terms of trade[2] (1980 = 100)	-	103	93	96	95	64

Source: UNCTAD
Notes: [1] *Average annual rate*
[2] *Ratio of export unit value index to import unit value index*

139

Trade performance is partly determined by conditions in major markets. Africa's exporters are more dependent on buyers in developed market economies than are other developing regions. Among the developed market economies Western Europe and North America are the main buyers for Africa's exports and the principal sources of supply. Import sources, however, are more diversified than export destinations. Asia has declined as a source of imports owing to the strong appreciation of the yen relative to the dollar and the fall in private bank lending and commercial credits for import finance.

Table 6.3 shows that four-fifths of the region's exports go to developed market economies while only 14% is purchased by other developing countries. The same sort of trade pattern can be found in the case of imports: over 70% of Africa's imports come from developed market economies and roughly a fifth from other developing countries. The importance of developed market economies in the region's trade is partly the result of very meagre levels of intra-regional trade. Less than 5% of Africa's imports and exports are with other African countries.

Table 6.3   AFRICA'S STRUCTURE OF TRADE BY ORIGIN AND
             DESTINATION[1] 1970-1985

%	Developed market economies	Socialist countries	Developing countries	of which: Intra-region
Imports				
1970	76.8	8.4	13.5	5.7
1975	78.9	4.8	15.0	4.1
1985	72.2	6.6	20.3	4.3

Continued...

Table 6.3 cont'd

	Developed market economies	Socialist countries	Developing countries	of which: Intra-region
Exports				
1970	80.4	6.5	11.4	5.6
1975	77.2	6.0	14.7	4.9
1985	80.0	4.1	14.4	4.7

Source: UNCTAD
Note: [1] *Figures exclude trade with socialist developing countries*

African countries also tend to be more vulnerable to external forces than other Third World countries because of their heavy reliance on primary products and other commodity exports. The combined value of exports by countries other than oil suppliers rose by nearly 19% in 1986. Kenya, Ethiopia, Ivory Coast and Uganda all benefited from higher coffee prices. These gains, however, were more than offset by the weakening international demand for other commodities. Exporters of cocoa beans, tea and some cereals suffered owing to lower prices and volumes. Countries dependent on non-fuel mineral exports (for example copper in the case of Zambia and Zaire) have seen their exports fall sharply following a decline in prices.

Table 6.4 shows the composition of African trade in the 1970s and 1980s. Fuels accounted for one-third of the region's exports in 1970, but following the oil price hikes in 1973 and 1978-9, the share rose to over 70%. Africa's second largest export category is food items (13% in 1985) while all other categories are negligible in the overall export pattern. The region's fragmented industrial base is reflected by the fact that manufactures dominate among imports: more than 60% in 1985, although down from 69% in 1970. The volume of food imports has increased significantly owing to the extremely poor

141

performance of the agricultural sector and the rapid growth of the region's population. Altogether, Africa's balance of trade in goods and services was positive in 1970 but soon afterward turned negative and has remained so for more than a decade.

Table 6.4   STRUCTURE OF TRADE BY MAJOR COMMODITY GROUP
IN AFRICA 1970-1985

%

	Exports			Imports		
	1970	1975	1985	1970	1975	1985
Food items	29.1	17.4	13.0	14.4	15.4	19.1
Agricultural raw materials	10.9	5.4	3.9	2.4	1.8	2.5
Ores and metals	19.6	11.0	5.6	7.3	7.1	6.1
Fuels	33.7	60.9	70.5	4.7	7.7	9.1
Manufactures	6.6	5.0	6.6	69.3	66.6	60.3
TOTAL ($ million)	12,021	33,943	58,375	11,836	40,806	63,316

Source: UNCTAD

Two features of Africa's trade performance have become more pronounced in the 1980s. First, import levels and the capacity to import are now tied to the level of export earnings. The reason is that net capital inflows declined sharply after 1982 as private lending dried up and net aid was reduced. Second, the increasing import content of domestic import-competing and export industries has narrowed the extent to which a devaluation improves competitiveness. In other words, the relationships between trade, payments and growth on the one hand and debt and capital inflows on the other are now much closer.

II Agriculture - Living with Famine

Farming is by far the most important form of production in Africa. Nevertheless, there has been an inexorable decline in the region's production of many food staples and exports. This fact, coupled with some of the highest population growth rates in the world, poses a serious challenge to the region's economic future.

Table 6.5 summarises, by country, the region's performance in food production. Per capita output showed no growth whatsoever in the 1960s and contracted in the 1970s. Poor harvests in 1982-4 further reduced regional per capita food production. It was not until 1985 that per capita output actually rose. The 1970s were a particularly difficult period. Of the 38 countries shown in Table 6.5, 25 experienced a decline in per capita food output during that decade. And during the 1980s several countries, including Gambia, Kenya, Senegal and Uganda, encountered a drop of per capita food production of more than 25% in a single year.

Table 6.5   GROWTH OF PER CAPITA FOOD PRODUCTION IN AFRICA
1961-1986

%

	1961-70	1970-80	1980-5	1982-3	1983-4	1984-5	1985-6
Algeria	-1.1	-1.1	0.6	0.6	7.4	8.7	-1.0
Angola	0.7	-1.6	-2.0	-5.4	-8.6	9.8	-1.0
Botswana	1.3	-3.0	-2.2	-1.6	-2.3	-2.3	-2.5
Burkina-Faso	0.7	0.5	3.3	0.6	16.4	2.4	1.4
Cameroon	1.4	-0.4	-1.2	-2.0	-2.6	1.5	0.0
Chad	-1.3	-0.3	0.0	2.6	-10.2	20.5	0.1
Congo	-0.5	-0.4	-1.9	-7.2	-1.4	0.8	-0.8
Ethiopia	-0.7	-0.7	-3.3	-8.9	-11.6	6.8	0.4
Gabon	-0.3	-0.8	-0.5	1.4	-1.5	-3.4	0.3
Gambia	0.2	-4.7	2.7	-27.8	7.1	18.6	-4.4
Ghana	1.3	-3.9	1.8	-11.1	40.7	-7.4	7.3
Guinea	0.8	-0.6	-2.6	-8.0	-0.5	-3.5	-0.6
Guinea-Bissau	-2.7	-1.6	4.4	-12.1	11.8	3.2	7.1
Ivory Coast	2.0	2.9	0.5	-0.9	9.6	4.1	-6.6
Kenya	-0.1	-1.7	-3.6	-6.2	-26.2	25.1	2.6
Lesotho	-1.5	-0.8	-2.9	0.2	-2.5	8.0	-10.3
Libya	3.8	1.6	7.8	-2.6	-5.9	20.0	-1.6
Madagascar	1.0	-1.2	-0.5	2.7	-1.4	-0.8	-2.7
Malawi	1.2	0.6	-1.9	-5.2	-1.7	-2.9	-2.2
Mali	0.6	0.4	-0.4	1.6	-9.4	-5.3	8.6
Mauritania	-0.3	-2.2	-3.9	-9.6	0.0	2.0	8.0
Morocco	1.8	-0.9	-0.3	-12.5	-0.3	6.4	16.4
Mozambique	1.0	-4.2	-3.7	-7.0	-3.0	-1.0	0.2
Niger	-0.7	1.5	-4.0	-1.2	-21.1	21.9	0.3
Nigeria	-0.8	-2.4	-0.3	-4.5	1.6	5.2	1.2
Rwanda	1.2	0.7	-3.1	3.3	-20.8	2.3	-0.9
Senegal	-2.3	-2.1	0.0	-26.9	13.8	14.4	-6.9
Sierra Leone	2.3	0.0	-1.4	0.7	-10.4	-5.3	8.0
Somalia	1.5	-3.3	-2.4	-7.7	-3.9	3.3	-0.9

Continued...

Table 6.5 cont'd

	1961-70	1970-80	1980-5	1982-3	1983-4	1984-5	1985-6
Sudan	0.0	0.4	-2.3	-1.3	-10.9	20.3	4.2
Swaziland	4.2	0.7	-1.2	-2.4	2.6	-6.8	-1.9
Togo	-0.4	-1.3	-2.3	-8.8	8.2	-3.9	-7.2
Tunisia	-2.0	1.5	1.7	8.1	-1.9	21.4	-13.0
Uganda	0.6	-3.1	1.7	2.7	-26.2	52.4	0.1
Tanzania	0.3	2.1	-1.5	-0.2	1.3	-1.7	-0.9
Zaire	-0.2	-1.2	0.0	-0.5	-0.5	-0.4	-2.0
Zambia	0.2	0.9	-1.3	2.2	-2.4	5.6	-2.0
Zimbabwe	0.4	-2.1	-2.2	24.2	6.4	36.9	-7.2
Regional Average[1]	0.0	-1.3	-1.0	-3.8	-2.8	6.2	0.5

Source: FAO
Note: [1] *Regional averages include Egypt which, for the purposes of this publication, is treated as part of West Asia*

The dismal performance throughout Africa has gradually forced changes in agricultural policy. But at least one aspect of the African dilemma lies outside the control of the region's governments and farmers. Price support schemes for a dwindling number of farmers in Europe, Japan and North America have unnecessarily led to huge surpluses in these countries. In 1950 Western Europe harvested 234 kilos of grain per person while Africa produced 157. Thirty-five years later Western Europe was harvesting 501 kilos per person though the African figure was only 150. Developed countries' surpluses depressed world prices available to African farmers.

In 1981 a controversial study by the World Bank, *Accelerated Development in Sub-Saharan Africa*, argued that

"for most African countries, and for a majority of the African population, the record [of economic development] is grim and it is no exaggeration to talk of a crisis. Slow overall economic

145

growth, sluggish agricultural performance coupled with rapid rates of population increases and balance of payments problems ... are dramatic indications of economic trouble" (page 2).

The controversial aspect of the study lay not in its warnings of impending crisis but in its suggestion that "domestic policy was the source of the problem". These criticisms drew the attention of others and African agricultural policies soon came under close scrutiny from many sources.

Much of the criticism of African agriculture has been directed at the ubiquitous marketing boards set up to handle many crops. This method, however, has a long history. In the early days of European rule, foreign companies were set up to handle plantations. These were grafted on to the existing African system. Land was allocated by licence from traditional chiefs to herdsmen and shareholders, who marketed export crops (eg cotton, coffee, tea, hides, etc) through state purchasing agencies. Though misjudgements by marketing boards have inevitably led to poor agricultural performance at times, some of Africa's problems are more fundamental, involving methods of land ownership itself.

According to customary laws in most African countries, farmland is not privately owned. Traditionally, a sparse population would work the land and, when it lost fertility, move on to farm elsewhere. This process was controlled by local tribes who allocated plots to each family according to the number of women available for work. But as the population of Africa soared, arable land became a scarce resource. Trees, pastures and fallow land can no longer recover through natural regeneration. Farming land requires care and maintenance which the traditional African agricultural system does not provide.

To conserve and fertilise their land, farmers must know it intimately and have reason to preserve their asset. However, private land-ownership is common in only two countries - Kenya and Zimbabwe.

The UK imposed its own land-tenure laws in those countries because it was trying to settle its own people as owner-farmers. The dangers of individual ownership are obvious: when owners die, their farms may be subdivided among many sons into tiny, unproductive holdings. No system of agriculture can effectively resolve Africa's major problem: the population is too large for its farming base. However, the benefit of private ownership is that it allows many farmers to experience both success and failures. Inefficient collective farms will spread the penalties of failure wide.

Uganda

Recent failures in African agriculture cannot all be attributed to the role of ownership. Uganda offers a dramatic example of what can happen when exchange rate policies go awry and undermine a country's ability to export its agricultural produce. In mid-1987 the Ugandan schilling was officially set at 1,400 to $1 though on the black market its value was 12,000 per dollar. Uganda's farmers suffered more than others. Because the government's marketing board changed hard currency into schillings only at the official exchange rate, it could pay growers no more than a tenth of the world price. Farmers either did not bother to harvest or sold their coffee and other produce to smugglers for export to other parts of Africa.

Belatedly, the Ugandan government devalued the schilling by 77%. It simultaneously reduced public spending and raised producers' prices for major crops. The short-run response was encouraging. Prices of raw coffee trebled, diverting sales from smugglers to the official coffee marketing board. But Uganda's problems were far from being resolved. Aid donors were not impressed with the government's reform and refused to provide further financial support. The result was that inflation resumed and by mid-1988 had reached an official annual rate of 200%. The black market exchange rate rose to a level seven times higher than the government-determined value of only a year earlier. Soon the cost of only a few days' supply of food staples was more than a Ugandan's minimum monthly wage, and the country's agricultural exports plummeted.

Tanzania

The causes of agricultural failures in Tanzania were different but no less severe. In developing its doctrine of *ujamaa* ("an agenda for caring and sharing"), farming was the key. Tanzanian agriculture had been based on a nationwide network of small and widely dispersed settlements, around which women tilled plots of collectively-owned land. When the plot lost its fertility, the chief allocated a new one and the family moved. The system yielded no marketable surpluses but provided for self-sufficiency. The *ujamaa* called for all these scattered households to be resettled, forming villages that could be economically supplied with piped water, schools, clinics and roads. The new communities rarely obtained the amenities promised. More important, they were unproductive. Instead of their wives going out to work in the fields, the men were supposed to walk to a collective field several miles away. The lack of a rural banking system meant that they were paid in government credits, not money. Incentives were further reduced because workers had access to no shops in which to spend any income or to obtain the seeds and fertiliser needed for farming.

Kenya

Kenya is the most industrialised of the three East African countries though more than 85% of the population live in the countryside, most on farms. Much of the country is semi-arid or desert though favourable weather and a government guarantee of higher agricultural prices have led to a rejuvenation of agriculture since

1986. In recent years Kenya has grown more maize then it can consume and exported much of this. But the margin of agricultural success is tenuous. Kenya's population is growing by more than 4% a year, meaning that it will double every 16 years. The added pressure this places on the country's farming sector and the virtual certainty that the rains will fail again some day mean that Kenya faces food shortages in the future.

Kenya's prospects are dimmed by conditions in international markets that apply as well to other parts of East Africa. Part of the problem is that Western countries, by dumping cheap grain on world markets and supplying free grain to the hungry, have made it unprofitable for Africans (and others) to develop their agricultural sector. In international markets East Africa's farmers also face harsh competition from other developing countries for their major exports, especially in the case of coffee. Brazil, one of the world's major coffee producers, required cash desperately in 1986 and 1987 and sold its coffee cheap on world markets. The surge in Brazilian supplies led to a steep decline in coffee prices. The repercussions for East Africa were serious since coffee accounts for 40% of Kenya's and Tanzania's exports and 90% of Uganda's.

Ivory Coast

The Ivory Coast, like several other African countries, has an agricultural sector dominated by a very few products. The country's Ivorian beans for cocoa and coffee are of superior quality. Until a world surplus reduced prices, these demanded a premium of international markets. The government tried to force up world cocoa prices by stockpiling in 1988 but the move proved unsuccessful. Cocoa prices in mid-1988 were at their lowest level in 12 years. Thus it seems likely that the 600,000 tonnes produced in 1988 will be added to the 80,000 tonnes already in the country's stockpile. International institutions, along with the French government, have sought to persuade the country to cut the price paid to its cocoa growers since this is now higher than the beans fetch for export. The state marketing board, which absorbs the difference between domestic and world prices, was unable to pay banks for the 1987 crop. However, the October 1988 the government launched the new growing season by announcing that prices would remain unchanged.

Madagascar

Development of the agricultural sectors in Madagascar has been part of a wider programme of structural adjustment intended to bring prosperity to farmers. The country's main staple is rice and until the early 1970s it was a net exporter. The government's subsequent decision to nationalise the rice trade and control its price brought about a steep decline in output. By 1982 Madagascar was importing 350,000 tonnes of rice a year. At the insistence of the IMF, in 1986 the country liberalised its controls as part of the restructuring programme. The result was a rise in the price of rice from 500 to 900 Malagasy francs a kilo. This event had serious political as well as economic repercussions. The Madagascans eat more rice than any country in the world except Burma and the price is the key to prosperity and politics. When the price of rice soared, supplies from Western countries were rushed to Madagascar, the intention being to create a buffer stock which would be slowly released on the market to reduce prices but not to depress severely farmers' income. Use of the buffer stock has now become a delicate issue. In response to political pressure, the government has been forced to sell at greatly reduced prices.

Zimbabwe

Zimbabwe, sometimes regarded as Africa's storehouse, faces a quite different situation from Madagascar. The country's agricultural performance suffered because of a drought in 1987. Maize deliveries fell to 600,000 tonnes after totalling 1.6 million tonnes in 1986. But Zimbabwe, unlike almost any other part of Africa, can rely on ample surpluses from previous harvests to bridge this shortfall. The country has about 4,000 large-scale farms (mostly White owned). There are another 750,000 small-farm holders (mainly Black) of which about 10,000 are commercial farms. The government's price guarantees ensure profits in all but drought years. For small farmers, it provides credit schemes and assistance in crop collection. In good years, almost half of all maize and cotton deliveries to state marketing boards come from Black-owned farms though in drought years it is the larger, mainly White-owned farms which are much more important suppliers.

In contrast to other African countries, it is Zimbabwe's agricultural potential that poses a threat. Large surpluses can be expensive to store and difficult to sell at worthwhile prices. One the advice of the IMF, some food prices were cut in 1987. Other moves have been taken to diversify the country's agricultural sector. One worry is that about a fifth of Zimbabwe's exports (excluding gold) is high-quality tobacco shipped to rich countries where anti-smoking campaigns threaten sales. The country's varied climate makes diversification an attractive strategy. For example, the recent rise in world prices of oilseeds led to increased production of soya beans, ground nuts and sunflowers which, when processed as vegetable oil, saved much foreign exchange. Another of the country's agricultural goals is to use its grain surpluses as a reserve against emergencies in neighbouring countries such as Mozambique and Zambia. European negotiators have discussed a scheme under which they would help pay Zimbabwe to keep such stocks.

151

Ethiopia

If Zimbabwe represents one of the more successful African examples, Ethiopia is an example of one of its failures. Internal strife, one of the world's harshest climates and meagre amounts of foreign aid ($17 per capita) make starvation a widespread condition. Crop losses have been high following years of poor rains in the northern part of the country. At the beginning of 1988 relief officials were already estimating that between 3 and 6 million people were threatened by hunger. The danger is greatest in the more remote northern provinces that have only one harvest a year. Once they have used up whatever crops or reserves are on hand, farmers must rely on food aid until the next harvest.

Ethiopia's agricultural policies have come under harsh criticism from Western donors. According to the Swedish International Development Agency the government sets grain prices too low, price relationships between inputs and outputs are unfavourable, provision of inputs is irregular and biased toward producer co-operatives and state farms, and agricultural extension agents are misdirected. Much aid has been delayed by various agencies until they are assured that it will not be used to continue many of the policies followed in the last decade. Recent figures show that Ethiopia spends about a quarter of its budget on defence, while allocating only 2.8% for agriculture, industry and mining.

For several years Ethiopian authorities and Western donors had advocated resettlement of 1.2 million farmers from overpopulated and overgrazed highlands to more fertile areas in the south. But implementation of the programme at the height of the last famine drew sharp criticism. It diverted vital resources at the height of the relief effort, entailed human rights violations and reflected poor planning that only heightened misery. Donors agree that without aid there will be recurrent famines in Ethiopia. But without socio-economic change, the country will remain dependent on such aid indefinitely.

III African Industry

The industrial base in Africa is minuscule in comparison with either Latin America or South and East Asia. The sector is nevertheless crucial for the region's overall economic performance and its future prospects. Close links between agriculture and industry are essential for development and modernisation of the former. Equally important, the growth of manufacturing enterprises can provide an increasingly important source of savings, and therefore investment, which is vital in a poor region such as this.

Table 6.6 provides an overview of growth in the manufacturing sector of many African countries. A comparison of figures for 1975-80 and 1980-5 reveals a very erratic pattern. Growth of manufacturing output in Cameroon has been exceptional - an increase of nearly 18% per year in 1980-5. In several countries, however, the manufacturing sector has contracted or has grown only negligibly in this decade. Worst hit have been Sierra Leone and Mozambique, where manufacturing output declined in the 1980s by 8.8% and 8.7% per year respectively. Other countries with a negative annual growth rate during 1980-5 include Zaire (-2.8%), Botswana (-2.2%) and Kenya (-0.4%). Overall, the growth record in the 1980s has not been as bad as in the previous five years when numerous countries experienced drastic declines in manufacturing output.

Table 6.6   GROWTH OF MANUFACTURING OUTPUT[1] IN AFRICAN
COUNTRIES 1975-1985

	Growth rate %				Index		
	1975-80	1980-5	1981	1982	1983	1984	1985
Angola	-0.8	2.3	99	103	104	108	111
Botswana	1.8	1.6	124	115	119	114	117
Cameroon	7.2	21.1	141	195	211	248	269
Ethiopia	4.2	4.0	103	83	113	116	115
Kenya	11.9	3.8	104	106	111	115	121
Malawi	2.6	3.4	103	103	110	113	118
Mozambique	-2.1	-8.7	103	86	80	72	67
Rwanda	6.5	6.2	108	109	118	124	128
Senegal	-2.0	2.5	110	113	118	116	114
Sierra Leone	1.6	-7.1	120	99	106	92	69
Somalia	-14.8	1.3	110	135	121	108	113
Sudan	-2.4	0.4	91	90	92	96	99
Uganda	-14.8	5.4	95	108	111	118	126
Zaire	-5.9	-2.8	101	90	89	86	90
Zambia	1.4	1.2	112	108	100	102	109
Zimbabwe	1.4	0.9	110	109	106	101	112

Source: UNIDO
Note: [1] *At constant 1980 prices*

Table 6.6 also shows year-to-year movements in the production
index. The feature which stands out is the erratic nature of
manufacturing performance. Given the small initial size of the
manufacturing sector in most African countries, levels of output can
easily double in only one or two years. This is true for Cameroon
where output more than doubled in 1980-5. Conversely, output in

Sierre Leone fell by 25% in only one year (1985). Similar abrupt shifts can be noted in many other countries in particular years.

The reasons for such erratic performance are often country-specific and too numerous to consider here though some are examined in section II of Chapter 7. The consequences, however, are severe and are common to many African countries. In years when output plummets, rates of capacity utilisation fall and unit costs rise. This not only affects efficiency but also rates of saving and business investment. The implications for development of skilled and semi-skilled workers are much the same. Erratic levels of demand and production in manufacturing bring about similar swings in employment. Workers have little opportunity for learning-by-doing, which has traditionally been an important source of labour skills.

Some of those consequences are illustrated in Table 6.7, which shows manufacturing output per employee. Wide swings in the year-to-year levels of labour productivity are indicative of the types of problems described above. The most alarming case is Nigeria, where labour productivity has fallen drastically. In 1985 the index declined by more than 38%, reaching a level which was only 59% of the 1980 base. Here, the effects of demand variation have been magnified by the country's reliance on large-scale enterprises in hopes of reducing unit costs. More generally, Table 6.7 leads to the impression that manufacturing output per employee has been falling in most African countries. This is true for eight of the ten economies for which data are available. A reversal of this downward trend will be essential if African countries are to achieve levels of industrial efficiency necessary for balanced and stable development.

Table 6.7   INDICES OF REAL MANUFACTURING OUTPUT PER
EMPLOYEE IN AFRICAN COUNTRIES 1981-1985

1980 = 100

	1981	1982	1983	1984	1985
Algeria	99.1	97.1	98.3	100.2	106.0
Burkina Faso	105.6	91.5	91.4	101.1	104.3
Central African Republic	97.6	74.4	75.1	69.6	75.6
Kenya	89.4	88.4	89.8	90.0	91.9
Morocco	93.3	89.2	88.6	83.3	78.3
Nigeria	105.8	119.2	106.4	81.5	59.1
Tanzania	81.6	86.1	81.1	80.5	85.8
Tunisia	105.1	95.4	93.3	90.3	87.5
Zambia	111.8	106.4	98.0	91.1	80.2
Zimbabwe	101.2	100.5	93.2	85.2	79.6

Source: World Bank

CHAPTER 7

IMPEDIMENTS AND PREREQUISITES FOR ECONOMIC PROGRESS IN AFRICA

As the least advanced of the Third World's four regions, the constraints on African growth are somewhat different. Although Africa, like Latin America, has a debt problem, its foreign obligations are mainly to official creditors and not commercial banks. The emergence of the region's debt problem and possible remedies are explored in section I. The development policies of many African countries are now in a stage of transition, in part because of the numerous programmes of structural adjustment that have been urged by international institutions. The policy transition is most apparent in the case of industry, and is discussed in section II. A related issue, that of exchange rate policies and pricing reforms, is examined in section III. Finally, the rudimentary economic state of many African countries means that much of the region is lacking in infrastructure and educational facilities. These two aspects are analysed in sections IV and V respectively.

I African Debt

Africa's debts began to mount at the same time as economic performance waned. Commodity prices began falling on world markets in the late 1970s and have continued their decline throughout most of the 1980s. African governments nevertheless continued borrowing to finance their relatively large bureaucracies and domestic programmes. In 1981 Zambia signed an agreement to borrow $1 billion dollars from the IMF over three years, the largest sum the Fund had ever loaned to a Black African country. Nigeria,

Black Africa's biggest oil producer, found it owed $25 billion in foreign debts when Major-General Babangida took over in 1985. Many African countries used the foreign funds they obtained to establish big, new industries. Airlines, steel mills, hotels and other "high profile" projects were established without sufficient markets and sales to make them profitable.

The cumulative effect of the misjudgements eventually became clear. Black Africa's ratio of debts to annual export earnings, 188% in 1982, had risen to 351% by 1987. When African countries began to seek help, they turned mainly to international institutions. Teams of World Bank and IMF experts assembled numerous reform plans. These provided concessionary finance but also required stringent economic policies. In varying degrees, most African countries adopted reform programmes that included devaluing their currencies, cutting food subsidies, abolishing state marketing boards and reducing the civil service. Though austere, the reform programmes did not always achieve their goals. A major reason was that Africa's per capita income was falling. Figure 7.1 shows that Africa's real GDP per capita was lower in 1987 than in 1980. Behind the fall in income was a 40% decline in the region's terms of trade in 1981-6. By the beginning of 1988 it was clear that even the most virtuous of African countries would probably not be able to repay their debts - and if their debts were not repaid, they would become ineligible for new loans.

In September 1988 the finance ministers of the seven leading capitalist countries agreed to choose between three options to reduce Africa's debt burden: to write off a third of these debts; to cut interest rates by 3.5%, or roughly half the debt; or to extend repayments over 25 years. Unlike Latin America, which owes most of its debt to commercial banks, Africa owes three-quarters of its debt to governments, the World Bank and the IMF. The new efforts should save African countries around $500 million each year. Hopefully, they will be able to keep more of the foreign exchange which they earn; it will be vital that they make the best use of it.

158

Governments will need to pursue their reform programmes with additional vigour as debt-imposed discipline is relaxed.

Figure 7.1   REAL GDP PER CAPITA IN AFRICA 1980-1987

1980 = 100

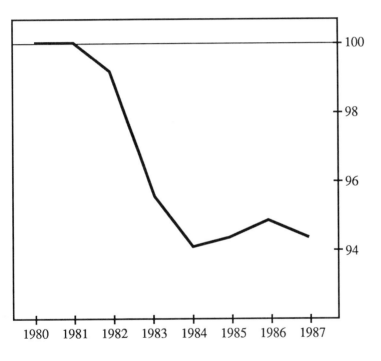

Source: World Bank

159

Table 7.1 shows long-term debt and debt service in African countries for 1970 and 1986. Nigeria is the region's largest debtor; in 1986 it owed nearly $22 billion to foreign creditors, and only two years later unofficial estimates put the debt at $35 billion. The Ivory Coast, too, is a relatively large debtor. Ivorians owed nearly $9.5 billion in 1986, a tremendous sum for such a small country. By 1988 the Ivory Coast was virtually bankrupt; with a national deficit of $280 million and world prices of its major export (cocoa) very low, payment of its external debts is impossible. Other countries with relatively large outstanding debts are Sudan ($7.1 billion), Tunisia ($5.3 billion), Kenya ($3.7 billion) and Zambia ($3.6 billion).

Table 7.1   AFRICA'S TOTAL EXTERNAL PUBLIC AND PRIVATE DEBT AND DEBT-SERVICE RATIOS 1970/1986

$ million

	Total long-term debt[1]		Debt service as a percentage of exports of goods and services	
	1970	1986	1970	1986
Burkina Faso	21	616	6.5	14.8
Cameroon	141	2,772	4.0	22.8
Central African Republic	24	393	5.3	9.6
Ethiopia	169	1,989	11.3	25.8
Ghana	494	1,413	5.5	10.8
Ivory Coast	266	9,455	na	na
Kenya	406	3,700	5.9	22.5
Liberia	158	1,002	8.1	6.4
Madagascar	90	2,635	3.7	27.7
Malawi	122	910	7.8	40.1
Mali	238	1,566	1.0	14.2
Nigeria	567	21,876	7.1	23.4

Continued...

Table 7.1 cont'd

	Total long-term debt[1]		Debt service as a percentage of exports of goods and services	
	1970	1986	1970	1986
Rwanda	2	439	1.2	7.6
Senegal	131	2,471	4.0	20.2
Sudan	307	7,057	10.7	7.7
Tunisia	541	5,251	19.7	30.7
Tanzania	265	3,650	5.3	15.3
Zambia	653	3,575	6.4	11.0
Zimbabwe	na	1,758	na	na

Source: World Bank
Note: [1] *Includes publicly guaranteed debt and private non-guaranteed debt*

The size of external debt, however, must be seen in relation to the country's ability to repay. Debt service as a percentage of exports of goods and services gives an indication of this capability. Increases in the percentage between 1970 and 1986 were dramatic, more than doubling in 11 of the 19 countries in Table 7.1. Equally ominous is the fact that by 1986 eight of these countries were expected to devote one-fifth or more of all export earnings to service their debt.

Ghana is one of the few African countries whose policies are presently looked on with favour by international lending institutions. The country was one of the region's first to obtain independence. When it began life in 1957 per capita GDP was roughly the same as in Mexico or South Korea. For the next 25 years Ghanaians' real income fell on average by 1% per year. Aid donors virtually abandoned Ghana and it was not until 1983 that the country's leader, Lieutenant Rawlings, persuaded the World Bank to help. By that time Ghana's economy was collapsing. The minimum wage was 13% below its 1975 level and investment was only 4% of GDP -

barely enough to replace depreciating capital stock and inadequate for growth.

Ghana adopted a three-pronged strategy to raise domestic revenues, liberalise trade policies and restore confidence in the banking system. Revenues were increased through higher taxes on luxury consumption, a general shift from direct to indirect taxes and improvements in tax administration. Liberalisation of trade eliminated the black market while the exchange rate was depreciated by about 90%. Money balances also increased once inflation abated, making it possible to ease credit restraints.

Figure 7.2 illustrates the results of this programme. The amount of arrears has declined significantly since 1982 but, more important, the value of external financial support available to the country rose from $1.6 billion to $2.2 billion in 1986. For Ghana this was critical in the initial phase before the exchange rate adjustment and domestic resource-mobilisation efforts could bear fruit. The bulk of lending was provided by the IMF and the World Bank but, significantly, the volume of funds supplied by other sources has now begun to increase. This could place Ghana in a position to continue to pursue a growth-oriented adjustment strategy.

By 1988 more than 30 of Africa's smaller countries (which number more than 40) have undertaken economic adjustment programmes similar to that of Ghana. Few have made such a successful recovery. Analysts estimate that if they are to carry through the necessary structural adjustments without disaster, African countries will need some $2 billion a year more than the $3 billion they received in 1988 in official external finance.

Figure 7.2   GHANA'S EXTERNAL DEBT TO OFFICIAL CREDITORS
1970-1986

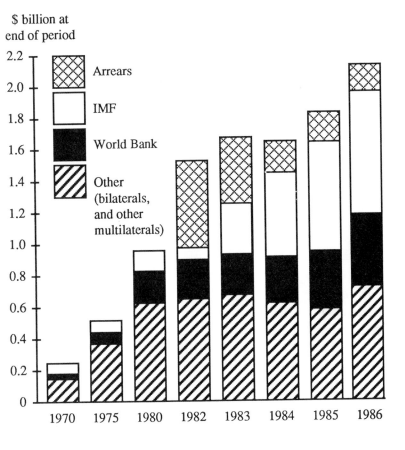

Source: World Bank

Nigeria's foreign debt is different from those of other African countries. It was amassed not by destitution but by incompetence and theft during the first half of the 1980s. Much of the debt was not borrowed from governments or official lenders trying to help Nigerians develop their economy. The debt is mainly owed for purchases made during the oil boom of the 1970s. In theory, it would not be hard to settle these obligations. Despite the fall in oil prices and Nigeria's difficulties in meeting its OPEC quota, the country still sells $7 billion worth of oil each year. The gap between these revenues and Nigeria's $25 billion debt could be easily bridged by a commercial loan. But bankers want to be sure that the borrower will use the money prudently before they lend it. The Nigerian government, on the other hand, understandably resents having to pay for the past misdeeds of others. For several years the IMF has been offering a loan coupled with various restrictions, which the Nigerians have rejected.

II Industrial Policy

The great diversity in the size and endowments of domestic markets in African countries has contributed to differences in policy approaches and industrial priorities. Nigeria is not only the region's largest country but also one of the richest in resources. Nigerian planners have attempted to make use of these characteristics to reap some of the benefits of scale economies enjoyed by industrialised countries. The government has spent much money to develop a steel industry. Progress, however, has been severely hampered because the steel plants are far away from raw materials, fuel and transport routes. Nigeria's other costly industry is petroleum. Although the country has reserves to last only another 20-35 years, it uses fuel lavishly and imposes very low prices. An unnecessary number of cars are imported and a sizeable proportion of the subsidised Nigerian petrol is smuggled into neighbouring countries. So much is wasted that the country can rarely meet its OPEC quotas for production of crude oil.

Africa's reform programmes have recently been extended to include aspects of privatisation. This is one of the tactics Nigeria and other African countries have employed to reduce the budget deficits. Nigeria has sought to sell dozens of state-run or parastatal companies including insurance firms, banks and breweries (though not steel or petrol). The Ivory Coast has sold holdings in 28 companies and hopes to sell 100 or more. Spurred by an IMF/World Bank austerity plan, Togo has also disposed of several state and parastatal holdings including the country's steel mill, food-processing plants, textile firms and plastics. Cameroon, Congo, Ghana, Liberia, Niger and Zaire have also taken steps toward disinvestment of state-run companies or are seeking investors for parastatals.

Despite this trend, privatisation of African economies is an art, not a science. Relinquishing state-owned industries to the private sector will not suffice to get African economies growing again. In many cases, there are few legitimate buyers. Some of the firms to be sold were ill-conceived in the first place, built in an era when every country wanted its own steel mill, car assembly plant or sugar mill and was not seriously concerned about economic viability. Other plants were over-built with a capacity far beyond actual market needs. Still others were run into the ground by a combination of poor maintenance and incompetence. Finally, governments are reluctant to sell off their profitable industries or those that deal with the primary sources of income such as Togo's phosphate industry of Nigeria's oil industry.

Today, Nigeria's efforts to develop large-scale industries are relatively unique within the region. Most African policymakers have been shifting their emphasis away from creating industrial capacity to encouraging more efficient resource use. The shift is partly in

165

recognition of the fact that the industrial sector has lagged well behind the rest of the economy in most countries. Many of the industries created in the 1960s and 1970s have not become internationally competitive and so have been denied export markets. Nor has the capacity created in this period been fully utilised; the shortage of foreign exchange has restricted the ability of firms to import necessary inputs. Industry's export earnings have more recently stagnated as a result of unfavourable trends in the world economy. Finally, inefficiencies and continuing subsidies of public industries have become a serious budgetary drain in a period when resources are increasingly scarce.

When the majority of African countries gained independence, they saw industrial development as the key to diversifying their colonial-based economies away from heavy dependence on imported manufactures and exports of primary products. Import substitution was the means by which this transformation was to be achieved with high levels of tariff production, overvalued exchange rates and investment incentives to produce for the domestic market. State ownership was a central feature of the socialist doctrine embraced by most African countries. Public investment was intended to increase capacity while reducing reliance on foreign capital. At the same time, government intervention discouraged private industrial investment, especially in countries such as Benin, Ghana, Somalia, Tanzania, Zaire and Zambia.

Capacity grew rapidly and production diversified during the 1960s. By the late 1970s, however, declining capacity utilisation was apparent while growth was still vulnerable to international economic conditions. Industrial production grew by only 1.4% and year in 1973-83 (one-tenth of the rate in 1965-73), well below the reduced GDP growth rate of 2.1%. Industry in many countries suffered another blow when their terms of trade worsened in the 1980s. Dependence on imports actually increased, partly because import-substituting industries relied heavily on imported inputs and partly because agricultural growth failed to keep up with population increases and led to a rise in food imports. Some of the failures were the result of economic stagnation and external factors such as drought and worsening terms of trade. But they also revealed that the strategy of import substitution entailed high costs.

These experience led many African governments to conclude that the industrial sector, by itself, cannot provide the basis for economic growth and recovery. An effective industrialisation strategy must be based on complementary agricultural development. The Ivory Coast's strong agricultural performance in the 1960s and 1970s, for example, helped to sustain industrial growth by increasing supplies of domestic raw materials and boosting rural demand. Freeing agricultural and industrial prices in Ghana since 1983 has likewise helped to rejuvenate the industrial sector. Zimbabwe, too, has avoided industrial decline partly through its agricultural success. In contrast, in other countries such as Nigeria and Senegal the momentum of growth has been snuffed out because a lagging agricultural sector has deprived industry of imports and domestic demand for its products.

Reforms have now been introduced in African countries at three levels: sectoral, subsectoral and firm. At the sectoral level, the emphasis has been on making the incentive structure more neutral. For example, policies in Ghana and Nigeria are now intended to induce resources to move from less productive, non-tradable activities (eg retailing and public administration) to tradable activities such as agriculture and exports. Exchange rate policies that are more responsive to the country's balance of payments position are being installed. These are being complemented by stabilisation programmes to reduce the inflationary pressures that led to overvaluation in the first place. Reforms in Ghana, Guinea, Nigeria, Sierra Leone, Zaire and Zambia have used foreign exchange auctions to make exchange rates more responsive to market forces.

Within industry, greater exposure to international competition is relied upon to encourage resources to shift into fields where they can be more efficiently used. Countries have relaxed quantitative reductions on imports, making tariff protection more uniform across industries. Many African industries have so much excess capacity that resources can be shifted out of them without necessarily reducing production: greater productivity can be achieved with the labour, capital and other inputs which remain. Zambia's adjustment programme, for example, brought capacity utilisation from under 40% to more than 50% in one year. Ghana, too, has undertaken institutional reforms to make it easier for firms to expand and contract, to begin or discontinue production, and generally to enhance the responsiveness of producers.

At the firm level, incentives favour the adaptation of technology to local resources and conditions. Positive real interest rates, the removal of tariff exemptions and the reorientation of investment incentives toward domestic output and away from imported capital have featured in these new programmes. Interest rates have been raised and investment lowered in some countries. Investment codes have also been revised in Ghana, Guinea, Madagascar, Togo and Zambia. Individual firms may also need substantial restructuring as well to be competitive in domestic and export markets. Costs may have to be reduced or quality raised. Improved marketing and a broader capital base are often required. As a consequence, policy reforms must be accompanied by funding and incentives for investment to replace outmoded equipment and to train management - as, for example, in Mauritius.

Reforms of such sweeping scope inevitably raise issues of implementation, one of the most contentious being the appropriate level of protection. The small size of most African markets limits the extent of competition, especially in industries characterised by economies of scale. Reduced protection must be offset by exchange-rate adjustments to avoid excess demand for imports. Devaluation, however, is not always a practical approach, being unsustainable in high inflation countries such as Uganda and Zambia. An increased consumption tax may also be required in order to compensate for any loss in revenues due to the reduction in tariffs.

The speed of adjustment to a more efficient industrial structure is another important issue. A rapid and complete change in the forces governing the allocations of resources is desirable. This requires substantial political will. However, sudden and large price changes can themselves hinder adjustment. Major policy changes therefore need to be co-ordinated with transitional measures to cushion the efforts of adjustment and permit phased changes.

Finally, responses to reform can be inhibited through economic constraints such as a shortage of credit, inadequate infrastructure, a primitive financial system or the lack of technology and technological expertise. Labour markets, for example, must be responsive to the new needs of firms, providing the flexibility to hire, fire and to develop a trained labour force through education and experience. Another likely source of problems comes from the public sector, which will control substantial resources. This is true even in countries such as Ghana, Ivory Coast, Madagascar or Senegal which are de-emphasising direct public sector investment in industry. Several types of measures are being used to remove constraints on public sector performance: conversion of debt to equity is intended to improve the financial soundness of these firms; decentralisation of operating decisions is another popular method used to free firms from political influence. In the field of finance, special criteria are being introduced for firms (both public and private) that are economically viable but financially weak. Foreign borrowing can also help to make reforms more acceptable by increasing supplies while adjustment takes place. Both Ghana and Nigeria have obtained loans for additional industrial inputs while restructuring their manufacturing sector.

Overall, many African governments have launched ambitious reform programmes in the last few years. Unlike previous strategies, the present ones put a greater emphasis on efficiency and complementary growth of agriculture and exports. Such programmes amount to a substantial departure from the forms of industrialisation in the past and, though difficult to implement, promise a stronger industrial base for the region in the 1990s.

III Exchange Rates and Pricing Reforms

Economic disaster at home and mounting foreign debts have driven more than half Africa's countries to seek financial help from the IMF and the World Bank. In return, they have usually been required to implement various types of economic reforms, often currency devaluation and price liberalisation schemes.

Ghana was one of Africa's leaders in the continent's early drive to free itself from economic dependence on developed countries. Eventually, however, the country found itself deeply in debt and with exchange rates that aggravated its economic plight. Ghana began life in 1957 with a GDP per capita roughly equivalent to that of Mexico or South Korea. However, real income declined by 1% a year during the next 25 years. Belatedly, the country introduced stringent economic reforms. More than 80,000 civil servants were released, petrol subsidies were abolished and realistic exchange rates installed. By 1988 the Ghanaian udi had fallen to a level against the US dollar 1/60th that in 1983. Economic difficulties abound though GDP has grown by 6% a year over the last five years. Economic reforms are beginning to show progress although the recent drop in world cocoa prices threatens these gains.

Nigeria, too, has embraced reform programmes, distinguished by currency devaluation and market liberalisation. In 1985 the country owed about $25 billion in foreign debt and had stopped paying its bills. On the advice of the World Bank, Nigeria has now devalued its currency to less than a quarter of the official rate in December 1985. The bureaucracies that controlled agricultural prices and supplies of imports were abolished. But riots occurred when the government raised the price of petrol by only 3% (though it is still less than $0.10 litre). Rising import prices have pinched the urban bourgeoisie while trade unions and students have violently opposed other reform steps. As opposition to Nigeria's reform programme mounts, prospects that the country's efforts can be kept on track have dimmed.

The new policies of countries like Ghana and Nigeria have created pressure on other neighbouring countries to undertake similar reforms. That pressure is greatest in the Francophone countries around the bight of Africa. The French African Community (CFA) is made up of 13 countries, all of which use the CFA franc. The franc, exchangeable at 50 to the French franc, is grossly overvalued. Although the financial system helped its members to avoid inflation and was sufficiently stable to encourage investment, its strength has been undermined by the long-term fall in commodity prices. Coffee and cocoa are West Africa's two main exports. However, the first now sells for two-thirds of the price of ten years ago while the price of the second has been halved. Smuggling, which is a good indicator of real currency values, used to drive Nigerians to buy cheap goods in Francophone countries. Now the illegal traffic goes the other way.

Both the IMF and World Bank have called for devaluations. Differential devaluation among members of the CFA would mean different currencies, a step which would destroy the monetary union. French supporters of the CFA are also reluctant to support devaluations. French companies with debts in French francs but earnings in CFA francs strongly oppose the move.

171

IV African Infrastructure

An adequate infrastructure is, of course, essential for the economic progress of any region. Africa's system of infrastructure is far less advanced than that of other developing regions. At this stage in Africa's development one of the most important types of infrastructure is a transport system that will not only link the region's economies but also help to integrate local markets within various countries. In theory, rail should be more economical than road for moving heavy freight over Africa's vast distances.

The origins of existing rail systems in Africa can be traced back to the colonial period. Cecil Rhodes dreamed of building a railway from the Cape to Cairo while the French had visions of a network stretching from Dakar in the west to Djibouti in the east. Fragments of these grand schemes still provide the major rail links for many African countries. Two important southern lines were built by the British through present-day Angola (the Benguela line) and Mozambique (the Beiru corridor). Another rib begins in Kenya at Mombasa and extends through Uganda. Uganda has an additional rail running to its copper mines while on the west coast the French-built line runs from the coast in Abidjan to Ougadougou in Burkina Faso. The most famous line is the Tazara Railway begun in the 1970s. With the help of China, Tanzania set out to build a railway which South Africa could not touch. The Tazara was to carry Zambia's copper to Dar es Salaam.

Altogether, these railways should represent a respectable start on a region-wide transport system. However, African governments have starved their railways of necessary investment whenever foreign exchange has run low. And in periods when traffic falls, they have insisted on maintaining workforces. Other lines have been handicapped by the provision of locomotives and equipment that were not suitable. The experience of Sudan Railways is typical. Rebels in the south and local disputes in the west have paralysed most of the country's 3,300 miles of track. The rail link between Khartoum and Port Said, which should be a key part of the country's transport system, has been weakened by mismanagement. The line's freight tonnage has declined from 3.5 million tonnes in 1972 to 600,000 tonnes in 1987. Nevertheless, Sudanese Railways continues to employ a workforce of the same size (33,000 workers) as in the early 1970s.

The Tazara Railway represents another example of a promising project gone awry. The Chinese equipment originally provided to supply the Tazara was not suitable: the locomotives would not pull their loads uphill. Although the line moves about 90% of Zambia's copper, it has never carried more than half the project's projected 2.5 million tonnes per year. A ten-year rehabilitation project was begun in 1985. Expected to cost about $227 million, much of it is for new locomotives to replace the original Chinese engines.

V Educational Development and External Aid

The role of educational and related development of skilled labour is vital for most African countries. Since their independence, African nations have invested heavily in education. The gains have been impressive. In 1960-83 the gross primary enrolment rose from 36 to 75% in sub-Saharan Africa. Adult literacy rates rose as well from 3 to 20% in that period.

More recently, these advances have been threatened by the region's economic decline and explosive population growth. If 1983 levels of school participation are to be maintained, primary school places would have to increase from 51 million to 91 million by the year 2000. Similarly, secondary school places would have to rise from 11 million to 20 million. The need for rapid expansion of education comes at a time when economic difficulties have led to a significant reduction in public spending in most countries. Recurrent public

173

expenditure on education, for example, declined from $10 billion in 1980 to $8.9 billion in 1983.

Yet the evidence drawn from African countries indicates that increased investments in education and training would yield substantial economic benefits in terms of increased labour productivity, economic growth and reduced fertility rates. African studies have found that, on average, investments in education can explain more than 30% of GDP growth. Moreover, there is a strong relationship between women's education and the number of children each woman has during her lifetime - the greater the educational level, the fewer the children.

The deterioration of African education is evidenced by stagnating enrolments and declining quality. The decline affects all levels of education but is most pronounced at the primary level. To some extent, this deceleration in the rate of expansion is a natural consequence of the rapid growth of enrolments in the 1960s and 1970s. Declines in enrolment, however, also reflect the current economic situation. Children who might have attended school in better times are kept out to work at home. In addition, many countries have introduced or raised fees just as family incomes have dropped. Finally, the quality of education may have fallen as a result of the recent economic stagnation.

The same sorts of problems plague higher education in Africa. Although the number of university enrolments has increased more than twentyfold since the early 1960s, higher education's contribution to African development is being threatened by three interrelated weaknesses. First, the quality of graduates in many countries has deteriorated: over-enrolment in less rigorous fields of study is one reason; the virtual disappearance of equipment, laboratory supplies, textbooks and other learning materials - all due to the enforced cutback in spending because of the economic crisis - is another. Second, the cost per student in African universities is

174

exorbitant; about 40 times that of primary education. By comparison, in Asia and Latin America the per student cost of higher education is 10 to 15 times greater than the cost per elementary student. Third, higher education - including student living costs - is entirely financed out of the public budget. Resources are inefficiently allocated and income inequality is exacerbated since higher income families are more likely to send their children to college.

There is much that African countries can themselves do to improve their educational systems. Necessary steps include the diversification of sources of educational finance, increased cost-sharing in public education and more rigorous control of cost. Alone, however, African countries are not likely to find the resources necessary for a revitalisation of their education programmes. The international donor community will also have to play a role. In the early 1980s international aid to education averaged about $1.3 billion annually - equivalent to 15% of Africa's domestic expenditures on education.

Education aid has tended to focus on discrete investment projects with little or no co-ordination between donors. Moreover, a disproportionate share of aid goes to higher education compared with primary schools: only 7% of all direct education aid is used to finance primary education against 34% for higher education. The lack of balance is even more dramatic among primary donors: less than 4% of bilateral direct aid is marked for primary education.

The neglect of primary education is partly explained by the failure (both by donor and recipient) to recognise the importance of primary education in African development. Since primary schools are usually widely dispersed, no single school enjoys high visibility or identifiable impact. Moreover, construction plus teachers' salaries typically account for more than 95% of expenditures on primary education. International donors, however, are hesitant to finance local salaries. There are relatively fewer higher and secondary technical institutions. Each is visible and has a discernible impact on the educational system.

Revitalisation of the African educational system is imperative if the region's workforce is to attain the skills necessary for progress in a competitive world. African countries must intensify their own efforts to offer high quality education and training. Following the example of developed countries, more on-the-job training and job-specific training will be needed. Higher education will have to focus on fields crucial to African development - for example agriculture, health and engineering. International donors can help in this endeavour by providing greater support for primary education and funding for applied research.

CHAPTER 8

ECONOMIC PERFORMANCE AND TRENDS IN WEST ASIA

The countries of West Asia are predominantly Arab. Most spent four centuries under the rule of the Ottoman Empire and regained their independence only after World War II. Altogether, West Asia comprises a population of nearly 160 million and claims more than half the world's proven oil reserves. Most of the region shares a common language and religion. More recently, several West Asian countries have attained a degree of wealth unimaginable only two decades ago. These conditions should result in an economically strong and politically influential region though, in fact, West Asia is not.

The countries making up this region are indicated in Table 8.1. Geographically, Egypt is part of Africa but is included here because of its close political and economic ties with the Arab nations to its east. The only non-Arab country in the region is Iran. That country shares a common religion (Islam) and similar resource base with its Arab neighbours though its stormy relations with other countries and the Iran-Iraq war mean that its links with other parts of West Asia are tenuous and difficult.

Table 8.1 illustrates some of the economic diversity within this seemingly homogeneous region. Countries such as Egypt and Iran have populations over 100 times larger than several of the tiny states in the Persian Gulf. The level and growth of per capita income are equally varied with countries like Qatar and the United Arab Emirates (UAE) being far richer than their neighbours. Patterns of trade performance in the region break down into two broad groups:

Table 8.1   KEY ECONOMIC INDICATORS FOR WEST ASIAN COUNTRIES 1985/1986

	Population 1985 (million)	GDP per capita[1] 1986 ($)	Growth of GDP[1] 1980-6 (%)	Trade balance 1986[2] ($ million)	Ratio of outstanding debt to GNP 1985 (%)	Direct investment in country 1985 ($ million)
Bahrain	0.4	11,850	-	177	21.1	-46.6
Egypt	48.5	1,100	3.4	-4,010	80.2	1,217.7
Iran	44.6	na	2.9	2,357 [3]	2.4	na
Iraq	15.9	2,800	na	na	32.5	na
Jordan	3.5	1,246	2.5	-1,424	80.4	24.9
Kuwait	1.7	8,850	-6.2	1,978	2.8	na
Lebanon	2.6	na	-	na	na	na
Oman	1.2	5,900	na	607	24.8	138.4
Qatar	0.3	16,550	na	-	4.1	-
Saudi Arabia	11.5	7,450	4.3	3,051	3.9	966.7

Continued...

Table 8.1 cont'd

	Population 1985 (million)	GDP per capita[1] 1986 ($)	Growth of GDP[1] 1980-6 (%)	Trade balance 1986[2] ($ million)	Ratio of outstanding debt to GNP 1985 (%)	Direct investment in country 1985 ($ million)
Syria	10.5	2,050	3.8	-1,952	16.6	na
United Arab Emirates	1.4	14,950	na	na	5.0	na
North Yemen	6.7	400	-2.9	-192	131.1	na
South Yemen	2.4	450	4.3	-780	56.8	5.4

Source: World Bank/UN/Arab Banking Corporation
Notes: [1] At constant market prices
[2] Exports (fob) less imports (fob)
[3] 1984

oil-poor countries have usually faced a negative trade balance while in others the trade balance depends mainly on the price of oil. Variation is equally great in the case of outstanding debt and foreign investment. Egypt received more than $1.2 billion in foreign capital in 1985 though its debt was equivalent to 80% of GNP. North Yemen's debt exceeds its GNP while Jordan is another large debtor. In contrast, countries such as Iran, Kuwait and Saudi Arabia have very little foreign debt.

Much of this diversity is attributable to oil wealth (or the lack of it). Income of the region's oil-producing countries began to rise at a dazzling pace immediately after the first price hikes in 1973-4. Saudi Arabia and some of its OPEC allies were soon earning foreign exchange at the rate of $115,000 per second. At 1974 prices they could have bought the equivalent of all the equities on the London Stock Exchange in only nine months. Within 22 months, they had earned an amount matching all the direct investments of American corporations outside the USA. Oil exports have brought the Arab states (excluding Iran) $1.5 trillion since the first round of price increases in 1973. But the flow of these vast amounts of annual income has slowed at least for now. In 1981 Saudi Arabia earned nearly $120 billion from oil but by 1987 its oil income was less than a fifth of that amount.

This survey of West Asia begins with a discussion of the region's trading patterns and export performance. During periods of high oil prices, the rapid growth of the region's wealth has created various types of imbalance: one of these, a shortage of labour, is examined in section II, which deals with the subject of immigrant workers. West Asian countries' fiscal policies and budgets are also a hostage to the price of oil. This aspect is considered in the chapter's concluding section.

I Trade in West Asia

Two distinct phases are evident in the trade of West Asia, both dominated by abrupt shifts in exports. Though the value of exports rose fivefold between 1963 and 1973, growth accelerated even more in later years. During the year immediately following the first OPEC price increase, Saudi Arabia and some of its neighbours began to record vast foreign exchange surpluses. By 1980 exports were $208 billion, representing nearly an eightfold rise over 1973, but they declined dramatically in the 1980s (see Table 8.2). The deterioration in 1981-5 was largely the result of lower export volumes but the 22.6% decrease in 1986 reflected weaker export prices. In fact, the volume of West Asia's exports is estimated to have risen by 15% in 1986 although the decline in prices more than offset these gains. The region's dramatic swings in exports had equally serious repercussions for its ability to import. In 1982 (two years after exports) imports reached a peak of $130 billion. The subsequent decline consisted largely of a reduction in volumes. Countries which were most dependent on oil exports cut back the volume of their imports sharply, sometimes by as much as 25%.

Table 8.2   GROWTH OF EXPORTS, IMPORTS AND TERMS OF TRADE IN WEST ASIA 1975-1986

% change	1975-86 [1]	1982	1983	1984	1985	1986
Growth of exports	0.0	-21.6	-23.3	-10.7	-10.6	-22.6
Growth of imports	8.7	4.7	-4.9	-8.0	-16.6	-8.5
Terms of trade[2] (1980 = 100)	-	120	106	107	104	54

Source: UNCTAD
Notes: [1] *Average annual rate*
[2] *Ratio of export unit value index to import unit value index*

181

Table 8.3 shows the structure of West Asia's trade. Oil accounts for more than four-fifths of the region's exports and manufactures nearly two-thirds of its imports. The four leading merchandise exporters in 1986 - Saudi Arabia, UAE, Iraq and Iran - supplied over 70% of all West Asia's exports, most of which comprised crude oil. The same four countries, together with Egypt, accounted for nearly 60% of the region's imports in 1986. The region is also competitive in some textile lines, leather and tanning products, metals and a few non-metallic minerals. However, the only significant exporters of manufactures - Syria and Jordan - both recorded declines in 1986.

Table 8.3   STRUCTURE OF TRADE BY MAJOR COMMODITY GROUP IN WEST ASIA 1970-1985

%

	Exports			Imports		
	1970	1975	1985	1970	1975	1985
Food items	5.9	1.5	2.8	14.1	11.5	13.4
Agricultural raw materials	3.9	0.8	0.7	3.0	1.8	1.5
Ores and metals	1.4	0.6	2.0	7.8	10.8	7.7
Fuels	84.5	94.4	81.1	6.5	6.5	10.8
Manufactures	4.3	2.8	8.7	63.6	65.2	63.2
TOTAL ($ million)	10,543	82,281	105,177	7,059	43,003	89,877

Source: UNCTAD

There are no indications that this pattern of country and product concentration will change in the foreseeable future. Non-oil exports have grown only marginally despite determined efforts by several countries to increase their shipments of these goods. The only product category where modest diversification is reflected is the increase in petroleum products in total petroleum exports. Until 1986 there was strong growth of investment and installed capacity in the region's petrochemicals industry. The move was mainly in response to incentives to diversify into downstream activities. These offered producers substantial cost advantages owing to the low price of feedstocks. Some oil countries also regarded the export of refined products as a means of augmenting foreign earnings held down by OPEC quotas on their crude petroleum exports.

Few changes have occurred in the product structure of the region's imports since the early 1970s. The share of manufactured goods, imported mainly from Western Europe, Asia and North America, remained stable during the 1970s and 1980s. In value terms, imports of primary commodities have been least affected by the region's rise and fall of imports. Food items are the second largest category in the region's import bill. While the share of these has risen slightly since 1975, the proportion of minor categories (agricultural raw materials and metals) has declined. Altogether, the division of primary and processed products in total imports remained broadly stable since 1970.

Table 8.4 shows the structure of West Asia's trade by origin and destination. The developed market economies are the region's major trading partners for both exports and imports although this group's share of West Asia's trade has diminished in the 1980s. Western Europe and North America accounted, on average, for over 50% of West Asia's petroleum exports during the 1970s but their combined share was reduced in the 1980s as Asian buyers increased their purchases to 46% of the total. West Asia's exports of petroleum products have been strongly influenced by exports of non-OPEC countries outside the region. The origin and destination of non-petroleum exports are largely a residual category and are subject to a much broader range of intra-regional and external factors than is oil.

Table 8.4   WEST ASIA'S STRUCTURE OF TRADE BY ORIGIN AND DESTINATION[1] 1970-1985

%

		Developed market economies	Socialist countries	Developing countries	of which: Intra-region
Imports					
	1970	68.4	11.5	19.1	11.1
	1975	75.8	5.9	17.6	9.2
	1985	62.7	5.7	29.6	16.2
Exports					
	1970	69.8	2.6	20.7	7.4
	1975	71.2	2.3	23.0	4.8
	1985	50.0	2.4	46.4	13.9

Source: UNCTAD

Note: [1] *Trade with socialist developing countries is not included*

West Asia's intra-regional trade accounts for a comparatively small portion of its total. Regional markets are also rather unreliable, being subject to the wide swings in trade as oil earnings fluctuate. In periods when oil exports were rising, the share of intra-regional trade (both imports and exports) fell as buyers shifted their purchases to goods supplied by industrialised countries. In 1985 West Asian producers themselves supplied just over 60% of the region's imports from all developing countries and accounted for 30% of total exports to developing countries.

Some West Asian countries have made efforts to boost their trade with one another. The six members of the Gulf Co-operation Council (GCC) - Bahrain, Kuwait, Oman, Qatar, Saudi Arabia and the UAE - recently agreed to co-ordinate their exchange rates in order to increase trade and capital flows within the Gulf. The GCC was originally a defence pact set up in 1981 but members now want to increase trade in order to strengthen economic integration. The drawback is that GCC countries trade very little with one another and their diversification into petrochemicals, fertilisers and cement is creating competitive, not complementary industries. Tariffs between GCC countries were officially abolished in 1983. Though many remain (unofficially), freer trade did not really stimulate greater integration of GCC markets. Most observers see the move as merely a formalisation of existing arrangements.

Three general sets of factors limit West Asia's export opportunities. First, and most important, is the level and rate of change in demand and consumption of oil in developed countries. The empirical evidence on the relationship between the growth of output in developed countries and their demand for energy suggests that growth rates substantially exceeding those prevailing since 1981 would be necessary for even marginal growth of West Asia's oil exports. Second, faster growth of non-oil exports is limited by domestic and foreign constraints that have restricted the efforts of West Asian countries to shift output towards more production of refined products. Finally, despite growth of investment and a build-up in productive capacity, industrial diversification in West Asia has proceeded only slowly. Much more rapid has been the development of services - including banking, financial and related services. This may be the reason for a noticeable rise in the share of services in total imports of several countries in the region.

II Immigrant Labour

The recession in the Gulf affects all corners of West Asia. In periods when oil prices were high, those countries with little or no oil of their own have still profited by sending workers to fill jobs their oil-rich neighbours would not take themselves. These migrants now work in a mature, even shrinking, labour market. In 1984 the oil-exporting countries of the Gulf cut the wages of foreign workers by up to 20%. In that same year roughly 700,000 migrant workers left the Gulf. The number of migrants is still large, however. Though oil prices have tumbled and Arab budgets are in deficit, more than 4 million immigrants (both Arab and Asian) are estimated to work in the Arabian peninsular alone. Table 8.5 shows receipts of workers' remittances by West Asian countries in 1970 and 1985. The value of remittances rose over 6,000% during this period. Egypt receives more than half these funds; in 1985 its foreign workers earned the country an amount equivalent to 11% of its GNP. Proportionately, the contribution of workers' remittances to GNP in other countries is even greater. Roughly 350,000 Jordanians, equivalent to 40% of the country's workforce, found jobs in Gulf countries after 1973. The remittances such workers earn have become an indispensable source of income and foreign exchange to the oil-poor countries of the region. The large numbers of foreign workers have had another important impact: they have done more to tie the economies of the region closer together than any efforts of Arab governments.

Table 8.5   RECEIPTS OF WORKERS' REMITTANCES BY WEST ASIAN
COUNTRIES 1970/1985

$ million

	1970	1985
Egypt	29	3,212
Jordan	-	1,022
North Yemen	-	897
South Yemen	60	494
Syria	7	293
TOTAL	96	5,918

Source: World Bank

It was expected that all these migrants would leave once the houses, hospitals, roads and telephone systems they built were completed. Although oil-producing countries cut spending when oil prices began to fall in 1982, they employed more migrants than ever before. By 1985, 72% of the 7 million workers in the GCC countries were foreign - up from 50% in 1975. Oil-producing countries underestimated how much labour they needed to maintain the things their foreign workers had built. More foreign workers are now employed in service industries in the GCC than in construction - a change which reduces the likelihood that they will eventually leave.

As the number of foreign workers has grown, their nationality and religion has become an issue in politically sensitive countries. Kuwait, which embarked on its development programme at about the time Israel was created, took many homeless Palestinians.

187

Today, they make up almost a quarter of the country's population and have risen to senior positions. Few, however, are granted citizenship and their loyalty is suspect. Based on Kuwait's experience, other, more conservative Gulf states became wary of Palestinians. They sought non-Palestinian Arabs as foreign workers because they had countries to return to. However, Jordanians and Egyptians created other problems: like Palestinians, they were well educated and brought free-thinking traditions with them. For these reasons, the rich oil countries began to turn to Indians and Pakistanis. These workers spoke little Arabic, did not assimilate easily and worked for wages half those of Arabs.

Management of the new workforce was not easy, however. A series of quarrels between Saudi Arabia and Pakistan over Pakistani soldiers hired by Saudi Arabia added to the difficulties. By the 1980s Thais, Filipinos, Koreans and Indonesians were replacing the sub-continent's workers. The new labourers were no cheaper but were easier to manage. Foreign contractors began to recruit the workers, transport and house them and then return them home when projects were completed. By 1985 Arabs comprised only a third of the foreign workforce in Gulf states, down from two-thirds a decade before; Indians and Pakistanis still accounted for more than two-fifths. East Asian workers, however, now make up a fifth of the foreign workforce though there were virtually none in 1975.

The new tactics have had a cost. Governments now worry that their countries are losing their Arab identities. The newcomers cannot speak Arabic and many are not Muslim. Qatar has now decided to "Arabise" its public sector and other Gulf states may soon follow suit. Whatever the source of labour supply, it is now clear that oil producers such as Kuwait and Saudi Arabia will not reduce their immigrant workforces by the amounts called for in their latest five-year plans.

III Fiscal Policies and Government Spending

In most West Asian countries the state assumes an especially important role. Among oil-producing countries the state's importance derives from the large revenues that accrue and the government's resulting involvement in virtually all economic and social matters. Oil-poor governments in West Asia can claim no similar financial leverage though the interplay between economic, religious and political forces can lead to numerous forms of government intervention. Most of these countries - both rich and poor - also share a scepticism for the free market and thus elaborate development plans are usually crafted by a bloated bureaucracy. The state's extensive role in West Asia means that decisions on government spending and fiscal policy carry especially important implications. Involvement of the government sector, in turn, is subject to the vagaries of the international oil market. This is true not only for oil producers but for other West Asian countries which depend greatly upon remittances from workers employed in oil-rich parts of the region.

Saudi Arabia

No West Asian country has experienced a more severe reversal in its fortunes than Saudi Arabia. In times of buoyant oil prices the country had acquired a habit of using money as a substitute for diplomacy. This ensured the loyalty of Shia Muslims in the eastern part of Saudi Arabia, helped to maintain relations with Syria and the Palestine Liberation Organisation (PLO) and, more generally, enabled the country to exert a stabilising influence throughout the region. Saudi Arabia's ability to sustain these policies will be undermined if oil revenues continue to fall. Domestically, a rising tide of unfulfilled expectations also poses a threat to the regime.

The combined effects of a weak dollar and low oil prices have already forced Saudi Arabia to reduce its 1988 budget to 141 billion riyals ($38 billion). The cut amounts to a 17% reduction over the previous year and is the lowest budget in 11 years. But even this austerity will not be enough: a budget deficit of 36 billion riyals is expected in 1988 - lower than 1987 but the sixth consecutive annual shortfall. The manoeuvrability of Saudi planners has been further reduced by a decline in the country's foreign assets, from an estimated $150 billion in 1980 to $70 billion in 1988, which had in the past helped to make up these shortfalls. The 1987 stock market crash alone erased $3 billion from the assets' value.

In response to the deteriorating financial situation the Saudi government has been forced to take several steps which go beyond a simple budget reduction, the most dramatic being to borrow money for the first time since the early 1960s. The government's issue of $9 billion in bonds is intended to meet its budget deficit but also raises the question of interest, which is forbidden under Islamic law. A second step is to freeze public sector recruitment despite the fact the fact that government employment accounts for a disproportionate share of the country's workforce. Third, the government is raising import tariffs: the previous maximum was 7% but now almost all imports other than food and supplies from other members of the GCC will face tariffs of 12%. Another revenue-generating strategy was to have been the reintroduction of income taxes on the country's 4 million foreign workers. That plan, however, was discarded only two days after it was announced owing to a wave of resignations by expatriates.

Egypt

Saudi Arabia's problems fade into insignificance compared with those of Egypt. For four years Egypt has struggled with a severe shortage of foreign exchange. A slump in worker remittances has been a main problem though the fall in oil prices has hurt as well. Simultaneously, Egypt's population has been growing by roughly a million inhabitants every eight months. Yet the country will be fortunate to manage a GDP growth rate of only 2% per year.

The Egyptian government has accepted the need for structural reform. After pressure from the USA, the IMF agreed on a standby arrangement in 1987 allowing the country to reschedule $8 billion of its foreign debt of $44 billion. The agreement, supposed to run for 18 months, was regarded as extremely lenient. The Egyptians have met some of their creditors' requests: they have consolidated several (though not all) of their various exchange rates and have raised prices for some agricultural commodities and energy. Egyptian officials, however, complain that these moves have been the main reason behind a rise in inflation - which reached 30% in 1987. At the same time, President Mubarak has pressured the US government to reduce the average rate of interest on the country's military debt of $4.5 billion. A part rescheduling has brought the average down from its 1987 level of 12.8%. More recently, the willingness of the US government to guarantee 90% of a commercial loan for prepayment of military debts should provide further relief. But despite all these moves Egypt was still having difficulty meeting its obligations in mid-1988.

Kuwait

At the other extreme is Kuwait, an emirate which is fast becoming the equivalent of a multinational corporation. Among Arab oil exporters Kuwait has followed a unique strategy, investing large amounts of its wealth overseas. The approach has proved so successful that, in 1987, the country's foreign investments yielded more income than oil exports ($6.3 billion against $5.4 billion). Until the mid-1980s the country's foreign investment strategy was passive but has gradually become more focused. To boost its income further, Kuwait moved to align its foreign investments more closely with its oil business. The purchase of overseas refining and marketing assets has become a means to integrate oil operations better. Kuwait now has 4,800 petrol stations in seven European countries and controls two European refineries. Altogether, Kuwait sells 250,000 b/d through its European outlets. These moves represent a further refinement of the country's initial tactic of acquiring second-hand downstream assets. Investments such as these have secured a market for Kuwait's oil accounting for 80% of the country's export revenues.

CHAPTER 9

ECONOMIC ISSUES AND POLICIES IN WEST ASIA

As discussed in Chapter 8, the economic, political and military circumstances at work in West Asia make for tenuous prospects and overshadow many of the more conventional forces which would otherwise determine progress. This chapter examines the more important of these unique but troublesome features. In Section I the region's efforts to move downstream from production of crude oil into refined products are considered. Given the limits on imports of refined products imposed by many industrialised countries, such a strategy is not so straightforward as might be expected. Substantial investment in foreign facilities for refining and distributing is required as well as close co-operation with the oil majors. Political and religious issues are the subject of section II. Iran's presence in the middle of the Arab world is a frequent source of tensions, and the Iranian revolution with all its religious undertones has greatly aggravated the intra-regional situation. Moreover, the ability of the two main protagonists in the Iran-Iraq war to re-establish their economic bases will greatly influence the region's co-operative efforts in coming years. Section III moves on to these broad issues of co-operation and conflict

I Oil Markets and Downstream Activities

In 1986 the price of a barrel of oil fell from $28 to $8.50 in only six months. Figure 9.1 shows a partial recovery in subsequent months although prices began to slide again in early 1988, soon reaching $12 a barrel - the lowest level since October 1986. OPEC's crisis in 1986 had been caused by its failed attempt to reclaim a larger share of the

Figure 9.1   MOVEMENTS IN REAL PRICES OF OIL[1] 1986-1988

January 1986 = 100

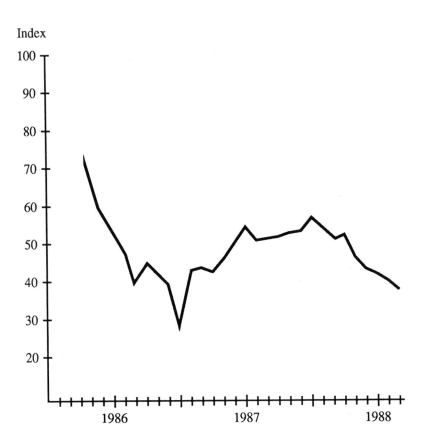

Source: Petroleum Finance Company
Note: [1] Adjusted for inflation and devaluation of the US dollar

world oil market. The cartel had supplied 60% of the non-communist world's oil in 1980 but five years later it was producing only 40% of a much smaller total.

The fall in prices hurt all OPEC members but the oil-rich countries of West Asia were among the hardest hit. Saudi Arabia, OPEC's biggest producer, suffered most. As the cartel's swing producer, Saudi Arabia regularly curbed output to defend oil prices, reducing it from 9.9 million b/d in 1980 to 3.2 million b/d in 1985. Oil prices declined steadily during the first half of the 1980s in spite of Saudi Arabia's efforts. The country has at least 110 years of proven oil reserves which can be pumped out at a cost of only about $0.50 per barrel. Yet it was producing only 43% of its capability in a futile effort to keep the price above $18 per barrel.

Saudi Arabia was finally forced to abandon its role as the swing producer. It turned to a form of "netback" pricing which linked the prices of crude oil and refined products thus guaranteeing a profit for oil refineries. The country simultaneously embarked on a full-scale price war which other cartel members soon joined. The results of this strategy were not impressive: OPEC's revenues fell from $132 billion in 1985 to $72 billion in 1986 and recovered only slightly to $84 billion in 1987.

Because of the deteriorating situation in recent years, OPEC countries were quick to react when oil prices weakened in January 1988. Arab producers (and Iran) had previously been flouting production quotas but they soon imposed a 1.5 million b/d cut. For a time the new quotas were taken seriously. Only six months later, however, the price of a barrel of Saudi light had slipped to $12.50 and most Middle Eastern producers decided to pump more. The UAE rejected its quota of 948,000 b/d as "unfair" and announced its intention to produce roughly 1.5 million b/d. Kuwait's output began to exceed its monthly quota by more than 25%. Saudi Arabia, on the other hand, sought to offer substantial discounts, pricing its oil as low as $12 compared with an official price of more than $17 for Saudi light.

With the latest round of OPEC difficulties a new strategy, largely influenced by Kuwait's experience, has emerged among other Arab producers. West Asian producers have grown weary of attempts to defend oil price floors while lacking the ability to enforce quotas or prevent discounting. Instead, they have turned to buying refineries and petrol stations abroad. By integrating their crude oil production with overseas downstream facilities, their goal is twofold: they hope to secure markets for valuable resources and to share in the refining and marketing profits which have since 1986 accounted for a third of the net earnings of international oil companies.

When oil prices are weak, downstream integration becomes more attractive. Refining and marketing operations prosper in such markets since the prices of oil products fall less than the price of crude. The opposite is true when crude oil is in short supply. High prices then favour oil producers since it is profitable to pump it from the ground. Another attraction of downstream integration is that ownership of foreign refineries and petrol stations guarantees outlets for the producer's oil when demand is slack.

Kuwait now owns two refineries and 4,800 petrol stations in West Europe which, together, are selling the equivalent of up to 250,000 b/d. Thanks to these investments, Kuwait was able to sell 25% more than its OPEC oil quota in 1987. Such benefits explain why Saudi Arabia is paying $12 billion in cash and oil to acquire half-ownership in three of Texaco's refineries and access to 11,500 US petrol stations. These acquisitions should provide a secure outlet for 600,000 b/d of Saudi oil. Other Arab countries have followed suit. The UAE has part ownership in Spain's biggest privately owned refinery and France's second oil company, Total.

Moves downstream are not without political complications as Kuwait's experience with BP suggests. After the UK government's unsuccessful sale of its 31.5% stake in BP in 1987, Kuwait stepped forward as a potential shareholder. The KIO brushed aside the British government's first request to limit its holdings in BP to 20%. Subsequently, the UK Monopolies and Mergers Commission recommended that the KIO reduces it stake in BP to 9.9% (down from 21.7% in October 1988). The recommendation was based on the argument that oil is a strategic business and should not be subject to foreign sovereign ownership. Though Kuwait had promised not to interfere with the company's day-to-day running, its voting rights are to be reduced to the 9.9% level immediately.

There are other implications, in addition to questions about foreign sovereign ownership, which make the downstream strategy of some OPEC countries intriguing. For example, when Saudi Arabia was merely a producer of crude oil, it could impose embargoes relatively painlessly. But should it undertake large investments in overseas refineries and petrol stations, the country will have less freedom to engage in such actions. Antitrust laws will restrict the ability of oil countries to manipulate downstream foreign markets while they would risk having their assets confiscated if they refused to supply oil to competitive refineries. The move downstream also raises issues which could undermine OPEC solidarity. Countries with big spending requirements (for example Iran, with a large population and war reconstruction to finance) can hardly contemplate overseas downstream investment. Producers facing these sorts of pressing financial problems will try to maximise their oil income with price discounting and overproduction. Owners of downstream facilities, however, will have other motives. They will be more content to restrain output in periods of weak prices, pumping more only when crude oil is in great demand.

197

II Iran - a Shia Power in a Sunni World

The religious and political factions that helped fuse the Iranian revolution have shown signs of splitting apart so long as the cease-fire has continued. The secular wing of the government wants to give policies a stronger egalitarian flavour. It argues that Islam is largely about social justice. Much of its reforming legislation, however, has been blocked by the Council of Guardians, a committee of conservative mullahs with constitutional power to ensure that all parliamentary bills conform with the Koran. In January 1988 Ayatollah Khomeini issued an edict declaring that Iran's government could in some circumstances overrule Islamic writ. Secularists took the edict as permission for a variety of economic measures that the Guardians had steadfastly blocked. The secularists' list included land redistribution, a greater role for the state in the economy, more statutory rights for industrial workers and the promotion of worker co-operatives. A new assembly was subsequently created to settle disputes between Parliament and the Guardians. The assembly is weighted in favour of the government and will have some powers of arbitration which previously resided with Ayatollah Khomeini.

Until now, egalitarian objectives have been suppressed in favour of more general goals such as the "liberation" of Iran from foreign domination and the Islamic cast given to the country's laws and government. But there is mounting pressure among the population to provide a better distribution of material benefits. By revolutionary standards, no redistribution of wealth has occurred. The Guardians' veto has greatly slowed the dispersion of land. Only 2 million acres, 3% of Iran's cultivated land, have been transferred to poor farmers. The government claims it has brought water, telephones, gas and schools to villages that did not have them. But this has not slowed the drift of farmers to the cities where black market activities can bring incomes several times greater than the earnings of educated civil servants.

The regime has blamed many of its economic failures on the war against Iraq. Nevertheless, by most standards poor Iranians are worse off than they were before the revolution. Inflation in 1988 was running at 40-50% per year and unemployment was widespread. A census in 1986 revealed that only one in five had regular work. Meanwhile, the currency is collapsing: a black-market dollar cost 1,000 riyals in early 1988 compared with an official exchange rate of 67.5.

One of the few aspects of economic policy on which Iran's diverse revolutionaries agree is that priority should be given to agriculture in the country's future. The agricultural sector deteriorated rapidly in the pre-revolutionary drive to "modernise" and establish an industrial base. So long as Iran's ancient irrigation system functioned adequately the country was able to feed itself and even export a little. But by 1974 Iran became a net importer of farm products. In the next ten years it emerged as one of the largest food importers in the Third World. In 1988 Iran bought more than a quarter of its food supply abroad while only 10% of its 400 million acres of land was arable.

High levels of rural-to-urban migration have been a continuous source of agricultural problems. The Shah's successors failed to stem the population's move out of agriculture which had begun once the oil industry began to siphon off rural workers. Urban dwellers amounted to only a third of the population in the 1950s but were in a majority by the mid-1980s. The absolute size of the rural community actually declined in 1986 for the first time on record, making it harder for Iran to grow food while increasing the need for it.

As the Iran-Iraq war fades, issues such as inflation or the trade-off between agricultural and industrial development will be subsumed in the drive for reconstruction. The government will be under pressure to produce some benefits from peace quickly. This can be done most effectively by relaxing controls on industry and by encouraging more imports of basic consumer goods. Iran may well start its post-war liberalisation programme with food and agriculture. In 1987 it spent nearly $4 billion on food imports alone and agricultural improvements could help to stem the rural-to-urban migration in the country.

Iran will have the option of obtaining much of the aid to rebuild by borrowing abroad, if it chooses to do so. As a borrower, Iran has a sound financial record. In the post-Shah period the country paid off the bulk of its foreign debts, which amounted to $6.5 billion, because of Islam's ban on usury. Since then Iran has financed imports with letters of credit and has paid when these fell due. Nonetheless, Iran has short-term debts of $6-8 billion although its liquid overseas assets would easily cover these. A major problem for reconstruction will be the fact that Iran's constitution forbids borrowing. When the country does begin to rebuild, it will start with its oil industry. Iran lost perhaps $30 billion in oil earnings during the war and the industry accounts for 90% of its export earnings. The next section looks more closely at regional elements of co-operation and particularly the region's efforts to rebuild following the war.

III Co-operation and Conflict within the Region

The leaders of the Arab revolt against Turkey in World War I foresaw the creation of a single Arab country with its capital in Damascus. That continued to be the dream of later leaders, inspiring a whole generation in the 1950s. Unification remains a formal goal of most Arab governments but its prospects have steadily dimmed in the 1970s and 1980s. As the outlook for political unity has waned, attention has turned to less demanding but more realistic forms of co-operation. The countries' shared culture and language, coupled with their growing military power and immense oil wealth, should have made the Arab states one of the world's more important power blocs. But more than most regions West Asia lacks any balance of power. One reason for the region's failure to achieve international stature is that countries have been unsuccessful in their attempts to integrate their economies or to co-ordinate their foreign policies.

Geography, as well as the distribution of wealth and population, works against co-operation. The region is dominated by two large countries: Saudi Arabia and Egypt. Saudi Arabia has a population of only 12 million, who live comfortably and depend completely on oil. Egypt, on the other hand, has a population of nearly 50 million. Its inhabitants, with a per capita income which is a seventh of Saudi Arabia's, scrape out a modest living mainly along the Nile. To the south of Saudi Arabia are the two small Yemens, which are the region's poorest countries.

The contrasts are equally apparent in the case of the Gulf countries. Some of these tiny states can boast of a per capita GDP more than twice that of Saudi Arabia. The conservative Gulf states were long concerned about the dangers of a radical Iraq but now agonise over the prospect an even more radical Iran might pose now that its war has wound down. Tiny Kuwait has adopted a pro-Western approach and has an overseas investment programme that yields it more income than its oil exports. But to the north of Kuwait are Iraq and Syria, whose people share a belief in the obscure ideology of Baath socialism but have incomes only a quarter that of Kuwait.

A bewildering array of political beliefs further complicates efforts at co-operation. Syria and Iraq have militantly secular governments though others claim their mandate from the Koran. Egypt and Jordan have close links with the USA and depend on that country for economic and political support while others - Syria and South Yemen - are Russian clients. The Gulf states and others are conservative monarchies embracing free market philosophies. Altogether, these sorts of imbalances involving wealth, population and political systems represent a poor framework for pan-Arab co-operation.

Arab countries have still continued their search for a common ground in the face of this diversity. But the collapse of the Egypt-Syria merger in the short-lived United Arab Republic in 1958 is still ruefully remembered. That merger fell apart because the Syrians thought they were being neglected by the more powerful Egyptians. Lacking another charismatic leader such as Nasser, similar experiments in merger are unlikely in the future.

Of course, none of these efforts has included Iran, and throughout the 1980s Arab leaders have been preoccupied with ways to reduce the intensity of the Iran-Iraq war rather than more ambitious schemes for greater co-operation. But even as the war concludes, the aftermath of reconstruction and rebuilding will have to be considered before any more ambitious efforts are made at pan-Arab co-operation. Since both Iran and Iraq will focus their reconstruction efforts on their oil industry, the repercussions for other Arab producers can be considerable. Iraq, at least, can rely on reconstruction aid from its neighbours. This should match the 300,000 b/d of oil pledged by Saudi Arabia and Kuwait to Iraq's war effort. However, the bulk of post-war finance for both countries will have to come from new loans or increased oil exports.

Iraq's chances of obtaining substantial new loans are slim. Because it is such a resource-rich country, with 100 billion barrels of oil resources and deposits of sulphur, phosphates and bauxite, credit for export finance will be obtainable. However, Iraq ended the war with debts of perhaps $70 billion. About half is owed to Saudi Arabia and Kuwait, which may forget them, but other commercial banks will not do so and will be reluctant to lend more. This leaves the country with little choice but to obtain the needed capital through increased oil revenues.

Iraq lost its two offshore export terminals during the war. But since then it has rebuilt export capacity by laying pipeline across Saudi Arabia and Turkey. In mid-1988 the country was producing nearly 3 million b/d and exporting 2.6 million b/d. Its export capacity could rise by a further million b/d when another pipeline through Saudi Arabia comes on stream in 1989. This would give it an export capacity of 3.6 million b/d, far above its OPEC quota. Even more exports could be obtained if Iraq resumes supplies via the Gulf. All this is far above Iraq's demand for an OPEC quota of 2.37 million b/d (the same as Iran's). The prospect of such a surplus of oil on the market will cause problems within OPEC though pan-Arab solidarity may mean that Iraq's plight is viewed with some sympathy.

Iran, too, may follow a similar strategy though this prospect is by no means certain. The country has a policy of conserving its resources. Moreoover, Iran may wish to avoid further annoying Saudi Arabia by large increases in oil production. But even if it does choose to increase output, Iran lacks the scope of Iraq. It has frequently found it difficult to pump its OPEC quota of 2.3 million b/d because of war damage. Iran was exporting 5 million b/d from Kharg Island before the war. However, damage to its oil fields, through neglect as well as Iraqi air attacks, has drastically reduced capacity. Iran's search for new oil was also cut back significantly during the war. It had only 20 rigs looking for oil in mid-1988 compared with 50 in the mid-1970s. Finally, Iran will need to repair its refineries. After destruction of its 600,000 b/d refinery at Abadan, the country was forced to import up to 300,000 b/d. A reduction in refined oil imports would immediately save foreign exchange.

Once the two countries' oil industries have been rebuilt, their subsequent reconstruction priorities are likely to differ. Iran is likely to try to rebuild its military forces - mainly its non-existent air force and navy. Iraq, by contrast, ended the war better armed then it began. Both governments, however, will be under added pressure to supply their populations with some of the benefits of peace. Iraq has already set the stage for this with a wave of economic liberalisation in 1987 which brought down food prices. Both countries want to produce more of their own food. Iran, as noted earlier, is now a major food importer. Iraq's agricultural sector, however, suffers not so much from the effects of the war as a shortage of labour. Once these demands are met, the two countries will turn to repair their infrastructures. Communications will be a priority, which will involve much business for foreign road-building and trucking companies. Only then will non-oil industries begin to receive attention.

Despite the problems the two countries obviously face in rebuilding their oil industries, the fact that each has 100 billion barrels of proven crude oil reserves has prompted many foreign manufacturers and contractors to look forward to the reconstruction era. Companies in Britain, France, Italy, the Soviet Union, China and elsewhere provided Iran and Iraq with arms and maintained commercial ties with them during the war. Many companies took large losses on earlier projects by extending lengthy credits to combatants and often accepting oil in lieu of cash. Those who maintained a presence throughout the war will now have a favoured position. Japan's Ministry of International Trade and Transport has offered both Iran and Iraq low-interest loans denominated in yen to help foster reconstruction and, in the process, help win contracts for Japanese companies. South Korea, too, is planning to provide cheap loans.

CHAPTER 10

ECONOMIC PERFORMANCE AND TRENDS IN SOUTH AND EAST ASIA

Major economic indicators for South and East Asia are found in Table 10.1. Countries vary markedly in terms of population: China and India together account for over 1.8 billion people while others such as Fiji and Singapore are minuscule in comparison. Population figures are not a particularly reliable indicator of market size in this region, however. Though China is the world's most populated country, the buying power of its inhabitants is low, with an average per capita income of only $300. Extremely low levels of per capita GDP are also found in other large countries such as Bangladesh ($160), India ($270) and Pakistan ($350). In contrast, several of the smaller economies in the region enjoy exceptionally high levels of income. South Korea, Malaysia and Fiji all have levels of per capita GDP which qualify them as relatively advanced developing countries while Singapore's and Hong Kong's standards now match those in developed countries. In Singapore income levels are now so high that they pose a problem. Economic success has driven the city-state's wages up to a point where it has difficulty competing directly with Thailand, Malaysia and other South and East Asian countries.

With regard to economic growth, the 1980s have been a good period for South and East Asian countries. China has enjoyed an exceptional rate of growth (10.5%) though other economies - particularly Hong Kong, Pakistan and South Korea - have also reported growth rates far above the average for the Third World. Rapid growth of income has sometimes spurred unexpected increases in domestic demand, which have spilled over into imports.

Table 10.1   ECONOMIC INDICATORS FOR SOUTH AND EAST ASIA[1] 1986

	Population (million)	GDP per capita ($)	Growth of GDP[2] 1980-6 (%)	Trade balance[3] ($ million)	Ratio of debt to GNP[4] (%)	Direct investment in country ($ million)
Bangladesh	103.1	160	3.7	-1,373.3	32.0	na
Burma	33.7	200	4.9	-198.3	42.7	na
China	1,054.7	300	10.5	-11,024.0	-	na
Fiji	0.7	1,810	na	-124.4	28.5	34.4
Hong Kong	5.6	6,720	6.0	74.1	11.7	na
India	781.0	270	4.9	-5,618.9 [4]	15.2	-215.3 [4]
Indonesia	165.4	500	3.4	2,490.6	38.1	259.3
Malaysia	15.9	1,850	4.8	3,369.3	63.5	530.3
Nepal	17.0	160	3.5	-297.9	23.8	-
Pakistan	99.0	350	6.7	-2,826.2	36.0	110.3
Papua New Guinea	3.6	690	1.8	75.7	71.2	100.1

Continued...

Table 10.1 cont'd

	Population (million)	GDP per capita ($)	Growth of GDP[2] 1980-6 (%)	Trade balance[3] ($ million)	Ratio of debt to GNP[4] (%)	Direct investment in country ($ million)
Philippines	56.1	570	-1.0	-208.8	52.4	126.7
Singapore	2.6	7,410	5.3	-2,328.7	19.2	673.4
South Korea	41.6	2,370	8.2	4,122.5	44.6	428.2
Sri Lanka	16.1	400	4.9	-559.2	55.8	30.0
Thailand	52.7	810	4.8	319.8	36.9	264.0

Source: United Nations/World Bank
Notes: [1] *Countries included in this region but not shown here are: Afghanistan, Bhutan, Brunei, Democratic Kampuchea, Maldives, Mongola, New Caledonia, Tonga and Vanautu*
[2] *Based on data at 1980 prices*
[3] *Exports (fob) less imports (fob)*
[4] *1985*

China's large trade imbalance ($11 billion in 1986) is an example of the consequences of pent-up demand, combined with income growth and the relaxation of trade restrictions. Overall, the countries' trade balances do not reflect the region's much discussed export drive. Several countries, including major exporters such as Pakistan and Singapore, have substantial trade imbalances. Most countries - even those achieving remarkable export successes - are large importers, which explains the frequently modest (or even negative) trade balances within the region.

The last two columns in Table 10.1 clearly distinguish the South and East Asian region from other parts of the Third World. The ratio of debt to GNP is generally low. Papua New Guinea's debt is highest (71% of GNP) followed by Malaysia (64%) and Sri Lanka (56%). Direct investment in most countries is modest to large: Singapore has been the major recipient, followed by Malaysia and South Korea. Only Hong Kong experienced a net outflow of investment ($215 million) in 1986 and this can be attributed mainly to investors' fears of the Chinese takeover rather than any genuine lack of confidence in economic matters.

The general impression is that South and East Asia represents an economically vibrant and rapidly growing part of the Third World. Although success does not mean that the region has been free of economic problems, the nature of these difficulties is necessarily distinct from those of other regions. Trade and trade-related issues feature prominently in most of the region's economies and continue to grow in importance. This subject is examined in section I. The manufacturing sector has provided the impetus for much of the region's economic success. Industrial growth and industrial policies are the focus of section II.

I Trade Performance in Export-Based Economies

In the years between 1970 and 1986 the growth of trade in South and East Asian countries far exceeded the corresponding global figures. The region's exports rose spectacularly: volume grew at 9% per year, double the world average. This achievement can be attributed largely to the success of four East Asian economies - Hong Kong, Singapore, South Korea and Taiwan - which have specialised in exports of manufactures. Exports resumed their torrid pace of growth in 1986 after a decline in 1985 due mainly to a slowdown in the US economy (see Table 10.2).

Table 10.2   GROWTH OF EXPORTS, IMPORTS AND TERMS OF TRADE IN SOUTH AND EAST ASIA 1975-1986

% change	1975-86[1]	1982	1983	1984	1985	1986
Growth of exports	13.5	-2.9	5.4	15.4	-2.9	9.0
Growth of imports	12.3	-1.6	2.5	6.6	-5.5	5.2
Terms of trade[2] (1980 = 100)	-	97	96	98	93	87

Source: UNCTAD

Note: [1] *Average annual rate*
        [2] *Ratio of export unit value index to import unit value index*

The growth of imports was slower in the 1980s than in the 1970s. Import volumes declined by 5.5% in 1985 when several countries experienced serious setbacks. The slowdown was pronounced in the case of Singapore, Taiwan and some of the region's heavily indebted countries. Though terms of trade have deteriorated, the decline has

209

been negligible in comparison with Africa or West Asia. Prices of manufactures in international markets have remained relatively stable or even risen and the large share of these goods in the region's exports have helped to keep the terms of trade relatively constant during this decade.

Table 10.3 shows the structure of trade by major commodity group. The driving force behind the region's success has been a rapid increase in exports of manufactures. This category accounted for 42% of exports in 1970, rising to over 60% by 1985. Among non-manufactures, the shares of food, agricultural raw materials and ores and metals all fell substantially between 1970 and the mid-1980s. Manufactures also represent more than half the region's imports: those into East Asia and China (mainly machinery and transport equipment) have grown particularly rapidly. The region's balance of trade was negative as recently as 1975 but ten years later South and East Asia's exports were $14 billion greater than imports.

Table 10.3   STRUCTURE OF TRADE BY MAJOR COMMODITY GROUP IN SOUTH AND EAST ASIA 1970-1985

%

	Exports			Imports		
	1970	1975	1985	1970	1975	1985
Food items	21.2	19.6	10.6	16.2	15.5	8.9
Agricultural raw materials	19.1	9.7	5.1	7.5	5.2	4.4
Ores and metals	10.1	5.7	4.2	9.3	7.6	6.4
Fuels	7.1	19.8	17.5	7.3	17.4	21.6
Manufactures	41.8	44.3	60.5	56.6	52.5	54.1
TOTAL ($ million)	14,278	44,972	180,234	17,779	54,281	166,228

Source: UNCTAD

210

Table 10.4 gives a breakdown of the region's trade by destination and source. The bulk of South and East Asia's exports gains can be traced to two markets: North America and intra-regional trade. The dollar value of exports to developed countries other than North America stagnated or declined as did exports to West Asia and Africa. Over 50% of imports come from developed market economies. Imports from Western Europe have been most dynamic while purchases from US suppliers rose only weakly. West Asia has been the main source of imports from other Third World regions.

Table 10.4   SOUTH AND EAST ASIA'S STRUCTURE OF TRADE BY DESTINATION 1970-1985[1]

%	Developed market economies	Socialist countries	Developing countries	of which: Intra-region
Imports				
1970	69.2	2.8	23.7	14.3
1975	62.4	2.6	31.0	15.5
1985	53.1	2.3	38.1	23.2
Exports				
1970	63.5	5.4	28.6	20.3
1975	65.4	3.0	30.2	18.7
1985	62.4	1.5	29.9	21.4

Source: UNCTAD
Note: [1] *Excludes trade with socialist developing countries*

By 1986 many Asian economies had experienced a decoupling of the long-term relationship between growth of trade volume (both imports and exports) and growth of real GDP. This departure from the long-run pattern reflects the different ways in which South and East Asian countries were affected by large changes in major economic parameters. Hong Kong, South Korea and Taiwan have all benefited from new economic opportunities provided by the dollar's depreciation, lower oil prices and a rise in interest rates. The region's exporters of primary products, on the other hand, were severely affected by weak commodity prices and their trade performance was disappointing.

Several factors offer promise for the region's exporters of primary products despite their presently discouraging circumstances. Product diversification is under way in many countries, making exporting more resistant to adverse developments in foreign markets. Indonesia is one example: in 1986 the price of its main export, oil, was halved, but when oil prices fell, the rupiah was devalued by 31% against the dollar. With a sustainable exchange rate, newly competitive exports - tropical commodities such as timber and rubber - have brought diversification from oil. In the year to April 1988 the volume of Indonesia's non-oil exports climbed 24%, earning $9.7 billion of foreign exchange. Second, tariff cuts and other trade-liberalisation measures are being implemented in several countries.

Thailand, too, is using its cheap labour to diversify its exports. The share of the country's seven largest traditional exports fell from 61% in 1976 to 34% in 1986. In their place have come labour-intensive light manufactures, made profitable by wage rates which are sometimes less than $3 per day. One beneficiary has been the footwear industry (especially sports shoes). Rising wages in South Korea and Taiwan have left the cheaper end of the market to Thailand. Textiles and integrated circuits are other export successes for Thailand.

The red tape that has hindered exports in countries such as Indonesia and Thailand is also being reduced. Other measures being taken by South and East Asia's export-conscious governments include new regulations making it easier to hire foreigners and providing tax benefits for export-oriented companies. Such moves will eventually boost both imports and exports and, consequently, economic growth. Finally, more open policies toward foreign investment have been proposed or are being undertaken in a number of countries. These policy changes should encourage the private sector to venture into new export activities and contribute to product diversification of exports.

II South and East Asia's Industrial Engine of Growth

The industrial base in South and East Asia is neither as large nor as sophisticated as that of Latin America. However, the drive to industrialise has been unprecedented, providing the major impetus for the region's impressive economic growth. Significant structural changes have occurred as South and East Asian industries have developed and launched their export drives.

Table 10.5 shows production indices in mining and in major fields of manufacturing. Though mining output has fallen significantly, this sector has never been of major importance in many of the region's countries. The decline in mining can be attributed partly to the weakness in commodity prices dating back to 1975. Similarly, the modest recovery in world prices for some minerals and metals in 1986 helps to explain the gains in mining output in that year. Trends since the late 1970s have been quite different. By 1986 output of the region's manufacturing sector was 78% above the 1980 level, having grown steadily in every year of this decade.

Food

Output of food, beverages and tobacco rose rapidly in 1980-4. Though the pace of growth slowed in later years, output in 1986 was still 56% above the 1980 level. One of the distinguishing characteristics of the food-processing sector in South and East Asia is the heavy levels of protection and harsh import restraints imposed by most governments. These policies mean that food prices are relatively high and that the industry is not as efficient as it might be. South Korea imposes some of the most stringent restraints on imports of food and related products. The country is striving to develop a domestic wine industry and severely limits foreign supplies. Until recently the ban on foreign cigarettes has been virtually complete. Workers found smoking overseas brands were even threatened with the loss of their jobs.

Other price distortions resulted from the decision to build hothouses to enable the country to grow its own bananas: the cost of heating the hothouses means that home-grown bananas are double the price of the imported variety.

Food processing and related activities are of special importance for densely populated countries such as China and India. Because only 10% of China's land is arable (compared with 57% in India), the need for an efficient agro-processing subsector is a crucial element for economic progress. The extent to which China has overcome this drawback is miraculous. After nine years of Deng Xiaoping's reforms, China has become the world's biggest agricultural producer. Given the limited amount of arable land, China turned to large-scale farming. More important, however, have been the gains of greater professionalism and specialisation necessary to make large-scale farming a commercial possibility. The country's emergence as a major agricultural producer is part of a much wider reform programme, which is discussed in Chapter 11.

Table 10.5   INDUSTRIAL PRODUCTION IN SELECTED SOUTH AND EAST ASIAN INDUSTRIES 1977-1986

1980=100	1977	1978	1979	1981	1982	1983	1984	1985	1986
Total industrial production	109	110	111	92	86	89	95	96	112
Mining	125	119	119	82	69	68	68	63	73
Manufacturing of which:	87	95	97	108	114	126	141	151	178
Food, beverages and tobacco	87	92	97	111	127	131	146	157	156
Textiles	89	98	96	105	103	112	114	115	123
Wearing apparel, leather and footwear	90	96	95	111	112	126	138	134	155
Wood products, and furniture	87	94	94	98	103	133	132	147	169
Paper, printing and publishing	83	91	95	112	116	123	145	146	159

Continued....

Table 10.5 cont'd

	1977	1978	1979	1981	1982	1983	1984	1985	1986
Chemicals, petroleum coal and products	89	94	96	104	113	124	133	134	143
Non-metallic mineral products	86	94	95	109	117	125	137	147	162
Basic metals	82	92	99	110	116	122	138	147	161
Metal products	81	95	97	112	117	134	160	168	210

Source: UNIDO/UNCTAD

India's approach to food-related issues is distinct from China's and has had very different implications for development of a food-processing industry. A third of the world's poor live in India and food-related issues are inextricably tied to the government's welfare programmes. Though agricultural production has grown impressively, the development of processing facilities has not kept pace. India has instead striven to develop a network of fair-price grain shops to distribute food to the poor or to pay workers in kind and has sought to develop new seeds, fertilisers and irrigation and flood-control schemes. India's agricultural successes have created a "grain mountain" of 23 million tonnes testimony both to the country's success as a food producers and its failure in processing and distributing or exporting its food surpluses.

Some South and East Asian economies are heavily dependent on one or two crops and their agro-processing facilities reflect this concentration. The Philippines, for example, produces much sugar and conditions in the food-processing sector depend on domestic supply. Though sugar traditionally accounted for up to 20% of annual export earnings, the country is presently importing sugar for refining and re-export. Previous governments had encouraged the build-up of refining capacity. The decision proved to be unfortunate when world prices fell to record lows in 1985 (3 US cents per pound compared to 30 cents in the mid-1970s). More recently, President Aquino's plans to include sugar farms in the land-reform programme have led farmers to turn to other crops. This has further reduced the supply of raw sugar and contributed to substantial excess capacity in the processing industry.

Thailand stands out among the region's countries as a model agro-processing economy. Sometimes described as a "newly agro-industrialising country", Thailand is now one of the world's largest food exporters. To achieve this surplus it had to develop an impressive food-processing sector. Once the economic laggard of East Asia, Thailand has combined its traditional strength in

217

agriculture with growing industrial expertise in fields such as tropical fruits, tapioca and shrimp farming. The strategy relies heavily on taking what is grown in the country and processing it before shipping it out as finished products. Five of Thailand's seven big traditional exports are agro-based: rice, tapioca, maize, shrimp and sugar (the others are tin and rubber). In 1986 these five products accounted for nearly a third of all the country's exports.

Textiles and clothing

One of the most important categories of industry shown in Table 10.5 is textiles and associated industries such as wearing apparel, leather and footwear. Inspired by the post-war experience of Japan, many South and East Asian countries made textiles and clothing a preferred industry when they launched their development drive. Their textile industry grew rapidly in the 1960s and 1970s but the rate of expansion has slowed in the 1980s as other parts of the manufacturing sector have developed. The region's production of textiles has grown by only 23% in the 1980s. However, production of wearing apparel and related products has boomed as manufacturers move downstream from textiles to increase earnings and to avoid overseas trade barriers.

South and East Asian producers of textiles and clothing are predominantly export-oriented but the system of import restraints developed by Western countries is the most extensive applied to the products of any industry. Rich countries protect themselves from cheap clothing from poor countries but trade freely among themselves. Known as the Multifibre Arrangement (MFA), the system restricts trade in textiles and garments. Virtually all the region's countries (as well as other Third World countries) face quotas on the bulk of their production. These are bilaterally negotiated and the developing country is told that it can send so many shirts, trousers, anoraks, etc to each country.

As the MFA has been extended to new products and suppliers, its impact on the pattern of South and East Asian production of textiles and garments has become more apparent. Figure 10.1 shows rates of growth and value of garment exports in the first half of this decade. The poorest countries, rather than Hong Kong, Singapore or Taiwan, have been the most rapidly growing suppliers. Businessmen from Hong Kong and South Korea quickly saw that they could shift production in response to the MFA quotas. The textile and garment industry uses little capital and is very mobile. Some South and East Asian governments are now helping to sell the attractions of their cheap labour and preferential market access by offering special deals to companies which plan to export. Bangladesh, for example, allows duty-free processing for companies which export 100% of their production, and gives them easy access to foreign exchange for their imports. Smaller countries are the most vulnerable to quotas as they grow. Small suppliers receive more generous terms under the MFA than larger ones. Hong Kong, for example, is allowed only a 0.6% annual increase in its shirt exports to the EC, yet Sri Lanka is allowed 7%.

China is an exception to the pattern, having been allowed extraordinary expansion for an exporter of its size, principally because rich countries hope to secure access to the country's domestic markets for other goods in return. China is already the world's second largest producer of textiles (after the USSR). The industry's labour-intensive nature and the priority accorded textiles in the country's industrial zones promise rapid growth of output and further development of exports.

Figure 10.1   AVERAGE ANNUAL GROWTH RATE OF SOUTH AND EAST
ASIAN APPAREL EXPORTS TO DEVELOPED COUNTRIES
1981-1985

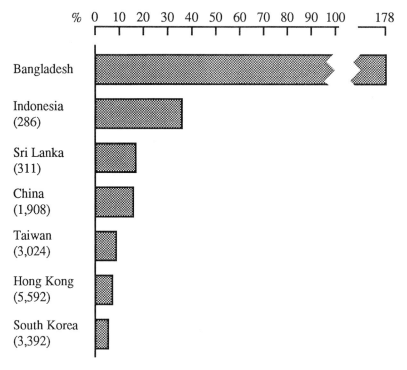

Source: GATT

Note: The figures in brackets are the 1985 value of such exports in $ million

After China, India ranks third in the world as a textile producer and intends to become a much bigger exporter. So far, 95% of the 13 billion metres of cloth produced in India is sold domestically. The textile exporters' target is to double overseas sales and to increase the country's meagre 2% share of the world textiles market. India's export of ready-made apparel is already growing as part of a more general programme to boost exports. Fifteen years ago India exported very few ready-made garments; now it is taking customers from Hong Kong, the Philippines, South Korea and Taiwan. India hopes to benefit from its cheap labour, which provides a competitive advantage in clothes with labour-intensive pleats, tucks and frills. Indian exporters also offer flexibility. For example, they are often willing to accept orders in much smaller lots than producers in other South and East Asian countries will supply.

Some parts of the Indian textile industry are not healthy, however, Cotton mills, for example, have suffered from competition by producers of polyester. Past government policy unintentionally encouraged the growth of polyester production (which is made from petroleum) at the expense of cheap, home-grown cotton. Although India's polyester producers pay high government levies, they are compensated by a domestic price for their products that is four times the world price. Polyester sells well because it is more durable than cotton and, in India, more fashionable.

To summarise, the South and East Asian textile and apparel industries have undergone dramatic changes in recent years as producers have responded to the more stringent trade barriers in Western countries and to the overall slowdown in world demand. Key elements in this adjustment process include the movement of production facilities for cheap products out of South Korea and Taiwan to Bangladesh, Sri Lanka and Pakistan, improvements in fashion content (and thus value added) and major efforts to raise efficiency and productivity in existing facilities.

Wood and wood products

Wood-based industries, including paper and related products, represent one of the fastest growing fields of manufacturing. Output of wood products and furniture in 1986 was 69% above its 1980 level while the corresponding increase in paper and products was 59%. These gains, however, were from a relatively small base. Though several Asian countries have valuable timber reserves, the industry is not large relative to others. The biggest producers (and exporters) of wood and wood products include Malaysia, Indonesia and the Philippines. Most of the production, however, is in very simple form - timber and sawn logs. These are exported to other South and East Asian countries which lack the natural resource but have built up substantial processing capacity. The major importer of semi-processed wood and timber is Japan, which uses the wood in its furniture and paper industries.

Some of the largest pulp and paper factories in developing Asia are found in South Korea and Taiwan. Paper consumption has traditionally been closely linked to the pace of economic growth. As a result, the industry has been one of the beneficiaries of East Asia's rapid development. This fact, together with a tolerance for polluting factories, has enabled South Korea and Taiwan to build up big paper factories. Each country produced close to 3 million tonnes in 1987. The only Asian country with a larger industry is China, which in 1986 produced 10 million tonnes of paper and paperboard. China's industry, however, has been hobbled by an irrational pricing system resulting in domestic supply falling far short of demand. As a result, China's neighbours are hoping it will become the next big market to be exploited.

Chemicals

Chemicals and related operations (eg petroleum refining, fertilisers and plastics) form one of the larger industries in South and East Asia. The industry's output spurted in 1981-3 but growth has slowed as oil prices weakened. In 1986 chemicals and related industries were producing at a level 43% above 1980 output. Chemicals have never been regarded as a prime candidate around which the region could build an export-oriented strategy, but in countries with large domestic markets, chemicals naturally play an important role as one of the backbones of an ample manufacturing sector. Nowhere is this feature more apparent than in China where the high priority accorded to agricultural development has required the country to support the development of the chemicals industry.

Nitrogenous and phosphate fertilisers are two of the more important chemicals produced in China. Their prominence reflects the priority the country places on large-scale, commercial farming. China, however, is short of sulphur deposits and sulphuric acid is vital in making synthetic fertilisers. Fertiliser production slumped badly in 1985 and, though recovering in 1986-7, shortages persist. The lack of phosphates and fertilisers has been acute, resulting in a deterioration in soil fertility due to over-application of nitrogen. With different ministries involved in the production, transport, distribution, import and research of chemical fertilisers, it is not surprising that China has been slow to react to the changing conditions.

China's producers of petroleum and refined products have also suffered some difficulties since 1986. Although production has grown steadily, export revenue has declined and foreign interest in exploration has slackened. China is emerging as one of the region's leaders in the petroleum industry while becoming one of the largest consumers. It has good reason at this stage of development to process more crude oil for home use and, if it can find the capital, to continue to expand production development and exploration. The depressed state of today's international oil markets and the increasing ability of some Chinese consumers to pay hard currency make these tactics even more attractive. The country's seventh five-year plan aims to have refiners processing 110 million tonnes of crude oil by 1990 from a total production targeted to reach 150 million tonnes. About 70 new petrochemical projects were launched in 1987 alone. Most of the new projects are intended to increase yields of lighter distillates, supply more sophisticated products and raise product quality.

Production of chemicals and related products is capital-intensive and depends on large volumes of output for the economies of scale needed if costs are to be controlled. Another important characterisitc is that chemicals and petrochemicals are inextricably mixed as roughly 90% of chemical products are now derived from petrochemicals. Only a limited number of South and East Asian countries - Indonesia, Brunei, China and perhaps Thailand, India and Vietnam - seem likely to have sufficient crude oil deposits to form a base to develop the type of chemicals industry common in other parts of the world. Aided by Japanese investment, Singapore has established a relatively large chemicals industry with no natural resources whatsoever, and India pressed ahead in this field long before the possibility of petroleum deposits was realised. Today, India's publicly owned chemicals industry does well but mainly because the government keeps prices high.

Metals and minerals

The production of basic metals, mineral products and metal products represents one of the fields of most dynamic growth in South and East Asia. Rapid expansion is partly due to the construction boom much of the region has undergone since 1980. Growth in other parts of the manufacturing sector has also spurred demand for metals and metal products. Of all these types of manufactures none has received the generous degree of government support steel producers enjoy.

No South and East Asian country can match the size of China's steel industry: in 1986 its iron and steel companies produced more than 51 million tons, making it the world's fourth largest steel producer after the USSR, Japan and the USA. Production of heavy industries has raced ahead since 1985, growing at 10% each year. China's steel industry lies at the heart of the heavy industrial complex and has been responsible for much of this growth. But even this rapid progress has not been sufficient to meet China's steel needs. The country had over 100,000 projects under construction in 1987, far beyond the needs which could be accommodated by its domestic steel industry.

Though China can claim to have the largest steel industry in the Third World, South Korea has Asia's largest and most impressive steel firm: Pohang Iron and Steel Co (Posco), now 20 years old. The firm produced two-thirds of South Korea's steel in 1987 and runs at 95% capacity. By any measure, Posco has progressed far since the World Bank turned down a loan request 20 years ago, saying that South Korea's plans for getting into steel were too risky. Instead, the South Koreans used reparations from Japanese colonisation to build what is now the world's fifth largest steel company outside the communist world.

Led by Posco, South Korea's steel industry has been feverishly expanding while steelmakers in West Germany, Japan and the USA have been shutting down. Though steel exports are booming, domestic industry - especially cars and machinery - has spurred the growth of Korean steel: domestic demand for steel grew by 31% in 1987 alone. In that year South Korea completed a second integrated steel mill which added 2.7 million tonnes to Posco's capacity and brought the state-owned firm's total capacity to 11.8 million tonnes. Yet Korea's steel makers could still supply only three-quarters of the country's domestic demand. A second stage was scheduled for completion by the end of 1988 and will add another 2.7 million tonnes to capacity. A third, equally large stage is set to be completed in late 1989. These additions would make South Korea the world's sixth largest steel producer.

Even with huge additions to capacity, the country's self-sufficiency ratio dropped from 82% in 1986 to 77.5% in 1987. The decline is not due to any loss in efficiency. Production costs in early 1988 were only $418 per tonne compared to $570 in Japan and $475 in the

USA. Though the recent rise in the Korean won has reduced this cost advantage, South Korea remains one of the world's most efficient steel producers.

Korea's steel exporters have exploited the price advantage that an undervalued won afforded. Japan replaced the USA as Korea's largest foreign buyer as steel producers boosted their sales to the world's most expensive market. The Japanese construction sector is responsible for most of these purchases with demand for pipes, tubes and bar-steel exports growing most rapidly. Japanese competitors have substantially improved their own efficiency but Koreans doubt that Japan's contracting industry will prove capable of meeting the country's domestic demand for many years.

Domestically, Posco is much in the news because of the programme to sell part of the state-owned enterprise on the open market. The part privatisation leaves control of Posco in government hands but is the first in a series of planned stock offerings of publicly owned enterprises. The shares are being sold by the government and the state-owned Korean Development Institute (KDI). Three-quarters are reserved for farmers, fishermen and middle- and lower-income workers. Another 20% are marked for Posco employees so only 5% will be sold freely.

The programme will make South Korea one of the few Asian countries where the government has made serious efforts to reduce its involvement in the steel industry. Throughout most of South and East Asia the state operates the steel industry. This ownership pattern reflects the widespread priority governments have accorded to the industry and the belief (generally held in the 1960s) that state ownership was necessary in embryonic industries which depended on economies of scale. That strategy is typical of India whose planners had considerable influence on their counterparts in other South and East Asian countries. India's considerable steel industry continues to be state-owned today, but heavy reliance on the sort of centralised planning this entails can have its costs. For example, India's Heavy Engineering Corporation has the capacity to service a steel industry five times larger than the country has actually established. The firm reported losses of 55 billion rupees in 1987.

Even the Taiwanese government has retained ownership of its steel industry. Although the share of state-owned enterprises in total industrial output fell from 46% in 1972 to 10% in 1988, virtually all Taiwan's steel industry is still publicly owned. Indonesia, too, has a large, publicly-operated steel industry which acts as a monopoly. Because inefficiency is so widespread, the government has now voiced hopes of dismantling it.

Automobiles

The ownership pattern is quite different in metal-using industries. Among this set of manufacturers the most important is the automobile industry, which is dominated not by local or state-run interests but by multinationals. South Korea's carmakers are the largest in South and East Asia. The Korean industry's expansion has been miraculous, even in a country noted for its high rates of economic growth. In 1983 the car industry accounted for less than 4% of the value of South Korea's industrial production. By 1990, it is expected to produce over 9% of the total - and that is during a period when the volume of total industrial production is expected to double.

South Korea exported only 65 cars to the USA in 1985 but just one year later these were about 140,000. With such success, the fears of the Korean automobile industry that its exports will soon prompt protectionist responses are not surprising. Another effect of the Korean surge in exports is that the country's imports from Japan have risen. Korea's car makers find that Japanese parts are essential for them to comply with America's safety and emission standards.

The Daewoo Research Institute has calculated that the value of South Korea's imports of car parts from Japan rose from $124 million in 1984 to $400 million in 1986. Overall, imports of car parts jumped from $172 million to $650 million in the same period. Japanese car makers have followed these imports to Korea where they now produce cars for export. Mitsubishi owns 15% of Hyundai, Korea's biggest producer. Hyundai relies on Misubishi for technical help. Mazda, a medium-sized car maker in Japan, owns 8% of Kia, another Korean company.

The Korean government wants its car makers to buy fewer parts from Japan and more from America. That way, it could stifle protectionist pressures in the USA while at the same time reducing its deficit with Japan. To some extent, this is happening. Hyundai now fits Goodyear tyres, Libbey-Owens-Ford windscreens, and Champion spark plugs to the Excel cars it exports. These initiatives may not be enough, however. A safer policy would be to build assembly plants in the countries to which the Koreans sell. Hyundai took this step in 1987 when work began on an assembly and components plant in Canada.

Korea's car makers have only recently begun to look at their home market more carefully. The Koreans jealously protect their own market for cars: tariffs on imported cars are 60% and a steep domestic tax is then added. American officials calculated that in 1987 a $20,000 imported luxury car cost its Korean buyer $55,412. With such high domestic prices, the Korean market is lucrative but also underdeveloped. Daewoo and Hyundai have both announced plans for a minicar with an engine capacity of 800cc or less. Sales are scheduled to begin by 1991 and are expected to be almost 200,000 per year in the 1990s. The government is encouraging this step by slashing registration and consumption taxes and by loosening pollution standards for small cars.

In the long term China is by far the most exciting prospect in South and East Asia - despite the obvious political imponderables. The country is also committed to building up its own production capacity. Volkswagen was the first multinational to set up operations in China. The Chinese were anxious to link themselves with a European manufacturer because of a fear that they were becoming too dependent on the Japanese. In 1984 Volkswagen concluded its joint venture agreement with the Chinese, which will run for 25 years. Initially, the local content (that is, the share of locally-produced components in the selling price of the car) was 30% but ambitious plans call for this to rise to 90% in the 1990s.

India's automobile industry, like China's, has potentially a large domestic market. However, cars are seen as luxuries in India and little scarce foreign exchange can be spared for such use. This attitude has led some Indian car makers to look to exports as a way of justifying their hard currency expenditures on imported machinery and components. The Indian car industry's main advantages for competing in export markets are cheap labour and India's special trading relations with Eastern Europe. The fact that this trade must be balanced enables the two sides to swap goods that could not be sold easily for hard currency.

The Indian public sector car maker, Maruti, recently announced plans to manufacture a new car and to export up to 10,000 per year. Maruti was started by Sanjay Gandhi in the early 1970s but quickly went bankrupt. In 1980 it was nationalised and given a generous infusion of cash. The company then arranged a deal with Suzuki to make 100,000 vehicles per year. Maruti has consistently met its production targets and now wants to expand its output and product range. The government has approved a proposal for it to manufacture a subcompact in direct competition with Hindustan Motors and Premier Automobiles. Suzuki has agreed to increase its equity to 40%. The balance of the $35 million required for expansion will come from foreign borrowing.

229

Malaysia's efforts to develop an automobile industry have been partly inspired by South Korea's success. In 1983 it was decided to produce a "national car", the Proton Saga, which was to be the showpiece of industrialisation. A plant with an annual capacity of 80,000 units was built near Kuala Lumpur in 1988. Exports, it was assumed, would follow. One of the company's major problems has proved to be its dependence on parts from Mitsubishi, which owns 30% of the project. These became wildly expensive as the yen appreciated against Malaysia's ringgit.

Thailand has joined Malaysia as an exporter of cars. Thai-assembled Mitsubishi Lancer compacts, rebadged as Dodge and Plymouth Colts, began to be exported to Canada in January 1988. The country hopes these will be the first of 100,000 to be shipped to Canada in the next six years. Thailand's achievement is underscored by growing foreign sales of car parts and accessories. Investments by Japanese and Taiwanese car-parts manufacturers were strong in 1987, surpassing those in other parts of South and East Asia.

The entry of Thailand and Malaysia as car makers has raised the question of the automobile industry's role in the Association of South East Asian Nations (ASEAN). The group, which consists of Thailand, Malaysia, Singapore, Indonesia, Brunei and the Philippines, had earlier proposed the idea of an "Asian car". The intention was to spread out car-component manufacturing among ASEAN members so that each would reap industrialisation benefits while not competing with its neighbours. All were expected to benefit by supplying parts not just to their own car market but to those of other ASEAN markets, free of duties applied to parts made outside the region.

Planning the division of capacity among ASEAN members has proved difficult. A 90% reduction in import duties for ASEAN suppliers was proposed. Thai car-parts producers, being significantly ahead of their neighbours, have said they will agree to only a 50%

reduction, however. But other, unexpected events have given a new impetus to the car industry in these countries - without ASEAN guidance. A strengthening of both the yen and the new Taiwan dollar has pushed these two countries' parts producers southward and has forced ASEAN car assemblers to scour the region for cheaper components. Even Indonesia, despite a car industry lagging far behind that of Thailand or Malaysia, has been able to take advantage of the currency shifts. Indonesia exported nearly 2,000 truck units to Thailand in 1988. The major difficulty, if an ASEAN car is to be realised, is the location for the source of the heaviest and most technology-intensive components. Each ASEAN member is pressing hard to get foreign car makers to produce engine transmissions, chassis and axles in their own countries. So far, no Japanese car maker has made a commitment to build engines in ASEAN.

Electronics

The last, and in many ways most important, industry to be covered in this survey is electronics. South and East Asian economies at all levels of development were first drawn to the industry because of its labour-intensive production technologies and the fact that multinationals came to the region searching for cheap-labour sites where they could produce mature, standardised electrical products for export. The region began with consumer electronics but within a comparatively short period its manufacturers moved on to more sophisticated items such as semiconductors and components for computers and other electronic products. Today, both industrial and consumer electronics provide the backbone of the manufacturing sector in many South and East Asian countries and account for a large share of the region's exports.

South Korea, followed closely by Taiwan, has led the region's rush into electronics. The rich American market has been the prime target for virtually all South and East Asia's electronics industry but none more so than for the Koreans. Exports of televisions, microwave ovens and personal computers are the products on which Korea's electronics firms depend. Few foreign buyers of Korean electronics would recognise the names of the large firms such as Lukey-Goldstar, Samsung or Sunkyong (SKC) which make these products. The reason is that to avoid a protectionist backlash, the Koreans have sold their products under the brand names of US firms.

This tactic worked well in the consumer electronics markets where products are mature and competition on the basis of price is paramount. But to move upmarket, Korean companies must win recognition on their own. Spending on advertising is heavy but few Korean companies have managed to set up reliable distribution networks. Even the largest firms have trouble keeping their outlets stocked. Japanese companies can perfect a product in their own market before beginning an export push. But lacking a large domestic market South Korea (and other South and East Asian countries) are obliged to discover problems through trial and error with foreign customers.

South Korea's approach depends heavily on US technologies. The largest Korean firms participate in a growing network of joint ventures, licensing arrangements and other forms of collaboration with American counterparts. To help companies boost their high-tech expertise, the government is encouraging the creation of research teams from among groups of companies. It also plans to double the number of engineers between 1988 and 1993. Another Korean strategy, typical of the large Daewoo conglomerate, is to combine the latest in foreign technology with creative designs to develop innovative products at competitive prices. This, of course, requires ample in-house expertise in engineering and design.

Korean export successes in important markets such as personal computers have intensified competition with other South and East Asian rivals such as Taiwan. To capture greater market share, Korean and Taiwanese manufacturers have slashed prices to lock in foreign customers. The contest pits two vastly different approaches. Taiwan's electronics firms have been building components for US firms since the 1960s while Korean firms have been in the business for a shorter period. The Koreans have often cut their prices drastically to build up market share. The Taiwanese, too, have reduced prices but Korean conglomerates are much larger; they can afford to extend credit to customers and have other resources to help them against the Taiwanese. The Taiwanese also complain that the Korean government has subsidised the high-tech end of its electronics industry with low-interest loans.

Hong Kong provides key inputs for China's push in the high-technology end of the electronics business. China has concentrated on items such as production of disk drives, which are one of the most labour-intensive parts of the computer industry. Foreign investors - frequently from Hong Kong - have opened electronics factories in southern China and state-operated plants are moving into the export of electronics items as well. The attraction to foreign investors is great: the wages paid to Chinese workers in electronics firms were only about a fifth of Hong Kong's wages in 1988. One drawback is that cheap labour is not always reliable. The country's exports often suffer from poor quality and numerous defects. Another difficulty is that foreign firms in high-tech businesses are reluctant to transfer technologies to China.

Like most of its other industries, India's electronics firms depend mainly on their domestic market for growth and are little concerned with exporting. The country's reliance on import substitution policies and the easy-to-acquire technologies for consumer electronics made it easy to enter that portion of the industry. Television producers make up a large portion of this sector.

Government policies helped to create a television industry with 120 firms by 1986. The government encouraged every aspiring producer of televisions to take out an industrial licence. But in line with the country's preference for small scale industry, most licences were for production of no more than 10,000 sets per year. When Rajiv Gandhi came to power, the policy was changed. The government approved capacity for around 10 million sets per year. Foreign investment followed with Toshiba, Hitachi, Mitsubishi and Philips having joint ventures.

Though India has only three television sets for every 1,000 persons (as against ten per 1,000 persons in China), the potential market is big. The problem is that the income of poor Indians is not rising fast enough to keep up with capacity expansion in television production and other parts of consumer electronics. Prices of several electronics products have begun to fall and some manufacturers are selling below cost. Exports could take up some of the slack but quality is not yet good enough though competition is improving it.

In industrial electronics India has begun to make use of its many trained (and often unemployed) engineers as a way of injecting more momentum into the industry. The government has made a serious effort to prod its computer industry into action by liberalising many policies. Since it adopted a package of tariffs and incentives for domestic computer makers in November 1984, production has more than tripled. Greater competition has also led to price cutting. In 1984 only 3,000 personal computers were made in the entire country; two years later the number was 20,000. A personal computer which cost 40,000 rupees at the beginning of 1986 was priced at 24,000 rupees two years later. Despite these improvements, India's prices are three times world levels and the domestic market for computers remains small.

Industrial electronics account for the largest share of India's collaboration agreements with the USA. One of the pioneers is Tata

Unisys (formerly Tata Burroughs), which began making computers in the mid-1970s. The venture began because it was the only way to get computer hardware into the country. By 1987, however, Tata Unisys was a major supplier of mainframes and personal computers and exported $30 million of software. Texas Instruments is another important collaborator with its own software-design centre in India. Altogether, more than 50 Indian companies are assembling computers in collaboration with firms such as Digital Equipment, Hewlett Packard, Tandy, Commodore, Data General and Motorola.

Meanwhile, the Indian government has attempted to boost demand. It instructed all government-owned banks to computerise their 40,000 branches. The railways, telephone system and state-owned manufacturing companies have also been told to automate their offices. At the heart of this strategy are many small, Indian-owned firms producing personal computers and software. However, India's best hope in other parts of the industry - for example production of larger mainframe computers - continues to be that foreign firms will help to produce the machines the government needs.

CHAPTER 11

ECONOMIC PROBLEMS AND PROSPECTS IN SOUTH AND EAST ASIA

The economic landscape of South and East Asia is rapidly changing. Major elements in this transformation are, first, the evolution of Japan's economic relations with its Third World neighbours and, second, the increasing importance of trade and foreign direct investment among countries of the region. The chapter begins with an examination of these particular trends. Section II looks at the importance of export-led growth in the region and the threat that protectionist forces in other parts of the world may gradually force some countries in the region to alter their development strategies. China's probable emergence as an international economic power is an issue of great regional significance and is considered in Section III. Other regional issues of particular importance include intellectual property rights and technology transfer and debt in selected Asian countries. These topics are examined in the last two sections of the chapter.

I The Regionalisation of Asia

In terms of their development strategies the countries of South and East Asia seem to be clustered around the extremes in the development spectrum, with some being heavily geared to exports while others are predominantly inward-oriented. Many East Asian economies have been influenced by the Japanese model of export-led growth. Countries like Hong Kong, Singapore, South Korea and Taiwan rely on exports as a major source of economic growth while others, such as Malaysia and Thailand, have recently embarked on this path. All these countries have aimed their export strategies primarily at markets in North America and Western Europe. Although they export to Japan as well, that country has not - until very recently - been an important market for their products.

At the other end of the spectrum are the region's more insulated economies. India has a long tradition of relying on its domestic markets for growth while few countries have been more insular than China. Until the late 1970s, other countries in South Asia - Bangladesh, Nepal, Pakistan and Sri Lanka - emulated their larger neighbours by following a strategy of zealous import substitution. This mixture of contradictory strategies meant that in relation to the size of South and East Asia's economies intra-regional markets were underdeveloped and received little attention, either from businessmen or policymakers.

All this is beginning to change. Many of the region's governments have come to realise that neither of the two policy extremes is likely to bring economic prosperity to their countries over the next 20 years. The USA's ability to absorb an ever growing volume of cheap Asian manufactures is limited and its willingness to do so is waning. At the same time the region's more insular economies are becoming less comfortable with their reliance on import substitution in an era when the pace of technological development is accelerating and foreign investment is reaching new corners of the world. As the industrial base of Asia has grown, manufacturers have realised that they have potential export markets close to home.

Another, more important reason for the transformation is the change in Japan's relations with the Asian economies. Japan is gradually abandoning its export-dependent growth strategy. Several forces would seem to make the Japanese adjustment an inevitable one: first, Japan's wages are the highest in the region and are rising rapidly; second, the appreciation of the yen has magnified the country's cost disadvantage relative to its Asian rivals. As the richest country in Asia turns away from export-led growth, it is becoming a more attractive target for exporters elsewhere in the region. Finally, Japanese manufactures - like their American counterparts before them - are trying to cope with their rising costs by relocating factories to cheaper sites. Many of these relocational decisions involve developing countries within the region and help to create a much wider network for intra-regional trade.

Japanese companies have traditionally produced no more than 3 to 4% of their output abroad. In contrast, the corresponding figure for US companies is 18 to 20%. But with the high yen and uncompetitive wage rates, Japanese manufacturers of all sizes have poured into the rest of Asia. According to the data in Table 11.1 Japanese direct investment in the rest of Asia in 1987 was more than twice the 1986 level. On average, more than five Japanese companies set up shop every week in Taiwan alone. Hong Kong was the largest recipient of Japanese investment in 1987 (more than $1 billion) - possibly because a presence in the city-state is seen as a useful beachhead to establish Chinese markets. South Korea was second, followed by Indonesia and Singapore.

Table 11.1   JAPAN'S DIRECT FOREIGN INVESTMENT IN SELECTED SOUTH AND EAST ASIAN COUNTRIES 1985-1987

$ million	1985		1986		1987	
	No. of cases	Value	No. of cases	Value	No. of cases	Value
Hong Kong	105	131	163	50	261	1,072
Indonesia	62	408	46	250	67	545
Malaysia	60	79	70	158	64	163
Philippines	9	61	9	21	18	72

Continued...

Table 11.1 cont'd

| | 1985 | | 1986 | | 1987 | |
	No. of cases	Value	No. of cases	Value	No. of cases	Value
Singapore	110	339	85	302	182	494
South Korea	75	134	111	436	166	647
Taiwan	68	114	178	291	268	367
Thailand	51	48	58	124	192	250
TOTAL	540	1,314	720	1,632	1,218	3,610

Source: Japanese Ministry of Finance

Japanese manufacturers have been moving offshore to stay competitive. One result is that Asian economies are becoming vertically integrated. Developing countries are becoming the assemblers of Japanese-supplied parts and act as proxy exporters for Japan to the West. South Korean and Taiwanese manufacturers, whose currencies have also risen against the dollar, are moving offshore too. Investment flows throughout the region are on the rise and these flows do not originate only in Japan.

The counterpart to Japan's thrust into the other parts of the region is growth of consumption and investment at home. These developments are radically changing Japan's economy - and bringing in large quantities of the foreign goods that the country's trading partners have been clamouring for. As a result, Japan has become a big market for other South and East Asian countries. Its imports from Hong Kong, Singapore, South Korea and Taiwan rose by 30% per year in 1986-7 in yen terms and by 50% per year in dollar terms.

As the horizontal integration of Japan and other countries in the region continues, governments have begun to think more seriously

240

about their regional relationships. Some have turned their attention to the possible development of a South and East Asian trading bloc, centred on Japan and built on the yen. That sort of an arrangement would not be universally welcomed by all Asians. Many remember their countries' World War II relations with Japan and would be unwilling to see the emergence of peacetime trading blocs including that country. Others, however, have accepted that greater political and economic integration of the region is inevitable and that Japan's regional leadership could not be denied.

A yen-based trading bloc is still many years away. The economic disparities in per capita incomes and levels of development are great, meaning that a South and East Asian version of the European Monetary System would be out of the question. A loosely co-ordinated affiliation bolstered by collaborative projects in energy, telecommunications and research and development would be more probable. The growth of trade within the Asian Basin is starting to make such a bloc appear sustainable.

There is already some evidence that current trends are pushing South and East Asian countries in this direction. Japan, for example, has long conducted its trade primarily in US dollars but is gradually coming to accept the yen as a basis for trade. The proportion of Japan's exports invoiced in yen rose from 29% in 1980 to 33% in 1987. Likewise, only 2% of the country's imports were yen-based in 1980 but seven years later the figure was 10.6%. Greater use of the yen as an international currency will smooth the way for a South and East Asian trading system. Some companies and countries also wish to borrow in yen because Japan's interest rates are low and its saving ample. But to do so, they need to earn yen by exporting and therefore welcome the change in Japanese trading practices.

A supporting piece of evidence is found in the foreign exchange policies of Japan's Asian trading partners. More countries in the region are becoming interested in pegging their currencies to the yen. They do so to avoid inflation rates which are higher than Japan's. So long as these currencies are linked to the US dollar, South and East Asian exporters can gain a competitive edge over Japan as the dollar depreciates relative to the yen. But the resultant injection of inflationary pressure into their economies is harmful and could undo these gains. Although most South and East Asian countries still peg their currencies to the dollar, some, such as Thailand, have switched to a basket of currencies. Others may do so if the USA continues to press them to revalue. Another intangible factor which would hasten the formation of a South and East Asian trading bloc is if the USA were to impose more protectionist barriers on Asian imports. This possibility is the subject of the following section.

II Export-Led Growth and Protectionist Reprisals

Industrialists and politicians in North America and Western Europe regard the Japanese inroads into their home markets as one of their major challenges. Though most see the Japanese problem as a lasting one, the developing countries in South and East Asia pose a more serious threat of additional market disruption in the next decade. By 1990 four countries - Hong Kong, Singapore, South Korea and Taiwan - are expected to have combined exports of manufactures greater than Japan. Close behind these supercompetitors are others such as Malaysia and Thailand. Meanwhile, the possibility that China and India might become ambitious exporters is daunting: if their 2 billion people were to export only $100 of manufactures per capita (currently the level of Turkey's exports) the two countries' share in world manufacturing trade would nearly match that of Japan.

Most South and East Asian developing countries continue to be net importers from the rest of the world but the situation is changing fast. The combined trade deficit of 25 countries tracked by the

Asian Development Bank fell from $12.7 billion in 1985 to $1 billion to 1986. As the region's trade balance moves into surplus, the prospects for further export gains will become more tenuous. Trading partners are likely to react by restricting their home markets just as they have tried to redress their trade imbalances with Japan. Trade wars have a habit of spreading and for almost all South and East Asian countries the USA is either the first or second (after Japan) major market for exports: it takes 20% of Thailand's exports; 13% of Malaysia's; 21% of Indonesia's; 18% of Singapore's; 36% of the Philippines'; two-fifths of Hong Kong's; over a third of South Korea's and about half Taiwan's. If the US market becomes more restricted - whether by tariffs, quotas or a slump in domestic demand - South and East Asian exporters will suffer, and by amounts that cannot be made up by increased exports to Japan.

The countries most obviously at risk are those which the USA has pressed to appreciate their currencies, to open up their home markets or both. At the forefront of this group are South Korea and Taiwan. South Korea has been liberalising its import controls since 1979, long before it achieved an external surplus. The government originally took this step to control inflation (46% in 1980) and later to reduce costs of its inputs. In 1987 and 1988 the pace of liberalisation accelerated when the government cut tariffs on 800 goods by an average of 40%. Trade officials point out that the import liberalisation ratio (the proportion of goods not subject to quota restrictions) has reached 95% for manufactures, though agriculture remains heavily protected. What worries Japanese and Americans is that the relaxations are highly selective. The Koreans have made little attempt to reduce import barriers in sensitive industries like automobiles. A bevy of tariffs and taxes means that the sale price of a foreign car is around twice that of a domestically produced vehicle with the same factory price. And even though imports of small cars are now permitted, Japanese models will be kept out.

Taiwan, too, has acted to reduce its import barriers. In 1987 the government cut tariffs on 2,900 items (though the cuts on 1,200 were only temporary). Reductions on another 3,700 were implemented in 1988. These steps brought the average tariff rate down to 16% from 20% in mid-1987. Many of the items concerned are insignificant, however, ranging from sweet apricots to boxes of chocolates. Taiwan's automobile industry has vigorously protested plans to reduce tariffs on imported cars from 55 to 30%.

In recent years both South Korea and Taiwan have allowed their currencies to rise against the US dollar by over 30%. The results were as expected. US exports to these countries increased by over 40% in the 12 months up to August 1988. Such moves give reason to hope that the region's major exporters might eventually be absorbed into the world economy without great difficulties. But this can be achieved only if both exporters and importers adhere to the existing international rules and market forces.

Co-operation applies not only to trade but to related fields such as finance. The four South and East Asian dragons are becoming financial leaders as well as manufacturing powers: together, their foreign exchange reserves are $100 billion, equivalent to a third of their combined GNP. The comparable ratio for Japan is only 3.5% while that of West Germany is 6%. Likewise, the capitalisation of the six largest stock markets in South and East Asia (excluding Japan) is $200 billion, roughly the size of the Italian and Swiss bourses combined. Yet most of the region's stock markets are tightly regulated and foreigners are not admitted. The dilemma is that no country can become an export leader without concomitant financial stature.

In the longer run, the emergence of stronger protectionist forces in the USA and Western Europe could force a response by South and East Asian exporters. The formation of a trading bloc centred on the yen runs the danger of provoking a breakdown in the GATT system. No South and East Asian exporter, of course, would wish to be excluded from the North American and Western European markets, but if trade with Western markets should be diminished significantly as a result of greater protection, a South and East Asian regional trading zone would be even more attractive. Creation of such a zone would restrict the gains from trade and slow the growth of world income.

III China - South and East Asia's Potential Economic Giant

China's role in the region's economic future would be difficult to overestimate. However, the country's insularity, political turmoil and erratic policies mean that its prospects are uncertain. The battle between the country's conservatives and its reformers has continued for several years with no clear outcome in sight. Meanwhile, China's economic ills have worsened. Prices are now rising faster than ever before in 40 years of communism. Depositors have threatened runs on banks at a time when factories are short of supplies and workers' strikes are becoming increasingly troublesome. Events such as these have strengthened the position of conservatives in their efforts to return to the pre-1978 period of central planning. For China, the biggest risk in its programme of economic reform is that an incomplete programme of modernisation, by increasing inflation, corruption and unemployment, will discredit the entire concept.

One cornerstone of China's reform policy has been the creation of 14 "open cities" along the coast, together with five "open areas" and five "special economic zones". These are all intended to operate with at least some degree of economic freedom. Three of the special zones were established in 1981 and the "open cities" have been in operation for four years. China's party chief, Zhao Ziyang, hopes to extend the concept eventually to all provinces along the country's coast. The danger is that the 400 million people living along the coast, instead of spreading ideas and wealth to the interior, will emerge as a separate and richer geographic group distinct from the rest of the country. This would occur at the expense of the unity and stability which China's rulers have always fought hard to maintain.

The special economic zones all repeat the formulas tried by almost every developing country eager for foreign investment, skills and technology. Cheap labour, low or no taxes, preferential customs treatment and minimal bureaucracy are the attractions. China's economists have assumed that the zones will succeed mainly because of their proximity to other economic centres such as Hong Kong, Taiwan and even Macao. But foreign investment has not flooded in. Shenzhen, close to Hong Kong, had only 334 new projects in 1987 compare with 454 in 1986. A second special zone, Shantow, has managed to attract only $80 million in foreign investment since 1980 while Ziamen (across from Taiwan) had less than $25 million in foreign investment in 1987. Moreoever, most of these investments have been low-grade, involving beer, soft drinks, cheap shoes and similar products.

China's programme of open cities and special economic zones is also coming under attack because of corruption. As the country broadens its contacts with the rest of the world, economic crimes proliferate, ranging from taking bribes to selling consumer goods on the black market to nepotism among high officials. Such corruption is common in other countries but is nevertheless discouraging many foreign investors. Inflation and rising expectations about living standards add to the temptation to make illicit profits. While consumption soars and prices are decontrolled in stages, many urban residents remain in low-paying jobs where the temptation for corruption is great.

Agricultural reforms

China's efforts at economic reform in agriculture have been more successful. Although there are sharp fluctuations in free market food prices and some rationing, the agricultural sector is in relatively good health. The volatility of free market prices stems from the changing nature of demand - in particular the rapid transformation of the rural economy and the need to reassess the role of the state - rather than being symptomatic of a deeper crisis. Assuring an abundant supply of cheap food has been an overriding concern of the Chinese government in the post-liberation period. Since that time the country has enjoyed steady increases in per capita food production despite its lack of arable land.

China's agricultural sector, however, has reached a turning point. The nature of agricultural demand is changing more rapidly. It is no longer a question of guaranteeing a basic minimum supply of food grain but of supplying feed-grain to commercial meat producers. As income levels have risen, diets have improved. Figure 11.1 illustrates the effect increases in income have had on spending and, in particular, the pattern of food consumption. The per capita amount spent on foodstuffs nearly doubled between 1983 and 1986. Little of this additional expenditure was on grains or non-staples, however. Because of the shift in consumption patterns, China's farms are now under pressure to ensure a sufficient supply of fibres and cash crops.

Fundamental changes are also occurring within the rural economy and its trading links with the urban sector. The changes are largely the product of reforms in the late 1970s. The most important has been a rapid increase in rural labour costs. From 1980 to 1986 the average value produced by each rural worker rose nearly 350%. Few of these gains, however, were due to increased agricultural production; they were primarily the result of the explosive growth of rural industry (which surpassed the value of agricultural output for

Figure 11.1   CHINA'S AVERAGE MONTHLY URBAN PER CAPITA INCOME
AND SPENDING 1983/1986

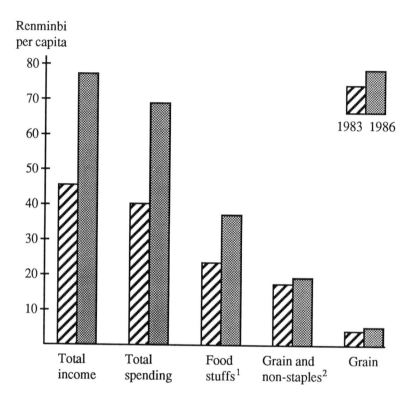

Source: *Chinese State Statistical Bureau (survey data)*
Notes: [1] *Including alcoholic beverages and tobacco*
         [2] *Largely meat, fish and eggs*

the first time in 1987). The implications of this shift have yet to be
fully understood. However, it is clear that in southern parts of the
country, in many suburban areas and in coastal provinces the
fundamental precondition of China's traditional small-scale

intensive agriculture - an inexhaustible supply of cheap rural labour - no longer exists.

In 1988 China's farming sector consisted of about 180 million household producers working plots of land averaging only 0.6 hectares. Under China's original system of small-scale farming and labour-intensive techniques, rising unit labour costs would eventually make the country's farm products the most expensive in the world. The changing structure of the rural economy requires a switch to large-scale commercial farming. However, simply enlarging farm size as excess labour is absorbed by other parts of the economy will not improve per unit yields. It is vital that farm incomes maintain a rough parity with other forms of rural employment. At the moment, the risks in large-scale, commercial farming are higher and the returns lower than other types of rural occupations.

Debt and foreign investment

Though the major impact of China's reform programme have so far been borne by the agricultural and industrial sectors, there have been other repercussions at the macroeconomic level. The most politically sensitive of macroeconomic issues concern debt, foreign investment and inflation. As China has modernised its economy, foreign debt has expanded in a chaotic fashion, growing at an annual rate of 30% in the period 1983-7. Many local governments and enterprises borrowed abroad without bothering to inform Beijing. International observers believe China borrowed about $4 billion in 1988, bringing its net foreign debt to more than $31 billion. As much as $12 billion of that will fall due between 1991 and 1993.

Most of China's foreign borrowing is done on concessionary terms from the Asian Development Bank, the World Bank or export-credit agencies. But in 1983 it turned to borrowing from commercial banks. In 1986 around 60% of the $3.3 billion China borrowed was from commercial banks, compared with nothing in 1982. The country's rapidly rising export revenues would seem to provide an ample cushion but the government worries that by the early 1990s it might not be able to keep up debt payments. Despite the growth in indebtedness, China's debt-service ratios appear manageable. Chinese officials are hopeful that they will soon be able to dictate terms to foreign bankers anxious for their business.

Chinese expectations for foreign investment are as optimistic as those with regard to foreign debt. Foreign investment in China has proceeded in spurts followed by periods of stagnation. It fell sharply in 1986 for the first time since China opened its doors in 1979. Tight credit controls had made it difficult for Chinese partners to obtain funds and contributed to the fall. The impact was amplified by a 10% cut in the country's budget and reductions of between 50 and 90% in state spending in fields such as energy, transport and communications. New investment rules led to an acceleration of foreign investment in the first half of 1988. The latest recovery in foreign investment represents the results of yet another shift in policymakers' attitudes. The new rules are less strict about ownership, allowing foreign companies 50-70-year leases - a feature which would have been unthinkable before. They also allow foreign companies more control over the management of factories.

China hopes much of the new investment will be channelled into its special economic zones. Table 11.2 shows the distribution of foreign direct investment by city in 1985, just prior to the slump as regulations were tightened. Over 27% was in Beijing alone, almost equal to the amount received by cities designated as special economic zones (27.5%). The remainder went to coastal cities, a pattern which reinforces Chinese fears that its society will become increasingly differentiated, with a rich coastal population and a poor hinterland.

Table 11.2   FOREIGN DIRECT INVESTMENT IN CHINA BY CITY END-1985

$ million

Beijing	904	Fuzhou[1]	44
Shanghai[1]	762	Qingdao[1]	35
Canton[1]	683	Nantong[1]	29
Shenzhen[2]	490	Qinhuangdao[1]	26
Xiamen[2]	242	Yantai[1]	8
Dailian[1]	142	Beihai[1]	5
Zhuhai[2]	128	Ningbo[1]	5
Zhanjiang[1]	109	Lianyungang[1]	4
Tianjin[1]	68	Wenzhou[1]	1
Shantou[2]	60		

Source: State Statistics Bureau
Notes: [1] *Coastal city designated as economic zone 1984*
          [2] *Special economic zone*

Inflation

The last and most politically sensitive consequence of China's reforms concerns the inflation the country has experienced. The official figure (which is probably low) puts the rate at 7% but prices in the first quarter of 1988 were 11% higher than for the same period in 1987. The burden of inflation has been greatest for China's urban population: in late 1988 prices in the country's largest cities were a third above their 1987 level.

Inflation is not supposed to occur in a proper centrally planned economy, yet China is experiencing price increases reminiscent of the war-torn economy during the pre-communist era. The reasons are several. For years queues served as a means of rationing scarce goods when prices could not. Now that some prices are allowed to move with the market, demand is strong and pushes them up. A construction boom, and bonuses 40% greater in 1987 and 1986 created a host of potentially new consumers. Imports, too, have become more costly as the Chinese, in effect, pegged their currency to a weakening dollar.

An even more important reason for inflation is that China's piecemeal introduction of market prices has revealed huge imbalances between demand and supply. Reformers argue that the gaps will be bridged only if the government allows prices to function as a rationing device - that is, to be determined by the market. Supply would eventually adjust and prices would stabilise. In the short run, this approach can be politically risky. More cautious economists therefore contend that reforms should follow, rather than precede, stable prices. The latter group wants the growth of industrial output to be slowed and public projects with long pay-back periods to be stopped. They also call for the People's Bank, which until now has served merely as the government's cashier, to become a real central bank with the ability to control the money supply.

In conclusion, China's bold reforms have set the country on a path towards greater economic power. The actual nature of these reforms remains tenuous and sometimes uncertain but the country will eventually emerge economically stronger. At that time China will begin to make its real mark on the outside world. Unsettled quarrels abound throughout South and East Asia and China has an interest in several. The nature of regional relationships is bound to change as China's economic strength grows. While today's relations with Japan, other Asian countries, the USA and Europe are partly based on China's potential as a market for outsiders, future relations will depend more heavily on its own economic self-interest.

IV Intellectual Property Rights and Technology Transfer

South and East Asia is home to considerable piracy of products and ideas. In the 1950s India had serious doubts about international conventions on intellectual property and led Third World forces in arguing that they had special needs with regard to the transfer of technological know-how. As Indian industries have matured the country has gradually taken a more favourable view towards international regulations. Other countries in the region are also slowly moving towards widespread acceptance of copyright as a concept and increasingly as a practice. China is considering copyright legislation and acceptance of major international copyright treaties. Singapore passed a stringent copyright law in 1986 and has now begun to enforce it with some vigour. Malaysia has also passed a law on copyrights which will soon to be implemented and South Korea is beginning to impose controls.

Taiwan was one of the major violators of intellectual property rights but it, too, has undergone a similar transition. As the country developed its own knowledge-based industries, there was greater acceptance of the need for regulation. Taiwan-based computer pirates, for example, were replaced by local companies developing their own technologies. For the new companies to deal with overseas firms, Taiwan had to shed its image as a "knowledge outcast". Thailand is one of the few countries which remains open to piracy, particularly for computer software and "brand name" consumer products.

Gradually, the concept of intellectual property has become better understood and accepted in South and East Asia. But despite this progress there are problems. South and East Asian countries have traditionally been critical of copyright treaties, pointing out that it is a Western concept created to maintain a monopoly over production and distribution of knowledge and knowledge-based products. Copyright protection was, historically, not part of the Asian cultural

253

tradition; instead, it has been imposed by pressure from major Western trading partners under threat of trade sanctions and legal action. Furthermore, countries without a copyright law, such as China, are not really violating anything since copying, translating and the like without permission from the copyright owners is not against their laws. Despite these conceptual and practical problems, copyright is becoming entrenched, both in law and practice.

There are a least two reasons for the recent progress in countries which until a few years ago were willing to disregard intellectual property rights. The first is that successful knowledge-based industries such as computers obviously require some kind of regulation. There is growing appreciation of the fact that knowledge is truly an international commodity and its transfer must be subject to some international regulations. Governments in South and East Asian countries have begun to take a long-term perspective while realising that they presently operate at a disadvantage in the international knowledge network. In short, South and East Asian nations aspire to become producers of knowledge as well as consumers.

The second major reason for progress is a combination of "carrots and sticks" from Western countries. The carrot in this instance is the willingness of Western countries to accept versions of compulsory licensing in various industries as a way of demonstrating that they understand the problems of the Third World. The stick is the pressure that has been applied to several major pirating countries to implement and enforce copyright laws. It is also likely that the Soviet Union's acceptance of the Universal Copyright Convention in the 1970s had an impact on Third World thinking. If the largest state still holding out could join the Western-dominated system and not be adversely affected, then perhaps Asian nations would have little to fear.

Despite progress, anything less than complete compliance with international regulations often gives rise to difficulties. South Korea's 1988 dispute with the European Commission (EC) illustrates the dangers of part compliance. The EC stripped South Korea of all its special trade privileges under the Generalised System of Preferences (GSP). The move was in retaliation for South Korea's refusal to give European exporters the same legal protection against violation of intellectual property rights as those granted to US firms. The EC action is aimed not only at South Korea but is also intended to discourage other South and East Asian nations from taking a more conciliatory trade line with the USA unless they are willing to extend it to the Community as well. The dispute arose when Seoul agreed to give retroactive patent protection to US companies. The EC, under pressure from its pharmaceutical and chemical exporters, quickly asked the Koreans for similar benefits and was refused.

Gradually, governments are recognising that they must fully regulate trade in knowledge, whether it applies to the licensing of computer technology, biomedical innovations or other fields. South and East Asian nations, including Japan, are still largely using technologies first developed in the West - primarily in the USA. Japan, however, has long been a leader in creating practical applications for basic research. This technological ability is spreading to other South and East Asian countries and Japan is becoming an important source of basic research. As the trend continues, support for international regulation makes sense. Piracy will, of course, continue to exist at the margin: fake Gucci handbags and Rolex watches will no doubt be available for a long time. Adherence to the new regulations may be fragmented and understanding of the complexities of the system incomplete, but in the most significant areas of international knowledge transfer, compliance is now established.

By accepting international agreements to protect intellectual property, South and East Asian governments have been able to pursue programmes to acquire foreign technologies (through joint ventures, licensing arrangements, etc) more agressively. India, perhaps because it led the region's resistance to these international regulations, has been slow to acquire foreign technologies through commercial channels. Not until Rajiv Gandhi became Prime Minister did India make the acquisition of technologies part of its new reform programme. A flood of foreign investment followed Gandhi's original decision to seek foreign technologies, much of it in electronic components and peripherals, food-processing equipment and pharmaceuticals. More recently the flood has slowed to a trickle as the programme met stiff resistance from entrenched bureaucrats and businessmen who wished to preserve their monopoly positions.

India relies heavily on the Soviet Union for defence technology but it clearly prefers Western alternatives in commercial fields. Suzuki Motors, Mitsubishi, Hitachi and Fujitsu are only a few of the Japanese giants which have established joint ventures and licensing arrangements with Indian companies since 1986. Ties with European companies are also growing, with chemicals and telecommunications among the leaders. The major attraction, however, is US technology. Many Indian businessmen were educated in the USA and are more familiar with American than with Japanese or European technology. American companies are also more welcome because they are generally more willing to accept equity stakes in India ventures.

The governments of several South and East Asian economies (eg Hong Kong, Malaysia, Singapore, South Korea, Thailand, Taiwan and others) have relied heavily on science-based industrial parks to attract foreign investors that will bring high technologies. The idea is that judicious government support and incentives - tax holidays of five to ten years, venture capital from the state, low-interest loans, no limits on foreign equity, etc - will attract the right kind of foreign businesses. Some countries have been disappointed, however: cheap, new facilities may bring in foreign investors but not necessarily their best technologies. Despite this drawback, such science parks are numerous: Taiwan alone has 71 and another eight under construction. As the number of foreign investors grows, the host country begins to achieve the critical mass essential for technology development.

The acquisition of foreign technologies is not without problems, even when governments offer generous incentives such as science parks. The purchase of licences from Japanese or other Western firms can be expensive and becomes a relatively high proportion of unit costs when production runs are long. South Korean firms, for example, pay a $10 licence fee to Japan for each video recorder they produce using the VHS standard. Production costs per unit fall as runs are increased. Large electronics companies throughout South and East Asia are realising, therefore, that the charges for technology purchased from foreign firms frequently make up a bigger share of their costs than labour.

Companies and bureaucrats also worry that supplies of foreign technology may be cut off. As South and East Asian countries close the technological gap with Japan and the USA, technology transfer becomes harder. The originators of the technology will be too intent on recouping their investment to be able to afford to license a rival. Technology transfer agreements continue to rise in countries such as Singapore, Taiwan, South Korea, Malaysia, Thailand and India. There is no way to evaluate how sophisticated these new technologies really are. But government officials everywhere complain that their countries' needs are becoming more difficult to obtain as they move up the competitive ladder. Ultimately, all the more successful economies will be forced to spend much more on their own research and development.

V Debt in a Prosperous Region

The bulk of the Third World's debt is concentrated in Africa and Latin America. The Philippines is the only South and East Asian country included among the World Bank's list of the most heavily indebted (see Table 2.13). Several countries nevertheless face serious problems associated with their overseas debt.

Table 11.3 shows external debt and debt-service ratios for South and East Asian countries in 1970 and 1986. Indonesia has the largest long-term debt, followed closely by South Korea and India. When debt service is expressed as a percentage of exports, the rise in Indonesian figures between 1970 and 1986 is substantial: from 7 to 28%. Like other oil exporters, Indonesia borrowed heavily in the past and then found that its ability to repay was eroded as the price of oil fell. In contrast, the two other large debtors - India and South Korea - have both managed to reduce their debt-service ratios between 1970 and 1986. Other countries included in Table 11.3 where the debt-service ratio is uncomfortably high are Burma (55%) and Pakistan (27%). The Philippines, on the other hand, has neither an excessive amount of debt nor an exceptionally high debt-service ratio. The severity of the country's debt problem reflects its dismal economic situation as much as its outstanding debt obligations.

Table 11.3   EXTERNAL DEBT AND DEBT-SERVICE RATIOS IN SOUTH
AND EAST ASIA 1970/1986

$ million

	Total long-term debt[1]		Debt service as a percentage of exports of goods and services	
	1970	1986	1970	1986
Bangladesh	0	7,282	0.0	25.1
Burma	106	3,664	12.2	55.4
China	na	17,193	na	7.8
India	8,118	34,511	25.8	17.9
Indonesia	2,904	35,729	7.0	27.8
Malaysia	440	19,650	3.8	13.7
Pakistan	3,069	11,794	23.6	26.8
Philippines	1,544	21,622	7.5	18.3
South Korea	2,015	34,504	19.5	16.7
Sri Lanka	317	3,554	10.9	17.5
Thailand	726	14,130	3.3	16.1

Source: World Bank
Note: [1] *Includes publicly guaranteed debt and private non-guaranteed debt*

The Philippines

The precarious situation of the Philippines is suggested by the fact that 30 years ago the country was arguably South and East Asia's richest after Japan. However, it is fast becoming one of the region's poorest economies, and since 1980 has experienced an absolute decline in living standards. Today, the Philippines is near bankruptcy, prompting major international donors to consider the formulation of a Philippine Marshall Plan to provide the country with up to $10 billion in new money. The case for such an approach is not as convincing as it might be. The new scheme would include development loans, rescheduled debt payment, debt-equity swaps and other benefits. But all these already exist in one form or another. The proposal's critics also note that the Philippines has been slow to disperse the aid which has been provided. Donors committed $3.2 billion in 1986 but only $770 million was actually used; in the next year commitments rose to $3.5 billion, of which £929 million was dispersed. The same pattern was continued in 1988 when, by mid-year, more than $2 billion in official development assistance was still unused.

Despite these criticisms, a joint Japanese-American rescue operation now seems likely. The three-country talks have focused on a multilateral economic aid package intended to run for five years. The aid package could set a new pattern. The Japanese seem to want to make it into a preliminary version of their more general plan for Third World debt relief. The Americans dislike two aspects of the Japanese strategy: known as the Miyazawa Plan, after the minister of finance, it proposes giving taxpayer subsidies to private banks and writing off some sovereign debt. These steps are counter to several of the principles in the USA's own proposal, known as the Baker Plan.

The Philippines enjoys a certain amount of leverage over its major creditor, the USA, because it plays host to the most important American military bases in the region. Other countries, Indonesia for example, have no similar leverage.

Indonesia

Indonesia has had to negotiate with its international creditors from a comparatively weak position following the drop in oil prices. The plunge in oil prices between fiscal 1985 and 1986 meant that the country's current account deficit rose from $1.7 billion to $4.1 billion. As a result of the deteriorating balance of payments the central government's budget deficit nearly doubled, reaching $5.1 billion in 1986-7. All this created tremendous pressure on the economy and forced the country to borrow even more. Foreign debt rose to over $43 billion in 1987.

A large, though undisclosed, proportion of Indonesia's total foreign borrowings are in yen and the fact that more than 60% of its exports are denominated in US dollars means that the sharp decline of the dollar against the yen has abruptly raised the debt-service ratio. None of this would imply that Indonesia is about to default on its sovereign debt, or even that it faces an urgent rescheduling of debt. The World Bank, the IMF and bilateral aid donors have all increased assistance and Japan has made Indonesia a preferred recipient of its newly expanded aid programme. Indonesian officials are quick to add that only 20% of the country's foreign borrowing is from commercial banks. The remainder is in the form of official development assistance and the concessional nature of these funds reduces the burden on the country.

China

China is a comparatively new entrant into international lending markets. Most of China's foreign borrowing is made on concessionary terms from international institutions and export-credit agencies, but in 1983 it turned to borrowing from foreign commercial banks. By 1986 about 60% of China's annual borrowing came from commercial sources, compared with none in 1982. Many of these loans were relatively innocuous, consisting of deposits with Chinese banks, project loans as part of export-credit programmes or loans to hotels or other projects under guarantees from the Bank of China. Nevertheless, the unexpected rapid growth of foreign debt became a cause of much concern. Preliminary estimates for 1988 indicate that China will borrow about $4 billion, bringing its net foreign debt to more than $31 billion.

The Chinese government was particularly sensitive to Japan's emergence as a major creditor. By the end of 1986 more than 1,700 enterprises, institutions and financial organisations had taken out foreign loans. Most of them borrowed in Japan, with the awkward result that 40% of China's foreign borrowing was in yen while more than 70% of its exports were in US dollars. When the yen soared, China faced a problem similar to Indonesia. However, the country reduced that imbalance in 1988 by repaying some yen debts early and by swapping other yen-denominated loans for those payable in dollars. China is now borrowing more from the USA and Europe. Chinese authorities simultaneously announced that all foreign loans were to be registered, foreign borrowing would become more difficult and yen borrowing in particular would be discouraged. By acting to head off the debt crisis well before it boiled over, China may prove to be a model for other borrowers. Only with the most reckless push for investment will debt become out of control. Given China's uncertainties about its current programme for growth and reform, that is unlikely to happen.

South Korea

Until it was recently overtaken by Indonesia, South Korea was the region's largest debtor. In a terrific gamble in the 1960s and 1970s, the government borrowed heavily and invested the proceeds in export industries and the infrastructure to support them. However, the legacy of debt remains. South Korea achieved a current account surplus only in 1986, when its debt peaked. It then began to repay its loans rapidly. Foreign debt was reduced from $44.5 billion in 1987 to $35.5 billion in 1988. Debt repayments are now likely to slow down. Most of the repaid debt has been held by public authorities who were ordered to make premature payments. Corporations are understandably reluctant to prepay dollar-denominated debt which, when won appreciation is taken into account, carried a negative interest rate.

Vietnam

Vietnam is one of the most capital-starved economies in South and East Asia. It has defaulted on almost all its debt, which exceeds $3 billion. Its foreign exchange reserves had fallen below $20 million by mid-1988. Apart from Sweden and Finland, most Western countries refuse to give any direct aid because of the country's Kampuchean occupation. Since Vietnam has yet to reach an agreement with the IMF, few banks will extend credit. The country depends on Soviet aid - between $1.8 and £2 billion in economic assistance in 1987 and an unknown amount of military aid. Even that donor, however, is now expecting repayments in some form. Soviet aid has been switched from huge dams and cement plants to export-oriented projects such as rubber, coffee and cocoa plantations.

Burma

Conditions are perhaps even harsher in Burma. The fact that the country's debt service requires 55% of all its exports is only part of the problem. Burma's ability to earn foreign exchange or to attract foreign investment is rapidly deteriorating. In 1982 the country's exports were $400 million but five years later they had dropped to $100 million. Moreover, Burma's exports are almost exclusively raw materials: 84% are made up of timber, rice and other farm products. Foreign demand and international prices for such simple agricultural products are weak and unlikely to improve.

CHAPTER 12

GROWTH PROSPECTS IN THE THIRD WORLD

The foregoing chapters of this *Handbook* have not painted an especially promising picture of the Third World's future. Large foreign debts, persistently high rates of growth in population and severe resource misallocations are only some of the reasons for the poor economic performance of the Third World. None of these constraints on growth can be removed in the near future though the direction of policy changes - at both the domestic and international levels - is promising.

The economic outlook for growth in Western countries is also improving and this, too, will make for brighter prospects for the Third World. The consensus of most analysts, for example, is that growth of world income will accelerate during the 1990s. A US recession in the next few years is still probable. This would have particularly severe consequences for Latin America which depends heavily on the USA for exports and investment. However, even these effects can be erased over the next ten years if the growth of world income for the decade exceeds that in the 1980s. Such an improvement will make it easier for the international community to deal with Third World problems such as debt, protectionism, stagnating foreign investment and dwindling foreign aid.

There are other reasons for this cautiously optimistic assessment of the Third World's prospects. One is that the prolonged and steady decline in international commodity prices now appears to have been reversed. The real prices of most minerals and agricultural products will stabilise or even improve slightly in the 1990s. Oil prices, too, will recover, though the OPEC of the 1990s will lack the cohesion to push them to the levels of ten years ago. The turnaround will be good news for many - though not all - developing countries. Resource-poor countries which specialise in exporting manufactures (for example, South Korea, Taiwan, Hong Kong and Singapore) will face a deterioration in their terms of trade. Another favourable factor is that levels of world trade should continue to grow despite protectionist pressures in rich countries. The developing countries as a group can expect to claim a slightly larger share of total world trade. Finally, although the international community has yet to agree on any coherent programme to deal with Third World debt, the flexibility being demonstrated by some of the major participants in this field gives reasons for optimism.

Table 12.1 gives the results of recent forecasts for income and trade in the Third World up to 1992. Real GDP should grow by 4.8% in 1990-92. This figure is moderately higher than rates recorded in 1986-8 though it will not be adequate to redress the most pressing problems in several regions. Africa, for example, can expect to recover from the severe slump it experienced in the mid-1980s though its anticipated rate of 3.4% per annum will merely match the pace of population expansion. Latin America, too, can look forward to a more rapid pace of expansion but it will not be sufficient for countries such as Argentina, Brazil and Mexico to "grow out of debt".

266

Table 12.1   OUTPUT AND FOREIGN TRADE - GROWTH AND FORECASTS
1986-1992

annual changes, %

	1986	1987	1988	1989	1990-92[1]
Developing countries[2]					
Real GDP	4.5	3.8	4.2	4.3	4.8
export volume	8.5	8.6	6.9	6.2	6.4
import volume	-1.6	5.0	8.7	6.4	6.6
Africa					
Real GDP	0.9	0.9	3.1	3.1	3.4
export volume	2.0	-1.7	3.6	2.5	2.3
Import volume	-12.3	-4.8	3.3	1.7	3.1
South and East Asia					
Real GDP	6.5	6.6	6.9	6.1	6.2
export volume	17.3	13.8	8.6	8.3	8.3
import volume	1.1	9.4	12.9	9.0	8.5
West Asia[2]					
Real GDP	4.1	2.4	5.5	2.9	3.2
export volume	15.3	0.9	11.7	6.0	5.7
import volume	-12.2	-0.8	1.9	1.6	3.5
Latin America					
Real GDP	4.0	2.3	2.1	3.5	4.5
export volume	-0.9	5.2	5.2	3.8	4.4
import volume	3.4	2.6	1.7	3.7	5.0

Source: IMF

Notes: [1] *Compound rates of change*
[2] *Excludes capital-exporting countries - Iran, Iraq, Kuwait, Libya, Oman, Qatar,*
Saudi Arabia and UAE

267

The outlook for trade in the Third World also shows some improvement. The volume of the developing countries' exports should rise slightly in the early 1990s. This implies that the Third World will expand its share of the world markets. Export-led growth, however, will not benefit all developing regions equally. Manufacturers, mainly in Asia, will account for a disproportionate share of these export gains.

African producers of commodities will continue to face supply constraints which limit their ability to respond to any rise in demand. In fact, Africa's growth rate for exports could be halved in 1990-92 in comparison with 1988. West Asia, too, will experience a decline in export volume though slight improvements in the price of oil should offset this drop. Similar comments apply to Latin America. The acceleration in growth of the region's exports represents a distinct improvement over 1986 but a slight fall in relation to later years.

The developing countries' imports will not grow exceptionally fast in the early 1990s. The volume, however, will have recovered from the period of severe contraction when foreign exchange was limited and domestic demand in several parts of the Third World was compressed. The most encouraging trend is the expected growth by Africa and Latin America. Both regions suffered greatly in the mid-1980s when the volume of imports declined absolutely.

These modest improvements in the economic outlook will help to alleviate other types of pressing problems. Table 12.2 shows recent levels of debt service payments as a percentage of total exports, along with forecasts up to 1992. Debt service obligations of all developing countries should decline slowly, dropping from nearly a quarter of total exports in 1986 to just over 15% in 1992. The downward trend applies to all four regions though the relative decline is only slight in West Asia (a drop of only 3.5%). Latin America should benefit substantially. That region's debt servicing

268

ıbligations would nevertheless still absorb over a third of its hard
ʼurrency earnings.

Table 12.2   DEBT SERVICE PAYMENTS[1] AND FORECASTS 1986-1992

% of exports of foods and services

	1986	1987	1988	1989	1990	1992
Developing countries[2]	24.3	20.9	20.9	18.7	17.5	15.4
Africa	27.8	25.5	26.6	24.9	23.2	21.5
South and East Asia	13.5	12.6	11.3	9.9	8.8	6.9
West Asia[2]	28.7	23.0	24.3	25.9	25.4	25.2
Latin America	45.1	37.8	42.1	37.9	37.3	34.0

Source: IMF
Notes: [1] *Interest payments on total debt plus amortisation payments on long-term debt*
[2] *Excludes capital-exporting developing countries. For a list, see Table 12.1*

Clearly, growth rates of the magnitude suggested here will not be
sufficient to bring any significant increase in standards of living in
the Third World. Much will also depend on investment. Net new
lending from private sources in Western countries fell significantly
in the last decade and will not provide much of a boost to growth in
the 1980s. Nor is lending from official sources likely to grow
substantially. This combination of factors means that domestic
sources of finance will be essential if developing countries are to
grow at satisfactory rates.

The ratio of investment to GDP has declined in most developing
countries since 1985 (mainly due to the costs of debt servicing).
Asian countries have the lowest amounts of external debt and
should be able to maintain their current pace of investment which is

presently at about 28% of GDP. In Latin America the share of investment fell as low as 17% in the early 1980s but is expected to rise to 21-22% by 1992. But without other structural adjustments the investment recovery will be in part offset by extremely low levels of productivity in the region. The proportion of African GDP going into investment also declined in the 1980s, falling from 28% in 1982 to 18% in 1988. It should rise in the 1990s but only slightly as African countries, too, will be constrained by their heavy foreign obligations.

Latin America

No acceptable solution to Latin America's debt crisis has yet to emerge. Should some form of debt relief be negotiated, the region's prospects would be greatly improved as it enjoys several advantages over other parts of the Third World. Latin America has a larger and more diversified range of natural resources than other parts of the Third World. Its domestic markets are also more developed and sophisticated than those in Asia or elsewhere. Other advantages are a relatively skilled work-force and the fact that the region remains solidly in the "dollar zone", making it appealing for foreign investors who wish to establish an export base aimed at the USA.

There are some grounds to expect progress on the debt problem in the first half of the 1990s. The original US strategy, known as the Baker Plan, was little more than a call for banks to pump more money into Latin America and other Third World debtors. This approach received little support from the banking community itself and its prospects for success were never bright. The current strategy, proposed by US Treasury Secretary Brady, calls for the banks to off-load more of their debt - at a cost - and so leave borrowers with less interest to pay. Known as "voluntary debt reduction", the new approach has better chances of success than its predecessor. The Brady proposal would also entail the active involvement of the IMF and the World Bank to guarantee "exit bonds" which would be issued by debtors. Banks could exchange their loans for these, at a discount, and thus avoid having to lend the debtor still more cash.

Many aspects of the plan remain to be worked out and it is unclear if it will ever be implemented. However, the mere fact that the USA has discarded the Baker plan and turned to other alternatives is promising. This step alone will help to prepare the way for a more effective method of dealing with Latin America's debt. Some bankers predict that the eventual solution will be a 1930s-style moratorium. Others dislike the thought of tampering with the legality of loan agreements. The multinational agencies see problems in rewarding ineptitude - whether in running countries or in managing banks. Despite the variety of objections, participants are moving closer to a workable solution to the debt problem. Once such a plan is in place, Latin America's growth prospects will improve significantly.

Africa

The economic outlook for the poorest region in the Third World depends mainly on events in commodity markets and agriculture. Farming dominates in most African economies and the greatest need is to reverse the steady decline in production and export of food products is urgent. The importance of this step lies not in the fact that Africa's economic future is inevitably tied to agriculture. A sustainable and acceptable standard of living will require much more extensive development of industry and services as well as transport and finance. But before real progress in these fields can be realised, Africa must be able to meet a much larger proportion of its own food needs.

The general impression in the 1980s was that Africa suffered more than other developing regions from events in the world economy. In other words, Africa's export prices - which are set in world commodity markets - were thought to have fallen by more than average prices. This was true for oil exporters but for the rest of the Africa it was not. The latest studies show the prices of African exports fell in the last decade by less than half of world averages. Prices of tea, coffee and cocoa stayed relatively high while cereal prices (which matter less) tumbled. Thus, the region was relatively lucky in the commodity mix of its non-oil exports.

Africa's poor export performance was due not so much to lower prices but to dwindling volumes. The volume of the region's non-oil exports was virtually unchanged between 1970 and 1990. This characteristic is important for any assessment of Africa's export prospects: if volumes rather than prices have been the source of the problem, much of Africa's distress can be attributed to poor policy formulation. Some improvement can be expected because many of Africa's governments are now focusing on policy reform in the agricultural sector. These reforms, which were discussed in Chapter Seven, include currency devaluation, liberalised pricing systems, lower fiscal deficits and other initiatives.

West Asia

The outlook for growth in this region depends heavily on two factors - the price of oil and the prospects for peace between Shia-led Iran and its neighbours. As Iran's efforts to establish itself as leader of the Islamic movement have faltered, a shaky peace has returned to the region. The growth prospects for Iran itself are not bright. The country's foreign policies continue to isolate it from the Western capital markets which it so desperately needs to begin reconstruction. But for the rest of West Asia, oil will then be the crucial determinant of growth. The economic links between Arab-speaking countries are now much closer than only a few years ago so even the non-oil producers of the region will be affected by events in this market.

Though oil prices have begun to recover from their lows in 1986-88, many western analysts have predicted a continued deterioration in the influence and stability of OPEC. If that prediction proves correct, the consequences for the cartel's members - and West Asian countries in particular - will be dramatic. A minority of forecasters hold a different opinion. This group sees OPEC's troubles as being directly related to its spare oil-producing capacity. Spare capacity amounts to 8 to 10 million barrels per day and could be absorbed by rising demand within a decade.

Such a turnaround in OPEC's fortunes seems unlikely, however. Several forces are combining to check world demand for OPEC's oil. One is conservation. The investments made to conserve oil in days of higher prices are still coming on stream. Energy-efficient factories, houses and forms of transport will continue to depress demand until well into the next century. Second, ecologists' warnings about the environmental damage caused by fossil fuels is adding a new emphasis to conservation - even when oil prices are low. Greater fuel efficiency is seen as the cheapest way to reduce the damage done by fossil fuels. Finally, both Europe and the USA remain concerned about "energy security" and increasing reliance on oil imports from the Gulf. Together, these circumstances mean that the real price of oil is not likely to approach the high levels of the early 1980s for the rest of this century.

Relationships between OPEC producers will certainly be transformed during this decade. Some countries have moved aggressively into downstream refining and will grow more like multinationals. As they do, their interests will diverge from those OPEC members which have not taken this route. Coincidentally, the GCC, which was forged by the Gulf war, includes among its members those OPEC countries which have most aggressively pursued moves into downstream ownership. These include Saudi Arabia, Kuwait and the UAE (along with smaller producers such as Bahrain, Qatar and Oman). Their moves downstream will bring them closer together, and widen the gap between the GCC and other OPEC countries, particularly Iran.

Many of the European and North American refineries that would have been closed in the 1990s have been kept in operation because OPEC producers which want to go downstream are ready to buy them. This overcapacity, coupled with the fact that oil producers will be able to feed their out-of-date refineries with cheap oil and still make a profit, promises problems. Any price war between cartel members will likely spill over into markets for refined products. Added value from refined products is the main reason why certain countries have moved downstream and a price war would destroy the purpose of these investments.

The cartel also faces greater internal dissension in the future. Several OPEC members outside West Asia (Algeria, Gabon, Libya and, perhaps, Venezuela) will be producing at full capacity by the mid-1990s. These countries will be pitted against others such as Iraq, Kuwait, Saudi Arabia and the UAE which will still have vast overcapacity. Pressure on the latter group to curb production will intensify as the decade continues. Other oil producers - notably Egypt and Qatar - will not be exporters by the end of the 1990s. Their dwindling reserves will permit them to do little more than service their own domestic needs.

Together, all these circumstances mean that governments will not have the tremendous revenues to spend that they did in the last two decades. Many states will be forced to reduce significantly their spending on infrastructure and social services. These cutbacks will have serious repercussions for some of the more conservative states. For more than a decade, these countries have bought social peace by spending heavily on hospitals, schools and other public works and

274

by offering generous social benefits to all. Reduced public spending will hit the middle classes in these countries hard but will not affect the ruling families. Resentment between these two groups is already rising. Political instability will be the result unless the smaller pool of petrodollars is shared more equally.

South and East Asia

As the most dynamic of the Third World's regions, the economic landscape of South and East Asia will probably undergo the greatest change during the 1990s. The most significant of these changes will involve patterns of trade.

Although the region will continue to be dominated by export-led growth, directions of trade will change. Japan and other major exporters will begin to trade more extensively among themselves rather than selling to the USA and Western Europe. This transformation reflects several factors. One is the growth in income in countries such as South Korea, Taiwan, Singapore, Thailand and even China. Aggregate demand grows as incomes rise but demand for imports grows disproportionately.

Another factor is the result of policy changes in Japan. In order to deal with its trade imbalance, the Japanese government will continue its efforts to encourage imports. The major gainers from this programme will be other Asian countries rather than the USA or Western Europe. Japan's foreign investment is also rising rapidly and neighbouring countries will be among the major recipients. Finally, China's cautious emergence as a borrower and trader will help to solidify the region's economic relations. This change in trade patterns will have at least one beneficial effect for the international community: they will help to deflect some of the protectionist pressures which are so strong today in other Western countries.

Developments in China will be of particular importance for the region but can hardly be anticipated. The pace of China's reforms will be reduced but not stopped. Greater caution should prevent the country from accumulating excessive foreign debts though it will also mean that the inflow of new technologies and managerial methods will be restricted.

Excessive rates of inflation, high levels of unemployment and structural bottlenecks will continue to plague China's planners. The country is already suffering from growing income disparities between regions. These threaten to undermine the unity and stability which the Chinese regard as essential. Together, these factors will force the government to step in to slow the pace of reform. The biggest risk is that problems such as these will discredit China's modernisation programme and thus prevent its completion.

Two of the larger economies in the region - India and Indonesia - will see a modest reduction in the role of the state as an owner of business enterprises. This process, however, will proceed more slowly than in China and its full effects will not be experienced until the end of the 1990s. The future of several other important economies in the region - Hong Kong, South Korea and Taiwan - will be clouded by political relations with their neighbours. An added complication for these countries, as well as Singapore, is that inflation will pose a greater threat in the 1990s. All four countries are resource-poor and the expected rise in commodity and oil prices will have a major impact on their competitiveness in international markets.

APPENDIX ONE

DEMOGRAPHICS

The data presented in this section are drawn from the Euromonitor Database. Original sources include the UN, IMF, OECD, ILO and national statistical sources, where available.

TOTAL POPULATION (MID-YEAR FIGURES)

Unit: Thousands

	1982	1983	1984	1985	1986	1987
LATIN AMERICA						
Argentina	29158	29627	30097	30564	31030	31496
Belize	153	158	162	166	171	176
Bolivia	5919	6082	6253	6429	6547	6665
Brazil	126807	129662	132580	135564	138493	141422
Chile	11519	11717	11919	12122	12327	12532
Colombia	26965	27502	28056	28624	29188	29752
Costa Rica	2324	2435	2417	2489	2666	2843
Ecuador	8607	8857	9115	9378	9647	9916
El Salvador	4662	4724	4780	4819	4913	5007
French Guiana	74	77	80	83	84	85
Guatemala	7315	7524	7740	7963	8195	8427
Guyana	900	918	936	970	971	972
Mexico	73122	74980	76792	78524	79563	80602
Nicaragua	2955	3058	3162	3272	3385	3498
Panama	2044	2089	2134	2180	2227	2274
Paraguay	3358	3468	3580	3693	3807	3921
Peru	18226	18707	19198	19698	20207	20716

Continued...

Table cont'd

	1982	1983	1984	1985	1986	1987
Puerto Rico	3262	3265	3282	3283	3502	3721
Suriname	364	365	370	375	380	385
Uruguay	2947	2968	2990	3012	2983	2954
Venezuela	15940	16394	16851	17317	17791	18265
CARIBBEAN						
Anguilla						
Antigua	77	78	79	80	81	82
Aruba	66	67				
Bahamas	219	224	229	232	236	240
Barbados	250	251	252	253	254	255
Bermuda	55	55	56	56		
British Virgin Is	11	12	12	13	13	13
Cayman Islands	19	19	20	21	22	23
Cuba	9801	9897	9994	10098	10246	10394
Dominica	79	81	82	76	77	78
Dominican						
Republic	5744	5962	6102	6243	6416	6589
Grenada	109	110	111	112	113	114
Guadeloupe	328	329	330	331	333	335
Haiti	5041	5119	5185	5273	5358	5443
Honduras	3955	4092	4232	4372	4514	4656
Jamaica	2200	2268	2301	2337	2372	2407
Martinique	327	327	327	328	328	328
Netherlands						
Antilles						
St Kitts	45	46	46	46	47	48
St Lucia	129	131	134	130	132	134
St Vincent/						
Grenadines	105	107	108	104	105	
Trinidad and						
Tobago	1129	1149	1166	1181	1204	1227

Continued...

Table cont'd

	1982	1983	1984	1985	1986	1987
SOUTH AND EAST ASIA						
Bangladesh	92585	94651	96730	98657	100616	102575
Burma	35910	36747	37614	37153	37872	38591
China	1026504	1038419	1049705	1059521	1072218	1084915
Fiji	663	672	686	697	703	709
Hong Kong	5265	5345	5398	5456	5533	5610
India	705000	720000	736000	750859	766135	781411
Indonesia	153048	156446	159895	163393	166940	170487
Malaysia	14456	14823	15193	15681	16109	16537
Nepal	15375	15738	16107	16625	17131	17637
Pakistan	87758	90480	93286	96180	99163	102146
Papua New Guinea	3094	3190	3252	3329	3426	3523
Philippines	50740	51956	53170	54378	55576	56774
Singapore	2472	2502	2529	2558	2586	2614
South Korea	39326	39929	40513	41056	41569	42082
Sri Lanka	15195	15416	15599	15837	16117	16397
Taiwan						
Thailand	48490	49459	50396	51301	52094	52887
MIDDLE EAST						
Bahrain	369	384	400	417	412	407
Egypt	44525	45915	47191	48503	49609	50715
Iran	40773	42071	43414	44212	45914	47616
Iraq	14110	14824	15356	15898	16450	17002
Jordan	3129	3250	3380	3515	3656	3797
Kuwait	1497	1566	1637	1712	1791	1870
Lebanon	2638	2635	2644	2668	2707	2746
Oman	1088	1142	1193	2000		
Qatar	257	276	295	315	335	355
Saudi Arabia	10231	10658	11093	11542	12006	12470
Syria	9298	9611	9934	10268	10612	10956
United Arab Emirates	1137	1206	1267	1327	1384	1441

Continued...

Table cont'd

	1982	1983	1984	1985	1986	1987
Yemen Arab Republic	6307	6480	6660	6849	7046	7243
Yemen PDR	2093	2158	2225	2294	2365	2436
AFRICA						
Algeria	19857	20517	21052	21718	22421	23124
Angola	8142	8339	8540	8754	8981	9208
Benin	3618	3720	3825	3932	4042	4152
Botswana	976	1012	1049	1088	1128	1168
Burkina Faso	6306	6415	6526	6639	6754	6869
Burundi	4310	4422	4537	4718	4857	4996
Cameroon	9279	9575	9871	10186	10446	10706
Cape Verde	306	312	319	334	333	332
Central African Rep.	2405	2460	2517	2608	2740	2872
Chad	4681	4789	4902	5018	5139	5260
Comoros	406	421	431	444	476	508
Congo	1609	1651	1695	1740	1787	1834
Djibouti	372	383	405	430	456	482
Equatorial Guinea	367	375	383	392	401	410
Ethiopia	40395	41390	42441	43350	44927	46504
Gabon	1095	1112	1131	1151	1172	1193
Gambia	635	618	630	643	656	669
Ghana	12244	12700	13151	13588	14045	14502
Guinea	5659	5793	5931	6075	6225	6375
Guinea-Bissau	849	863	875	890	906	922
Ivory Coast	8799	9300	9464	9810	10165	10520
Kenya	18044	18775	19536	20333	21163	21993
Lesotho	1425	1465	1470	1528	1559	1590
Liberia	1977	2043	2109	2189	2223	2257
Libya	3330	3469	3624	3605	3742	3879
Madagascar	9200	9400	9731	9985	10303	10621
Malawi	6408	6618	6839	7059	7279	7499
Maldives	163	168	173	177	189	201
Mali	7509	7741	7973	8206	8438	8670

Continued...

Table cont'd

	1982	1983	1984	1985	1986	1987
Mauritania	1727	1779	1832	1888	1946	2004
Mauritius	982	991	1012	1021	1030	1039
Morocco	20359	20878	21408	21941	22476	23011
Mozambique	12909	13257	13602	13961	14336	14711
Namibia	1425	1465	1507	1550	1595	1640
Niger	5612	5772	5940	6115	6298	6481
Nigeria	86126	89022	92037	95198	98517	101836
Reunion	518	527	537	531	536	541
Rwanda	5551	5757	5871	6070	6257	6444
Sao Tome e Principe	89	92	94	108	108	108
Senegal	5985	6316	6400	6444	6674	6904
Seychelles	64	64	65	65	66	67
Sierra Leone	3411	3472	3536	3602	3670	3738
Somalia	4293	4420	4539	4653	4760	4867
South Africa	30044	30802	31586	32392	33221	34050
Sudan	19795	20362	20945	21550	22178	22806
Swaziland	585	605	626	647	670	693
Tanzania	19782	20412	21062	21733	22462	23191
Togo	2705	2787	2872	2960	3052	3144
Tunisia	6726	6886	6937	7081	7234	7387
Uganda	13997	14468	14961	15477	16018	16559
Zaire	27396	28163	29671	30363	30850	31337
Zambia	6029	6242	6445	6666	6896	7126
Zimbabwe	7477	7740	7980	8379	8426	8473

POPULATION PROJECTIONS 1985-2010

Unit: thousands

	1985	1990	1995	2000	2010	% change 1975-2010
LATIN AMERICA						
Argentina	30564	32880	35073	37197	41507	59.3
Belize						
Bolivia	6371	7314	8422	9724	12820	162.0
Brazil	135564	150368	165083	179487	207454	92.0
Chile	12038	12987	13922	14792	16348	58.2
Colombia	28714	31820	34940	37999	43840	89.2
Costa Rica	2600	2937	3271	3596	4239	115.7
Ecuador	9378	10782	12314	13939	17403	147.4
El Salvador	5552	6484	7531	8708	11188	170.0
French Guiana						
Guatemala	7963	9197	10621	12222	15827	162.8
Guyana	953	1040	1119	1196	1351	73.2
Mexico	78996	89012	99165	109180	128241	113.2
Nicaragua	3272	3871	4539	5261	6824	183.4
Panama	2180	2418	2659	2893	3324	90.2
Paraguay	3681	4231	4807	5405	6653	147.7
Peru	19698	22332	25123	27952	33479	120.8
Puerto Rico	3451	3707	3954	4185	4595	53.5
Suriname	375	403	435	469	534	46.7
Uruguay	3012	3128	3246	3364	3581	26.6
Venezuela	17317	19735	22212	24715	30006	136.9
CARIBBEAN						
Anguilla						
Antigua						
Aruba						
Bahamas						

Continued...

Table cont'd

	1985	1990	1995	2000	2010	% change 1975-2010
Barbados	253	261	271	284	309	25.6
Bermuda						
British Virgin Is						
Cayman Islands						
Cuba	10038	10540	11152	11718	12584	34.8
Dominica	421	450	481	516	591	56.8
Dominican Republic	6243	6971	7704	8407	9945	101.1
Grenada						
Guadeloupe	334	340	346	354	380	15.5
Haiti	6585	7509	8596	9860	12868	149.5
Honduras	4372	5105	5953	6978	9394	203.7
Jamaica	2336	2521	2703	2880	3206	56.9
Martinique	328	331	338	346	366	11.2
Netherlands Antilles						
St Kitts						
St Lucia						
St Vincent/ Grenadines						
Trinidad and Tobago	1185	1283	1379	1473	1652	63.7
SOUTH AND EAST ASIA						
Bangladesh	101147	115244	130323	145800	177053	131.2
Burma	37153	40843	44665	48499	55842	83.4
China						
Fiji	691	748	793	834	904	56.9
Hong Kong	5548	6034	6458	6775	7205	63.9
India	758927	827152	896676	964072	1086344	75.0
Indonesia	166440	181539	196861	211367	238605	75.9
Malaysia	15557	17298	18987	20497	23349	89.7
Nepal	16482	18470	20686	23048	27651	112.7
Pakistan	100380	112226	126723	140961	170072	127.6

Continued...

283

Table cont'd

	1985	1990	1995	2000	2010	% change 1975-2010
Papua New						
Guinea	3511	3955	4430	4933	5981	121.8
Philippines	54498	60973	67591	74057	86344	102.9
Singapore	2559	2701	2834	2947	3141	38.8
South Korea	41258	44828	48059	50981	55942	58.6
Sri Lanka	16205	17451	18564	19620	21843	60.6
Taiwan						
Thailand	51411	55712	60509	65503	74795	80.7
MIDDLE EAST						
Bahrain	432	520	608	693	853	213.6
Egypt	46909	52536	58178	63941	75263	107.4
Iran	44632	51529	58204	65161	79044	137.1
Iraq	15898	18760	21928	25377	32866	198.2
Jordan	3515	4291	5269	6437	9186	253.3
Kuwait	1811	2230	2630	3007	3769	274.3
Lebanon	2668	2967	3291	3617	4246	53.5
Oman	1242	1457	1699	1973	2580	236.8
Qatar	315	413	494	569	722	322.2
Saudi Arabia	11542	13988	16742	19824	26397	264.0
Syria	10505	12634	15114	17809	23284	213.0
United Arab						
Emirates	1327	1578	1769	1939	2283	352.1
Yemen Arab						
Republic	6848	7925	9262	10881	14735	179.0
Yemen PDR	2137	2484	2908	3379	4367	164.0
AFRICA						
Algeria	21718	25494	29544	33444	40586	153.4
Angola	8754	10002	11493	13234	17439	167.5
Benin	4050	4733	5555	6532	8910	192.9
Botswana	1107	1332	1599	1917	2724	260.8
Burkina Faso	6924	7923	9116	10538	14096	153.2
Burundi	4721	5443	6281	7226	9262	147.2
Cameroon	9873	11359	13114	15168	20065	164.6

Continued...

284

Table cont'd

	1985	1990	1995	2000	2010	% change 1975-2010
Cape Verde	326	367	416	470	575	103.2
Central African Rep.	2576	2907	3297	3750	4799	133.3
Chad	5018	5668	6430	7308	9337	131.7
Comoros	444	518	603	695	857	166.1
Congo	1740	1994	2295	2643	3467	156.4
Djibouti						
Equatorial Guinea	392	440	496	559	708	121.9
Ethiopia	43557	50087	57765	66509	87795	155.9
Gabon	1151	1273	1433	1603	1978	97.2
Gambia	643	715	800	898	1129	115.5
Ghana	13588	16072	19048	22607	31460	221.0
Guinea	6075	6876	7807	8879	11430	135.6
Guinea-Bissau	889	987	1100	1229	1523	142.5
Ivory Coast	9810	11658	13657	16006	21567	218.7
Kenya	20600	25413	31375	38534	55801	307.2
Lesotho	1520	1731	1976	2255	2903	144.6
Liberia	2191	2577	3046	3615	5052	219.3
Libya	3605	4331	5162	6082	8068	232.0
Madagascar	10012	11575	13417	15550	20573	170.6
Malawi	6944	8198	9680	11387	15452	199.1
Maldives						
Mali	8082	9362	10878	12658	16992	170.0
Mauritania	1888	2202	2571	2998	4030	183.6
Mauritius	1050	1140	1223	1298	1439	65.8
Morocco	21941	24616	27162	29512	33835	95.5
Mozambique	13961	15972	18352	21104	27521	183.2
Namibia	1550	1793	2080	2415	3216	172.1
Niger	6115	7109	8313	9750	13266	184.4
Nigeria	85198	113343	135451	161930	227539	236.2
Reunion	531	573	616	656	728	51.0
Rwanda	6070	7179	8526	10123	14042	222.1
Sao Tome e Principe						

Continued...

285

Table cont'd

	1985	1990	1995	2000	2010	% change 1975-2010
Senegal	6444	7377	8479	9765	12837	169.1
Seychelles						
Sierra Leone	3602	3968	4388	4867	5957	95.6
Somalia	4653	5169	5801	6671	8778	169.9
South Africa	32392	36754	41623	46918	58525	129.5
Sudan	21550	24895	28703	32926	42002	162.3
Swaziland	650	760	892	1048	1435	197.1
Tanzania	22499	26998	32501	39129	55670	250.1
Togo	2960	3449	4030	4709	6344	181.7
Tunisia	7081	7894	8681	9429	10858	93.5
Uganda	15477	18425	21992	26262	36907	230.4
Zaire	29938	34852	40714	47581	64024	185.8
Zambia	6666	7912	9422	11237	15807	226.5
Zimbabwe	8777	10511	12612	15130	21456	245.0

BIRTH RATES 1982-1986

Births per '000 of the population

	1982	1983	1984	1985	1986	% change 1982-1985	
LATIN AMERICA							
Argentina	22.8	23.9					a
Belize	38.4	38.3	37.9	40.1		-2.2	c
Bolivia	44.0	44.0	44.0	44.0		-1.8	b
Brazil	30.6	30.6	30.6	30.6		-4.4	b
Chile	23.8	22.2	22.2	21.6		0.9	a
Colombia	31.0	31.0	31.0	31.0		-3.4	b
Costa Rica	30.7	30.0	31.4	33.9		9.0	a
Ecuador	36.8	36.8	36.8	36.8		-3.7	b
El Salvador	33.6	30.5	29.8				a

Continued...

Table cont'd

	1982	1983	1984	1985	1986	% change 1982-1985	
French Guiana	32.1	30.1	29.0	30.0		25.0	c
Guatemala	42.7	40.8	40.3	41.0		-8.3	a
Guyana	28.5	28.5	28.5	28.5			a d
Mexico	32.7	35.0	33.2	32.3		-14.1	a h
Nicaragua	44.2	44.2	44.2	44.2		-3.1	b
Panama	26.7	26.4	26.6	26.6	25.9	-9.5	a
Paraguay	36.0	36.0	36.0	36.0		-1.9	b
Peru	35.7	36.8	36.4	35.5		-6.6	e f
Puerto Rico	21.3	20.1	19.3	18.6		-24.1	a
Suriname	28.8	28.8	28.8	28.8		-2.4	d g
Uruguay	18.5	18.0	17.7				
Venezuela	32.0	31.4	29.9	29.0		-15.2	
CARIBBEAN							
Anguilla				25.3			
Antigua	14.9	15.0	14.2	14.8		-24.9	a
Aruba	15.7	16.9					a
Bahamas	24.2	23.6	22.6	23.4		-5.3	a
Barbados	18.0	17.9	16.7				a
Bermuda	14.7	16.5	15.1				a
British Virgin Is	20.7	24.2	21.0				a
Cayman Islands	18.2	20.2	20.5	17.4		4.2	c
Cuba	16.3	16.7	16.6	18.0	16.2	1.7	a
Dominica	22.1	22.9	20.8				a
Dominican Republic	33.1	33.1	33.1	33.1		-4.3	b
Grenada							a
Guadeloupe	20.2	20.4	20.2	20.4		5.7	a
Haiti	41.3	41.3	41.3	41.3		-1.2	b
Honduras	43.9	43.9	43.9	43.9		-6.8	b
Jamaica	26.9	27.1	23.4				a
Martinique	16.5	17.3	17.5	17.4	18.1	5.5	a
Netherlands Antilles							a
St Kitts	29.2	23.9	24.2				a

Continued...

Table cont'd

	1982	1983	1984	1985	1986	% change 1982-1985
St Lucia	31.4	31.0	30.1			a
St Vincent/						
Grenadines	31.8	30.8	26.2			a
Trinidad and						
Tobago	28.8	28.9				a
SOUTH AND EAST ASIA						
Bangladesh	44.8	44.8	44.8	44.8		-5.1 b
Burma	30.5	30.5	30.5	30.5		-7.3 b
China	19.0	19.0	19.0	19.0		-11.6 b
Fiji	30.6	29.5	28.4	27.9		3.3 a
Hong Kong	16.5	15.4	14.4	14.0	13.1	-20.0 a
India	33.8	33.7	33.9			a
Indonesia	32.1	32.1	32.1	32.1		-11.8 b
Malaysia	30.9	30.9	30.9	30.9		1.6 b
Nepal	41.7	41.7	41.7	41.7		-6.5 b
Pakistan	43.0	43.0	43.0	43.0		38.3 d
Papua New Guinea	38.8	38.8	38.8	38.8		-8.7 b
Philippines	33.3	33.3	33.3	33.3		-8.5 b
Singapore	17.3	16.2	16.4	16.6	14.8	0.6 a
South Korea	20.9	21.5	20.6	19.7	19.4	f
Sri Lanka	26.8	26.2	24.8	24.3		-12.9 a
Taiwan						
Thailand	28.0	28.0	28.0	28.0	28.0	-11.4 b
MIDDLE EAST						
Bahrain	32.2	32.2	32.2	32.2		-6.4 b
Egypt	36.0	36.8		37.5		0.5 a
Iran	40.8	40.8	40.8	40.8		-2.9 b
Iraq	44.4	44.4	44.4	44.4		-5.5 b
Jordan	31.7	31.3	30.3	30.3	29.8	-0.3 a
Kuwait	36.2	35.5	34.7			a
Lebanon	29.3	29.3	29.3	29.3		-2.7 b
Oman	47.0	47.0	47.0	47.0		-3.9 b

Continued...

Table cont'd

	1982	1983	1984	1985	1986	% change 1982-1985	
Qatar	38.3	38.3	38.3	38.3		28.1	b
Saudi Arabia	42.1	42.1	42.1	42.1		-8.3	b
Syria	46.5	46.5	46.5	46.5		0.2	b
United Arab Emirates	29.8	29.8	29.8	29.8		-2.3	b
Yemen Arab Republic	48.6	48.6	48.6	48.6			b
Yemen PDR	47.0	47.0	47.0	47.0		-1.3	b
AFRICA							
Algeria	42.9	39.6	39.6	38.9		-8.7	b
Angola	47.3	47.3	47.3	47.3		-0.4	b
Benin	50.7	50.7	50.7	50.7		-0.6	b
Botswana	49.9	49.9	49.9	49.9		-1.2	b
Burkina Faso	47.8	47.8	47.8	47.8		-0.6	b
Burundi	47.2	47.2	47.2	47.2		-2.1	b
Cameroon	42.9	42.9	42.9	42.9		-0.5	b
Cape Verde	36.2	36.7	36.7	33.8		-2.6	a
Central African Rep.	44.6	44.6	44.6	44.6		-0.7	b
Chad	44.2	44.2	44.2	44.2		0.2	b
Comoros	46.4	46.4	46.4	46.4	50.4	-0.4	b
Congo	44.5	44.5	44.5	44.5		-0.4	b
Djibouti	12.9	13.3	13.0	13.7		-18.0	c
Equatorial Guinea	42.5	42.5	42.5	42.5			b
Ethiopia	49.7	49.7	49.7	49.7		2.9	b
Gabon	33.7	33.7	33.7	33.7		9.4	b
Gambia	48.4	48.4	48.4	48.4		0.2	b
Ghana	46.9	46.9	46.9	46.9		-0.4	b
Guinea	46.8	46.8	46.8	46.8		-0.2	b
Guinea-Bissau	40.7	40.7	40.7	40.7		-0.5	b
Ivory Coast	45.6	45.6	45.6	45.6		-0.7	b
Kenya	55.1	55.1	55.1	55.1		-1.8	b

Continued...

Table cont'd	1982	1983	1984	1985	1986	% change 1982-1985
Lesotho	41.8	41.8	41.8	41.8		-0.2 b
Liberia	48.7	48.7	48.7	48.7		-1.8 b
Libya	45.6	45.6	45.6	45.6		2.5 a d
Madagascar	44.4	44.4	44.4	44.4		-0.7 b
Malawi	53.2	53.2	53.2	53.2		0.4 b
Maldives						
Mali	50.6	50.6	50.6	50.6		-0.6 b
Mauritania	50.1	50.1	50.1	50.1		0.2 b
Mauritius	22.4	20.7	19.7	18.8	18.3	a
Morocco	36.4	36.4	36.4	36.4		-7.6 b
Mozambique	45.1	45.1	45.1	45.1		4.6 b
Namibia	45.1	45.1	45.1	45.1		-0.2 b
Niger	51.0	51.0	51.0	51.0		0.2 b
Nigeria	50.4	50.4	50.4	50.4		-0.4 b
Reunion	23.1	23.7	24.4	24.8		-2.4 b
Rwanda	51.9	51.9	51.9	51.9		1.6 b
Sao Tome e Principe	37.4			36.3		-16.2 a
Senegal	46.4	46.4	46.4	46.4		b
Seychelles	24.1	25.8	26.9	26.5	26.2	2.3 a
Sierra Leone	47.4	47.4	47.4	47.4		-0.8 b
Somalia	47.9	47.9	47.9	47.9		-1.2 b
South Africa	38.7	38.7	38.7	38.7		1.3 b
Sudan	45.9	45.9	45.9	45.9		-2.3 b
Swaziland	47.3	47.3	47.3	47.3		-0.6 b
Tanzania	50.4	50.4	50.4	50.4		-1.0 b
Togo	45.2	45.2	45.2	45.2		-0.7 b
Tunisia	32.7	31.6	32.2	31.3	31.1	-15.9 a
Uganda	50.3	50.3	50.3	50.3		b
Zaire	45.1	45.1	45.1	45.1		-1.5 b
Zambia	48.1	48.1	48.1	48.1		-0.6 b
Zimbabwe	47.1	47.1	47.1	47.1		-0.4 b

Notes: *a Figures include more than 90% of occurences*   *e UN estimates 1977-78*
   b UN estimates 1976-80 and 1981-85   *f Figures of unknown quality*
   c Figures include less than 90% of occurences   *g UN estimates 1977-79*
   d UN estimate 1981-85   *h UN estimate 1977-80*

LIFE EXPECTANCY AT BIRTH

Latest available year

	Year	Male	Female
LATIN AMERICA			
Argentina	1982	68.2	74.6
Belize	1984	68.1	74.8
Bolivia	80-85	48.6	53.0
Brazil	80-85	60.9	66.0
Chile	1985	65.0	71.7
Colombia	80-85	61.4	66.0
Costa Rica	80-85	70.5	75.7
Ecuador	74-79	59.5	61.8
El Salvador	80-85	62.6	67.1
French Guiana			
Guatemala	1984	61.0	64.6
Guyana	80-85	65.8	70.8
Mexico	1979	62.1	66.0
Nicaragua	80-85	58.7	61.0
Panama	80-85	69.2	72.9
Paraguay	80-85	62.8	67.5
Peru	80-85	56.8	60.5
Puerto Rico	1983	71.6	78.3
Suriname	1985	63.6	71.7
Uruguay	1985	68.7	75.5
Venezuela	1985	66.7	72.8
CARIBBEAN			
Anguilla			
Antigua			
Aruba	72-78	68.3	75.4
Bahamas	1981	66.5	74.5
Barbados	1984	72.0	76.2

Continued...

Table cont'd

	Year	Male	Female
Bermuda	1980	68.8	76.3
British Virgin Is			
Cayman Islands			
Cuba	1985	72.3	75.5
Dominica			
Dominican Republic	80-85	60.7	64.6
Grenada			
Guadeloupe	75-79	66.4	72.4
Haiti	80-85	51.2	54.4
Honduras	73-75	53.4	56.9
Jamaica	80-85	70.3	75.7
Martinique	1985	70.6	77.1
Netherlands Antilles			
St Kitts			
St Lucia	1983	67.2	75.3
St Vincent/Grenadines	1985	67.5	70.8
Trinidad and Tobago	1983	67.2	71.4
SOUTH AND EAST ASIA			
Bangladesh	1984	54.9	54.7
Burma	1978	58.9	63.7
China	80-85	66.7	68.9
Fiji	1976	60.7	63.9
Hong Kong	1985	73.8	79.2
India	76-80	52.5	52.1
Indonesia	80-85	52.2	54.9
Malaysia	1984	67.6	72.7
Nepal	1981	50.9	48.1
Pakistan	76-78	59.0	59.2
Papua New Guinea	80-85	51.2	52.7
Philippines	80-85	60.2	63.7
Singapore	1986	71.0	76.4
South Korea	78-79	62.7	69.1
Sri Lanka	1982	66.9	71.9
Taiwan			
Thailand	74-75	57.6	63.6

Continued...

Table cont'd

	Year	Male	Female
MIDDLE EAST			
Bahrain	81-86	65.9	68.9
Egypt	80-85	56.8	59.5
Iran	1976	55.8	55.0
Iraq	80-85	61.5	63.3
Jordan	80-85	61.9	65.5
Kuwait	1986	71.9	74.9
Lebanon	80-85	63.1	67.0
Oman	80-85	51.0	53.7
Qatar	80-85	65.4	69.8
Saudi Arabia	80-85	59.2	62.7
Syria	76-79	63.8	64.7
United Arab Emirates	80-85	65.4	69.8
Yemen Arab Republic	80-85	46.9	49.9
Yemen PDR	80-85	46.9	49.9
AFRICA			
Algeria	1983	61.6	63.3
Angola	80-85	40.4	43.6
Benin	80-85	42.4	45.6
Botswana	1981	52.3	59.7
Burkina Faso	80-85	43.7	46.8
Burundi	80-85	44.9	48.1
Cameroon	80-85	49.2	52.6
Cape Verde	79-81	59.0	61.0
Central African Rep.	80-85	41.4	44.6
Chad	80-85	41.4	44.6
Comoros	80-85	48.3	51.7
Congo	80-85	44.9	48.1
Djibouti			
Equatorial Guinea	80-85	42.4	45.6
Ethiopia	80-85	39.3	42.5
Gabon	80-85	47.4	50.7
Gambia	80-85	33.5	36.5
Ghana	80-85	50.3	53.8
Guinea	80-85	38.7	41.8

Continued...

Table cont'd

	Year	Male	Female
Guinea-Bissau	80-85	41.4	44.6
Ivory Coast	80-85	48.8	52.2
Kenya	80-85	51.2	54.7
Lesotho	80-85	46.3	52.3
Liberia	80-85	47.4	50.7
Libya	80-85	56.6	60.0
Madagascar	80-85	48.9	50.4
Malawi	1977	38.1	41.2
Maldives	1982	53.4	49.5
Mali	1976	46.9	49.7
Mauritania	80-85	42.4	45.6
Mauritius	1986	65.0	71.5
Morocco	80-85	56.6	60.0
Mozambique	80-85	44.4	46.2
Namibia	80-85	46.6	49.9
Niger	80-85	40.9	44.1
Nigeria	80-85	46.9	50.2
Reunion	80-85	65.5	74.0
Rwanda	1978	45.1	47.7
Sao Tome e Principe			
Senegal	80-85	41.7	44.9
Seychelles	78-82	66.2	73.5
Sierra Leone	80-85	32.5	35.5
Somalia	80-85	39.3	42.5
South Africa	80-85	51.8	55.2
Sudan	80-85	46.6	49.0
Swaziland	1976	42.9	49.5
Tanzania	80-85	49.3	52.7
Togo	80-85	48.8	52.2
Tunisia	80-85	60.1	61.1
Uganda	80-85	47.4	50.7
Zaire	80-85	48.3	51.7
Zambia	80-85	49.6	53.1
Zimbabwe	80-85	54.0	57.6

URBANIZATION

Latest available year

	Average annual growth of urban population 1975-85	Year	Urban Population (000)	% Urban	% in Main City
LATIN AMERICA					
Argentina	2.1	1985	25874.9	84.7	11.6
Belize	2.3				
Bolivia	4.1	1986	3197.9	48.8	31.0
Brazil	3.9	1985	95914.0	70.8	10.5
Chile	2.2	1982	9316.0	82.2	44.0
Colombia	3.2	1983	17980.0	65.4	22.0
Costa Rica	4.5	1985	1107.3	44.5	
Ecuador	5.0	1986	5030.1	52.1	27.6
El Salvador	2.9	1985	2170.0	39.1	
French Guiana	4.3				
Guatemala	3.6	1981	1980.5	32.7	38.1
Guyana	2.9				
Mexico	3.8	1980	44929.7	66.3	19.7
Nicaragua	4.2	1980	1459.3	53.4	41.7
Panama	2.9	1984	1089.0	51.0	39.0
Paraguay	4.5	1982	1295.3	42.8	35.3
Peru	3.6	1984	13224.3	68.9	37.9
Puerto Rico	2.6	1980	2134.4	66.8	19.9
Suriname	0.5				
Uruguay	0.8	1983	2502.9	84.3	49.9
Venezuela	3.9	1986	14642.2	82.3	0.8
CARIBBEAN					
Anguilla					
Antigua	1.3				
Aruba					

Continued...

Table cont'd

	Average annual growth of urban population 1975-85	Year	Urban Population (000)	% Urban	% in Main City
Bahamas	1.3				
Barbados	1.2				
Bermuda	2.3				
British Virgin Is					
Cayman Islands	3.5				
Cuba	1.8	1983	6957.7	70.3	30.0
Dominica					
Dominican Republic	4.4	1982	2985.6	52.0	
Grenada					
Guadeloupe	1.1				
Haiti	4.5	1985	1340.5	25.4	34.4
Honduras	5.8	1985	1737.3	39.7	34.4
Jamaica	3.0	1985	1260.0	53.8	8.3
Martinique	1.6				
Netherlands Antilles	1.5				
St Kitts	2.0				
St Lucia					
St Vincent/Grenadines					
Trinidad and Tobago	4.4				
SOUTH AND EAST ASIA					
Bangladesh	5.4	1982	12237.0	13.2	28.3
Burma	2.0	1983	8455.8	23.9	29.1
China	1.5	1982	206309.1	20.6	5.5
Fiji	3.0				
Hong Kong	2.5	1986	5024.0	93.1	12.6
India	3.7	1986	194585.0	25.4	5.7
Indonesia	4.7	1980	32845.8	22.4	19.8
Malaysia	4.6	1980	4073.1	37.2	22.6
Nepal	7.0	1986	1224.0	7.1	19.2
Pakistan	4.2	1986	28060.0	28.3	18.4
Papua New Guinea	4.4	1980	393.1	13.1	30.1

Continued...

Table cont'd

	Average annual growth of urban population 1975-85	Year	Urban Population (000)	% Urban	% in Main City
Philippines	3.6	1986	22492.3	40.5	7.7
Singapore	1.2	1985	2560.0	100.0	100.0
South Korea	4.6	1985	26427.9	65.4	36.5
Sri Lanka	1.3	1981	3192.5	21.5	20.1
Taiwan					
Thailand	4.8	1980	7632.9	17.0	61.5
MIDDLE EAST					
Bahrain	4.9	1981	283.2	80.7	38.3
Egypt	3.2	1986	22230.0	44.8	26.4
Iran	4.2	1984	22310.2	51.4	25.7
Iraq	5.1	1982	9602.0	68.0	20.7
Jordan	4.5	1979	1266.7	59.4	64.1
Kuwait	7.0				
Lebanon	1.2	1985	2140.0	83.4	
Oman	8.5				
Qatar	6.6				
Saudi Arabia	6.8	1985	8360.0	72.4	
Syria	4.3	1986	5208.0	49.1	23.4
United Arab Emirates	9.4				
Yemen Arab Republic	8.6	1980	843.5	80.9	
Yemen PDR	4.1	1980	690.0	36.9	39.4
AFRICA					
Algeria	3.6	1985	9260.0	42.6	16.4
Angola	6.2	1985	2150.0	24.5	22.1
Benin	7.8	1976	1313.7	39.4	29.0
Botswana	8.5	1986	245.3	21.7	38.8
Burkina Faso	4.4	1985	550.0	7.9	56.0
Burundi	8.6	1986	242.9	5.0	32.4
Cameroon	7.2	1985	4190.0	42.4	24.6
Cape Verde	1.7				

Continued...

Table cont'd

	Average annual growth of urban population 1975-85	Year	Urban Population (000)	% Urban	% in Main City
Central African Rep.	4.4	1980	817.8	35.4	57.9
Chad	7.9	1978	792.0	18.4	
Comoros	4.9	1980	78.1	23.3	22.2
Congo	3.5				
Djibouti	6.6				
Equatorial Guinea	4.5				
Ethiopia	4.3	1985	4473.7	10.3	32.7
Gabon	4.3				
Gambia	4.0	1980	109.5	18.2	100.0
Ghana	3.8	1984	3825.4	31.3	
Guinea	5.4	1985	1350.0	22.2	
Guinea-Bissau	6.2				
Ivory Coast	6.4	1983	3950.0	42.5	36.0
Kenya	8.3	1979	2382.2	15.5	48.8
Lesotho	6.9				
Liberia	5.9	1986	936.9	42.2	45.0
Libya	7.2	1985	870.0	24.1	64.0
Madagascar	5.6	1985	2200.0	21.8	
Malawi	7.5	1985	865.6	12.3	
Maldives	4.4	1985	46.3	25.5	
Mali	3.5	1985	1450.0	18.0	27.6
Mauritania	8.5	1977	303.8	22.7	
Mauritius	1.6	1985	410.2	41.6	33.2
Morocco	4.1	1982	8730.4	42.8	27.6
Mozambique	11.8	1980	1539.1	13.2	
Namibia	5.4				
Niger	6.9	1985	990.0	16.2	
Nigeria	5.8	1985	6916.0	72.8	35.1
Reunion	2.8				
Rwanda	7.7	1978	224.9	4.7	51.6
Sao Tome e Principe	4.9				
Senegal	3.6	1985	2340.0	36.4	34.1

Continued...

Table cont'd

	Average annual growth of urban population 1975-85	Year	Urban Population (000)	% Urban	% in Main City
Seychelles	6.8	1977	23.0	37.2	100.0
Sierra Leone	4.6	1985	1020.0	28.3	48.7
Somalia	6.1	1985	1590.0	34.1	
South Africa	3.4	1980	13168.5	52.6	
Sudan	3.9	1983	4153.6	20.2	13.5
Swaziland	9.3				
Tanzania	11.4	1986	4086.0	18.2	
Togo	6.1	1985	650.0	22.1	
Tunisia	4.1	1984	3685.5	52.8	16.2
Uganda	4.7	1985	1470.0	9.5	
Zaire	4.9	1980	9101.3	34.2	
Zambia	6.3	1980	2440.4	43.0	22.1
Zimbabwe	5.9	1983	1823.0	23.6	23.5

UNEMPLOYMENT 1982-1986

Unit: Thousands

	1982	1983	1984	1985	1986
LATIN AMERICA					
Argentina	183.6	159.4	152.1	216.2	177.8
Belize					
Bolivia	200.9	277.6	303.2	370.9	415.5
Brazil	2533.0				1862.0
Chile	717.6	551.9	530.4	516.6	374.1
Colombia	311.6	406.5	503.5	499.9	482.2

Continued...

299

Table cont'd

	1982	1983	1984	1985	1986
Costa Rica	78.6	76.2	44.4	60.8	56.7
Ecuador					
El Salvador					
French Guiana	2.3	2.4	3.7	4.2	
Guatemala					
Guyana		7.2	11.7		
Mexico					
Nicaragua					
Panama	51.5	64.2	68.8	88.3	73.6
Paraguay					
Peru	417.0	565.9	666.9	773.2	554.1
Puerto Rico					
Suriname	7.4	10.7	12.9	17.0	13.4
Uruguay	60.9	89.7	83.7	77.9	64.2
Venezuela					
CARIBBEAN					
Anguilla					
Antigua					
Aruba					
Bahamas					13.5
Barbados	15.5	16.9	19.2	21.2	20.7
Bermuda					
British Virgin Is					
Cayman Islands					
Cuba					
Dominica					
Dominican Republic					
Grenada					
Guadeloupe	20.6	18.6	21.5	24.2	27.2
Haiti					
Honduras	128.3	254.2			
Jamaica	278.5	266.0	266.8	260.8	250.4
Martinique	23.1	24.6	25.6	29.5	33.9
Netherlands Antilles	15.5	20.1	15.8	17.2	17.9

Continued...

Table cont'd

	1982	1983	1984	1985	1986
St Kitts					
St Lucia					
St Vincent/Grenadines					
Trinidad and Tobago	44.1	50.0	63.2	72.8	81.2
SOUTH AND EAST ASIA					
Bangladesh			2400.0		
Burma	656.4	430.4	441.0	338.0	
China	2.2	2.1			
Fiji					
Hong Kong	91.1	113.8	101.0	785.2	855.0
India	18646.0	20802.0	23034.0	24861.0	28261.0
Indonesia					
Malaysia	86.4	68.0	71.4	76.0	85.7
Nepal					
Pakistan	980.0	1084.0	1115.0	49.8	79.6
Papua New Guinea					
Philippines	1083.0	1003.0	1465.0	1316.0	
Singapore	30.0	38.8	32.5	49.8	79.6
South Korea	654.0	613.0	568.0	619.0	611.0
Sri Lanka					
Taiwan	149.0	197.0	183.0	222.0	212.0
Thailand					
MIDDLE EAST					
Bahrain	606.2	812.7			
Egypt					
Iran					
Iraq					
Jordan					
Kuwait					
Lebanon					
Oman					
Qatar					
Saudi Arabia					
Syria		92.1	109.6		

Continued...

Table cont'd

	1982	1983	1984	1985	1986
United Arab Emirates					
Yemen Arab Republic					
Yemen PDR					
AFRICA					
Algeria					
Angola					
Benin					
Botswana					
Burkina Faso					
Burundi					
Cameroon					
Cape Verde					
Central African Rep.					
Chad					
Comoros					
Congo					
Djibouti					
Equatorial Guinea					
Ethiopia	57.7	57.2	54.7	56.4	52.7
Gabon					
Gambia					
Ghana	23.5	21.2	24.2	25.8	
Guinea					
Guinea-Bissau					
Ivory Coast					
Kenya					
Lesotho					
Liberia					
Libya					
Madagascar	25.9	29.5	29.0		
Malawi					
Maldives					
Mali					
Mauritania					
Mauritius	73.5	73.0	70.2	64.8	54.6

Continued...

Table cont'd

	1982	1983	1984	1985	1986
Morocco	20.8	23.3	59.8		
Mozambique					
Namibia					
Niger	16.0	19.5	27.4	29.0	27.7
Nigeria	16.3	31.0	34.3	28.3	33.0
Reunion	31.7	33.8	36.4	45.0	51.6
Rwanda					
Sao Tome e Principe					
Senegal	10.6	11.8	12.8	36.1	
Seychelles	2.9	4.0	5.6	5.7	
Sierra Leone	9.1	5.3	2.9		
Somalia					
South Africa	497.0	594.0	587.0	641.0	710.0
Sudan	48.8	38.8	63.4		
Swaziland					
Tanzania					
Togo					
Tunisia					
Uganda					
Zaire					
Zambia					
Zimbabwe					

APPENDIX TWO

ECONOMICS

GROSS DOMESTIC PRODUCT 1982-1986

Unit: Million units national currency

	1982	1983	1984	1985	1986
LATIN AMERICA					
Argentina	148	683	5281	39593	74309
Belize	332	352	368	385	393
Bolivia	0.4	1.5	21.5	2771	10559
Brazil	48150	118200	387970	1406080	3586290
Chile	1239100	1557700	1893400	2576600	3258600
Colombia	2497300	3054100	3856600	4865100	6407300
Costa Rica	97505	126337	163011	192425	238468
Ecuador	415720	605000	812630	115080	560270
El Salvador	8966	10152	11657	14331	19763
French Guiana					
Guatemala	8871	9050	9470	11180	
Guyana	1446	1468	1700	1964	2219
Mexico	9417100	17141700	28748900	45588500	
Nicaragua	29696	35783			
Panama	4279	4374	4566	4882	
Paraguay	737040	818110	1070440	1393890	1833800
Peru	14183	26313	59865	157977	
Puerto Rico	16988	18622	19683	21109	
Suriname	1849	1787	1745	1741	1751
Uruguay	128696	185006	294359	520158	945037
Venezuela	291270	290490	348450	372030	403860

Continued...

Table cont'd

	1982	1983	1984	1985	1986	
CARIBBEAN						
Anguilla						
Antigua	346	354	444	483	527	
Aruba						
Bahamas	1449		2216			
Barbados	1990	2113	2301	2474	2677	
Bermuda						
British Virgin Is	67.6	77.1				
Cayman Islands						
Cuba	12176	12926	13695	13952	12854	a
Dominica	194	211	231	221.3		
Dominican Republic	7981	8575	10706	14477	16157	
Grenada	291	253	275	311	348	
Guadeloupe	7649	8486				
Haiti	7425	8148	9082	10047	11218	b
Honduras	5762	6035	6462	6959		
Jamaica	5842	6897	9381	11263		
Martinique	8874	10114	11020	12577		
Netherlands						
Antilles	2558					
St Kitts	158	154	167	174	183.4	
St Lucia	363	380	408.2	416		
St Vincent/Grenadines	225	247	269	289		
Trinidad and Tobago	19176	18461	18918	18140		
SOUTH AND EAST ASIA						
Bangladesh	265140	288420	349920	418750	481620	
Burma	46811	49823	53597	56081	58442	c
China	426700	473000	563000	682200	779000	a
Fiji	1113	1142	1275	1340	1493	
Hong Kong	186328	207562	248728	261195	299826	
India	1651400	1940600	2143900	2435500	2762600	c
Indonesia	62476000	73698000	87055000	94492000	96489000	
Malaysia	62579	69565	79550	77547	71731	
Nepal	30988	33761	38184	41738	50124	d

Continued...

Table cont'd

	1982	1983	1984	1985	1986	
Pakistan	321840	362170	418200	477980	539540	e
Papua New Guinea	1749	1974	2171	2292		
Philippines	340600	384100	540470	609460	622870	
Singapore	32670	36733	40048	38521	37774	
South Korea	52913000	61003000	68867000	75511000	86510000	
Sri Lanka	99238	121601	153746	162375		
Taiwan	1859665	2041370	2255111	2357106	2675614	
Thailand	846100	924900	988900	1041400	1098400	
MIDDLE EAST						
Bahrain	1746	1822				
Egypt	20290	24820	27886	32516	38295	f
Iran	10756300	13749500	15029600	15305800		g
Iraq	12617	13096	14792	14547		
Jordan	1321	1423	1499	1573	1614	
Kuwait	6134	6292	6575	5943	4984	e
Lebanon						
Oman	2752	2881	3174	3575		
Qatar	27652	23542	11487	10814		
Saudi Arabia	524720	415230	372020	330880	286690	h
Syria	68788	73291	75342	79549	86364	
United Arab Emirates	112400	102900	101800	99400	78300	
Yemen Arab Republic	13111	16395	17729	19297	23707	i
Yemen PDR	311					
AFRICA						
Algeria	207600	233600	262300	292500		
Angola						
Benin	411900	385300	466200	499800		
Botswana	780	1029	1279	1524	2145	e
Burkina Faso	359600	381000	390600	461400		
Burundi	91190	100658	118170	138790	147733	
Cameroon	2172800	2618100	3195000	3216702		
Cape Verde	5358	5672		8623		e
Central African Rep.	246000	251100		318677		

Continued...

307

Table cont'd

	1982	1983	1984	1985	1986	
Chad	209325	229017		261920		
Comoros				38636		
Congo	712	799	920			
Djibouti	47274	48162	48162	48162		
Equatorial Guinea		25649	29532	40638	34540	
Ethiopia	9167	10031	9942	9999	10480	j
Gabon	1188900	1320000	1455600	1537000		
Gambia	451	522	599	749	990	e
Ghana	86450	184038	270561	344182		
Guinea				44924		
Guinea-Bissau				24479		
Ivory Coast	2484000	2497700	2557900	2827800		
Kenya	67959	76404	84381	96207	112304	
Lesotho	369	397	480	540		c
Liberia	890	835	835	811		
Libya	8846	8531	7921	7663		
Madagascar	996100	1220900	1369100	1553400	1806900	
Malawi	1244	1436	1705	2024	2275	
Maldives	432	466	537	596		
Mali	411700	421900	470200	479360		
Mauritania	42669	45921	44500	47099		
Mauritius	11750	12775	14360	16380		
Morocco	90090	94640	105540	119310	134330	
Mozambique				76894		
Namibia						
Niger	663000	687100	626400	682300		
Nigeria	55679	55226	56716	58814		
Reunion	12286	13675	14692	16337		
Rwanda	132400	142600	158900	173300		
Sao Tome e Principe				1400		
Senegal	844300	924900	1015500	118900		
Seychelles	968	989	1068	1205		
Sierra Leone	1597	1872	2716	3802	5932	e
Somalia	15265	19924		56624		
South Africa	79676	89875	105814	120141	139695	

Continued...

Table cont'd

	1982	1983	1984	1985	1986	
Sudan	8810	9981		9860		e
Swaziland	547	580	666	754	957	e
Tanzania	60508	65976	75658	108091	144682	
Togo	269700	281300	292100			
Tunisia	4804	5497	6237	6904	7112	
Uganda				24610		
Zaire	31110	59134	99723	147214		
Zambia	3595	4181	4931	7049	12098	
Zimbabwe	5149	5980	6696	8099		

Notes: Data refer to calendar years
   * Billions
   a Net material product
   b Year ending 30 September
   c Year beginning 1 April
   d Year ending 15 July
   e Year ending 30 June

f Year ending 30 June starting 1980
g Year beginning 21 March
h Fiscal year based on Hegira calendar
i Year ending 30 June before 1980
j Year ending 7 July

APPENDIX THREE

FOREIGN TRADE

IMPORTS BY COMMODITY (SITC CODES 0-4)

Unit: Million units national currency
For key to commodities, see notes

	Year	0	1	2	3	4
LATIN AMERICA						
Argentina	1986	313.9	6.0	426.7	427.1	4.7
Belize	1984	56.0	6.3	1.0	43.4	0.9
Bolivia						
Brazil	1986	2136.8	30.7	904.4	4164.5	129.9
Chile	1986	112.2	10.5	142.6	440.5	23.5
Colombia	1985	258.3	17.2	238.4	484.9	81.0
Costa Rica	1984	90.2	6.7	29.4	166.7	5.8
Ecuador	1983	4588.9	324.1	2641.5	1093.8	1487.1
El Salvador	1984	331.2	8.2	66.0	1242.8	84.5
French Guiana	1986	393.0	100.6	5.0	178.4	7.9
Guatemala	1984	74.1	7.2	30.7	485.7	23.0
Guyana						
Mexico	1985	818.2	4220.5	950.5	425.0	83.5
Nicaragua	1984	846.0	5.3	143.6	1467.0	195.8
Panama	1984	121.7	9.3	9.7	367.2	16.5
Paraguay	1986	4819.5	12380.9	3053.5	40923.1	38.6
Peru	1986	503.7	8.0	97.1	68.4	25.4
Puerto Rico						
Suriname						
Uruguay	1986	66.6	8.7	52.9	169.1	3.0
Venezuela	1985	4713.0	765.3	3847.9	1341.3	1361.8

Continued...

Table cont'd

	Year	0	1	2	3	4
CARIBBEAN						
Anguilla						
Antigua	1984	67.9	11.7	6.8	89.1	1.2
Aruba						
Bahamas	1985	154.2	29.8	14.9	2271.1	2.0
Barbados	1986	149.7	25.5	31.4	122.2	9.9
Bermuda	1984	67.7	14.3	3.6	50.7	
British Virgin Is	1982	12.3	3.1	1.1	6.2	0.1
Cayman Islands	1980	14.8	4.2	3.0	12.9	
Cuba	1984	807.1		252.1	2214.7	79.1
Dominica	1982	30.0	4.1	3.8	10.4	6.3
Dominican						
Republic	1984	20.6	0.7	15.3	126.3	18.4
Grenada	1982	41.9	4.0	8.0	20.3	0.3
Guadeloupe	1986	1005.2	227.3	91.3	416.3	37.6
Haiti	1981	409.9	36.7	48.5	270.7	137.7
Honduras	1984	154.3	9.3	18.9	201.3	13.5
Jamaica	1986	166.2	9.9	30.2	202.7	10.6
Martinique	1986	1121.1	199.7	85.3	589.2	40.6
Netherlands						
Antilles	1984	264.0	29.1		6168.3	
St Kitts	1983	27.0	3.8	2.6	14.0	1.8
St Lucia	1981	71.2	9.7	7.1	34.0	4.0
St Vincent/						
Grenadines	1980	46.2	7.8	4.9	13.7	14.8
Trinidad and						
Tobago	1986	783.2	34.1	200.0	139.8	37.8
SOUTH AND EAST ASIA						
Bangladesh	1986	6756.0	57.0	2918.0	6338.0	5350.0
Burma	1984	93.0	4.0	30.0	164.0	249.0
China	1986	5.7	0.6	11.0	1.8	0.7
Fiji	1986	77.7	3.5	2.9	82.1	5.9
Hong Kong	1986	22481.0	3944.0	9863.0	8860.0	684.0
India	1982	6396.0	12.0	7670.0	57584.0	4477.0

Continued...

Table cont'd

	Year	0	1	2	3	4
Indonesia	1985	556.0	21.0	729.0	1288.0	35.0
Malaysia	1986	2917.0	210.0	1018.0	2402.0	69.0
Nepal	1985	743.0	61.0	423.0	913.0	126.0
Pakistan	1986	9851.0	31.0	4941.0	17360.0	6874.0
Papua New Guinea	1985	154.0	10.0	7.0	156.0	3.0
Philippines	1986	459.0	75.0	259.0	920.0	15.0
Singapore	1986	3866.0	541.0	1905.0	10994.0	720.0
South Korea	1986	1422.0	44.0	4291.0	5052.0	124.0
Sri Lanka	1984	6620.5	171.7	940.3	12090.6	384.8
Taiwan	1986	50.4	3.9	120.9	119.2	2.1
Thailand	1985	9441.0	2254.0	15791.0	56718.0	493.0
MIDDLE EAST						
Bahrain	1986	75.6	15.3	9.7	383.0	2.6
Egypt	1986	1832.0	133.8	451.2	276.3	426.8
Iran						
Iraq						
Jordan	1986	165.6	6.7	28.6	116.5	9.4
Kuwait	1984	321.4	25.1	29.5	11.6	6.2
Lebanon						
Oman	1986	129.9	16.9	12.1	26.3	2.3
Qatar	1984	792.0	95.0	139.0	36.0	35.0
Saudi Arabia	1986	10396.0	925.0	985.0	187.0	297.0
Syria	1985	2658.0	19.0	528.0	4562.0	238.0
United Arab Emirates	1984	3412.0	382.0	484.0	1961.0	127.0
Yemen Arab Republic	1981	2182.2	103.9	39.9	608.0	45.0
Yemen PDR						
AFRICA						
Algeria	1985	10773.5	218.1	2108.5	955.7	1540.8
Angola	1981					
Benin	1982	17988.8	20791.0	1669.7	7403.0	

Continued...

313

Table cont'd

	Year	0	1	2	3	4
Botswana						
Burkina Faso	1983	20988.9	3551.1	3219.1	18807.3	3413.0
Burundi	1985	3200.2	128.7	281.0	4123.6	407.2
Cameroon	1982	31869.6	6257.5	11795.0	14840.3	1196.2
Cape Verde						
Central African Rep	1980	2377.2	1085.6	448.8	301.1	85.0
Chad						
Comoros	1980	2116.5			1355.2	
Congo	1985	42706.7	5261.1	2506.3	8161.8	1853.0
Djibouti						
Equatorial Guinea						
Ethiopia	1985	5005.7	84.6	675.9	3028.2	990.8
Gabon	1983	36313.0	8800.0	3858.8	4633.2	1937.0
Gambia						
Ghana	1982	289.9	11.6	29.9	990.7	9.2
Guinea						
Guinea-Bissau	1980	319.2	40.4	43.8	115.9	14.6
Ivory Coast	1985	116.3	14.8	13.6	170.3	1.5
Kenya	1983	771.9	44.2	531.5	6685.6	920.8
Lesotho						
Liberia	1984	78.4	7.8	4.9	71.7	4.7
Libya	1982	301.5	10.3	32.3	30.7	27.3
Madagascar	1986	34380.8	1180.9	5480.6	58355.8	2907.0
Malawi	1983	20.8	3.1	8.8	65.5	5.8
Maldives	1985	10.6	3.1	0.3	7.4	
Mali	1982	245.7	23.2	16.9	363.3	5.6
Mauritania						
Mauritius	1983	1147.7	23.2	230.8	987.3	157.4
Morocco	1985	4757.3	347.1	4504.7	10811.7	1517.2
Mozambique	1984	5781.0			4320.1	
Namibia						
Niger	1981	26853.3	4367.7	4473.4	20563.3	1334.8
Nigeria						
Reunion		1526.6	201.8	172.3	524.0	57.3

Continued...

Table cont'd

	Year	0	1	2	3	4
Rwanda	1980	1638.4	510.6	1049.9	2822.4	657.1
Sao Tome e Principe						
Senegal	1981	63348.9	3918.2	3875.8	89020.4	11769.8
Seychelles	1985	104.6	14.4	6.6	185.4	7.7
Sierra Leone	1984	54.4	6.9	4.1	162.7	4.5
Somalia	1981	582.5	22.4	206.3	70.7	49.5
South Africa	1984	1284.3	169.0	882.6	79.4	244.0
Sudan	1981	130.5	18.7	18.9	159.1	11.4
Swaziland						
Tanzania	1981	402.3		108.7	2212.4	68.5
Togo	1981	16931.5	13370.4	2659.0	9975.5	
Tunisia	1986	273.2	16.1	232.5	156.7	40.6
Uganda						
Zaire						
Zambia	1982	49.4		11.0	193.0	11.8
Zimbabwe	1984	83.6		38.4	256.9	10.9

IMPORTS BY COMMODITY (SITC CODES 5-9)

Unit: Million units national currency

	Year	5	6	7	8	9	Total
LATIN AMERICA							
Argentina	1986	1133.7	610.8	1542.6	255.9	2.3	4723.5 a
Belize	1984	21.7	32.8	51.9	44.7	1.5	260.3
Bolivia							
Brazil	1986	2461.3	1209.8	3835.3	677.0	4.9	15554.6 a
Chile	1986	486.4	452.0	1056.9	192.6	46.8	2964.0 a
Colombia	1985	859.6	747.6	1165.2	187.7	90.8	4130.7
Costa Rica	1984	248.5	250.1	221.0	66.2	1.7	1086.2 a

Continued...

315

Table cont'd

	Year	5	6	7	8	9	Total
Ecuador	1983	12774.9	15511.4	23595.5	4076.0	347.5	66440.5
El Salvador	1984	555.6	492.4	345.0	159.2		3285.0
French Guiana	1986	135.2	288.8	684.1	274.0	11.1	2078.3
Guatemala	1984	318.9	235.4	224.5	72.4	0.3	1472.2
Guyana							
Mexico	1985	1348.2	1193.3	4229.9	672.6	4.5	9730.0 c
Nicaragua	1984	1716.9	1240.9	2306.4	375.2	3.2	8300.3
Panama	1984	180.4	255.3	308.4	140.7	2.6	1411.8
Paraguay	1986	16655.1	26949.2	62131.7	23737.0	97.7	190785.8
Peru	1986	496.4	291.5	738.7	136.4	25.6	2391.2 a
Puerto Rico							
Suriname							
Uruguay	1986	197.1	109.6	223.1	39.8	0.1	870.0 a
Venezuela	1985	1056.2	6909.0	23520.2	5075.7	182.2	55638.1
CARIBBEAN							
Anguilla							
Antigua	1984	22.7	44.7	77.3	32.2		356.0
Aruba							
Bahamas	1985	119.6	139.2	199.6	150.5	0.3	3081.1
Barbados	1986	104.4	176.2	428.5	119.1	26.4	1193.2
Bermuda	1984	36.2	52.9	95.8	79.7	11.9	413.4
British							
Virgin Is	1982	2.5	6.6	19.3	5.0	2.1	58.5 a
Cayman							
Islands	1980	4.9	17.6	24.0	17.2	2.1	101.0
Cuba	1984	425.2	958.5	2193.1	260.2		7197.9
Dominica	1982	14.3	30.8	18.9	9.0	0.5	128.2
Dominican							
Republic	1984	37.3	46.7	45.1	7.4		317.9
Grenada	1982	15.3	25.5	22.5	14.7		152.4
Guadeloupe	1986	503.5	845.4	1455.3	842.7	29.4	5454.1
Haiti	1981	174.1	277.6	321.7	188.4	13.1	1878.4
Honduras	1984	329.5	402.7	404.5	92.5		1626.9
Jamaica	1986	107.8	107.8	168.9	174.6	105.7	976.4
Martinique	1986	670.7	921.4	1407.6	1006.4	73.5	6065.5

Continued...

Table cont'd

	Year	5	6	7	8	9	Total
Netherlands							
Antilles	1984	167.0	170.8	233.1	191.2		7243.9 b
St Kitts	1983	12.0	31.9	27.0	19.9	0.2	140.2
St Lucia	1981	34.2	90.0	69.4	29.3	0.1	348.9
St Vincent/							
Grenadines	1980		29.5	24.2	12.7		154.2
Trinidad and							
Tobago	1986	520.5	1014.0	1808.6	376.8	16.7	4931.4

SOUTH AND EAST ASIA

Bangladesh	1986	5943.0	12798.0	9962.0	1268.0	441.0	51831.0
Burma	1984	743.0	1207.0	2436.0	268.0	13.0	5207.0
China	1986	13.2	39.1	58.6	6.6	12.7	149.8 c
Fiji	1986	41.3	106.3	116.2	44.5	16.4	496.7
Hong Kong	1986	21227.0	80241.0	66247.0	60876.0	1532.0	275955.0
India	1982	9889.0	28218.0	25726.0	2908.0	47.0	142927.0
Indonesia	1985	1917.0	1718.0	3617.0	332.0	46.0	10259.0 a
Malaysia	1986	2749.0	4058.0	12519.0	1716.0	322.0	27980.0
Nepal	1985	924.0	2420.0	1727.0	456.0	7.0	7798.0
Pakistan	1986	11663.0	10039.0	27247.0	2583.0	350.0	90979.0
Papua New							
Guinea	1985	68.0	134.0	262.0	75.0	11.0	875.0
Philippines	1986	778.0	700.0	839.0	117.0	1232.0	5394.0 a
Singapore	1986	3246.0	7614.0	20781.0	4887.0	991.0	55545.0
South Korea	1986	3495.0	4558.0	10640.0	1655.0	304.0	31584.0 a
Sri Lanka	1984	3898.6	9286.0	11417.1	1989.1	174.3	46973.1
Taiwan	1986	133.0	130.2	296.9	57.8	2.0	916.4 c
Thailand	1985	35167.0	42835.0	70549.0	14043.0	3878.0	251169.0

MIDDLE EAST

Bahrain	1986	49.4	106.8	188.3	71.4	3.2	905.3
Egypt	1986	754.8	1832.6	2066.4	276.3	1.1	8051.4
Iran							
Iraq							
Jordan	1986	74.9	140.9	176.6	79.9	51.1	850.2
Kuwait	1984	97.8	442.4	791.0	310.8	5.8	2041.7

Continued...

Table cont'd

	Year	5	6	7	8	9	Total
Lebanon							
Oman	1986	42.7	175.7	377.3	107.3	26.3	916.7
Qatar	1984	246.0	772.0	1493.0	588.0	33.0	4230.0
Saudi Arabia	1986	5621.0	15914.0	24662.0	11342.0	453.0	70780.0
Syria	1985	1473.0	2744.0	2927.0	334.0	1.0	15570.0
United Arab							
Emirates	1984	1426.0	5551.0	8174.0	3794.0	153.0	25464.0
Yemen Arab							
Republic	1981	412.6	1632.7	1865.5	389.5	61.0	7340.3
Yemen PDR							
AFRICA							
Algeria	1985	3746.5	11621.5	16343.3	2032.0	156.6	49496.3
Angola	1981						
Benin	1982	8322.7	48448.7	34724.7	15434.5	1419.7	156426.6
Botswana							d
Burkina Faso	1983	264.1	17793.9	26051.1	4951.1		109739.3
Burundi	1985	1967.0	4473.8	6577.5	1422.9	761.5	23360.7
Cameroon	1982	53609.2	109745.8	140976.9	34745.8	179.3	405215.1
Cape Verde							
Central							
African Rep.	1980	2006.3	3254.3	5759.6	16593.0		17010.8
Chad							
Comoros	1980						6378.2
Congo	1985	21823.8	67842.4	92255.1	18285.4	12.1	260707.6
Djibouti							
Equatorial							
Guinea							
Ethiopia	1985	1504.3	2757.9	5881.8	535.1		20464.4
Gabon	1983	796.9	57933.2	100861.5	26221.4	1400.0	261666.8
Gambia							
Ghana	1982	305.2	299.9	577.5	134.2	147.2	2795.2
Guinea							
Guinea-Bissau	1980	105.5	449.0	681.8	68.5		1872.7
Ivory Coast	1985	98.7	135.8	171.9	44.5	5.7	773.0 c
Kenya	1983	2544.7	2127.0	4234.1	532.4		18398.0

Continued...

Table cont'd

	Year	5	6	7	8	9	Total
Lesotho							d
Liberia	1984	24.2	50.2	97.2	22.3	1.8	363.2 a
Libya	1982	82.7	576.0	781.4	282.2		2124.3
Madagascar	1986	299683.5	36479.5	72769.0	10944.2	533.0	252719.6
Malawi	1983	66.8	78.4	88.9	23.7		362.9
Maldives	1985	3.0	12.1	8.5		2.9	47.9 a
Mali	1982	122.0	248.4	242.4	47.1	5.7	1320.5
Mauritania							
Mauritius	1983	408.4	1319.1	634.2	341.4	5.6	5254.9
Morocco	1985	3131.0	5625.2	6933.6	1034.6	13.4	38675.8
Mozambique	1984	1074.7	817.9	4013.8			23155.6
Namibia							d
Niger	1981	9591.0	28040.5	35620.7	6516.0	1151.1	138511.7
Nigeria							
Reunion		744.3	1275.3	2084.4	1213.7	88.3	9961.8
Rwanda	1980	1357.1	7536.3	5723.4	1097.9	2.5	22570.2
Sao Tome e Principe							
Senegal	1981	22215.8	33923.9	51093.5	12414.1	1196.7	292777.2
Seychelles	1985	41.4	95.2	180.2	68.9	3.8	708.4
Sierra Leone	1984	21.4	66.7	80.4	14.7	1.9	417.6
Somalia	1981	67.0	205.5	1611.0	77.4	21.8	3228.8
South Africa	1984	2136.5	2687.9	9246.7	1742.4	3136.1	21635.8 d
Sudan	1981	99.2	178.6	183.5	30.5	3.7	834.1
Swaziland							
Tanzania	1981	715.2	881.7	2517.6	272.8	1.0	7187.3
Togo	1981	7538.6	36394.3	25216.0	6380.2		118422.8
Tunisia	1986	220.4	586.9	579.4	126.8	71.0	2303.7
Uganda							
Zaire							

Continued...

Table cont'd

	Year	5	6	7	8	9	Total
Zambia	1982	148.9	165.7	320.9	26.9		929.6
Zimbabwe	1984	178.1	177.9	373.6	24.2		1200.7

Notes: a Data reported in million US dollars
*   b Data for Netherlands Antilles refer to Aruba and Curacao only*
*   c Billion units national currency*
*   d Data for South Africa refer to Southern Africa Customs Union (SACU)*
*   ie Botswana Lesotho Namibia South Africa and Swaziland*
SITC codes: 0   Food and live animals
*   1 Beverages and tobacco*
*   2 Crude materials, excluding fuels*
*   3 Mineral fuels etc*
*   4 Oils and fats*
*   5 Chemicals*
*   6 Basic manufactures*
*   7 Machinery and transport equipment*
*   8 Miscellaneous and manufactured goods*
*   9 Others*

EXPORTS BY COMMODITY (0-4)

Unit: Million units of national currency

	Year	0	1	2	3	4
LATIN AMERICA						
Argentina	1986	3219.2	47.7	863.8	164.7	655.2
Belize	1984	116.2	2.1	3.5	5.8	0.9
Bolivia	1985	24.9	0.2	128.2	374.5	
Brazil	1986	2136.8	30.7	904.4	4164.5	129.9
Chile	1986	1144.1	20.7	1241.0	2.5	19.4

Continued...

320

Table cont'd

	Year	0	1	2	3	4
Colombia	1985	2079.1	25.9	198.5	578.3	81.0
Costa Rica	1984	682.9	0.7	20.2	18.1	0.4
Ecuador	1983	23651.5	114.6	806.4	72540.6	82.4
El Salvador	1984	1035.0	4.2	45.8	41.5	0.7
French Guiana	1986	185.3	100.6	15.5	4.4	7.9
Guatemala	1984	599.9	19.2	191.4	26.2	1.0
Guyana						
Mexico	1985	1118.3	94.7	461.4	9149.9	1.4
Nicaragua	1984	2045.8	53.5	1463.3	1467.0	195.8
Panama	1984	208.5	4.5	3.1	5.6	0.4
Paraguay	1986	17891.1	1805.9	47011.2	40923.1	3080.9
Peru	1986	503.7	8.0	97.1	68.4	25.4
Puerto Rico						
Suriname						
Uruguay	1986	437.2	4.4	125.7	5.0	8.6
Venezuela	1985	4713.0	765.3	3847.9	1341.3	1361.8
CARIBBEAN						
Anguilla						
Antigua	1984	1.6	1.1	0.3	5.5	1.2
Aruba						
Bahamas	1985	154.2	29.8	14.9	2271.1	2.0
Barbados	1986	67.8	11.8	2.3	0.1	9.9
Bermuda	1984	67.7	0.4	0.1	50.7	
British						
Virgin Is	1982	0.3	0.7	1.1	6.2	0.1
Cayman Islands	1980	0.8	4.2	0.3	12.9	0.3
Cuba	1984	4354.7	90.8	325.5	549.4	79.1
Dominica	1982	31.6	4.1	3.8	10.4	3.4
Dominican						
Republic	1984	140.8	11.9	1.1	126.3	6.7
Grenada	1982	45.1	4.0	8.0	20.3	0.3
Guadeloupe	1986	587.6	50.4	5.0	1.4	37.6
Haiti	1981	235.4	36.7	48.5	270.7	137.7
Honduras	1984	1077.2	32.0	171.6	9.4	23.1
Jamaica	1986	122.9	29.6	314.7	18.3	0.1

Continued...

Table cont'd

Year	0	1	2	3	4
Martinique	1986	799.5	158.5	7.9	266.3	40.6
Netherlands						
Antilles	1984	264.0	29.1	28.5	6599.5	
St Kitts	1983	30.5	2.8	0.3	14.0	1.8
St Lucia	1981	47.9	9.4	1.0	34.0	7.7
St Vincent/						
Grenadines	1980	33.6	0.9	0.2	0.7	1.1
Trinidad and						
Tobago	1986	160.6	48.8	23.8	3529.2	0.1

SOUTH AND EAST ASIA

Bangladesh	1985	4265.0	68.0	4026.0	537.0	4.0
Burma	1984	93.0	4.0	30.0	164.0	249.0
China	1986	15.6	0.4	10.2	12.9	0.4
Fiji	1986	174.0	0.6	6.0	82.1	4.3
Hong Kong	1986	1620.0	1146.0	1235.0	463.0	10.0
India	1982	18968.0	2488.0	8168.0	12404.0	260.0
Indonesia	1985	1565.0	49.0	1403.0	12575.0	414.0
Malaysia	1986	1970.0	37.0	7884.0	8060.0	3609.0
Nepal	1985	976.0	1.0	485.0	1.0	62.0
Pakistan	1986	8607.0	201.0	9579.0	519.0	6874.0
Papua New						
Guinea	1985	287.0	1.0	430.0	2.0	41.0
Philippines	1986	875.0	29.0	519.0	66.0	346.0
Singapore	1986	2626.0	332.0	2459.0	10147.0	880.0
South Korea	1986	1570.0	95.0	338.0	649.0	4.0
Sri Lanka	1984	18864.8	90.8	4369.5	3332.1	315.5
Taiwan	1986	90.0	0.3	24.3	15.6	0.1
Thailand	1985	86582.0	1648.0	19611.0	2448.0	583.0

MIDDLE EAST

Bahrain	1986	1.1	1.4	1.2	741.0	2.6
Egypt	1983	137.5	133.8	335.5	1052.8	0.1
Iran						
Iraq						
Jordan	1986	41.9	1.4	97.8	0.1	1.5

Continued...

Table cont'd

	Year	0	1	2	3	4
Kuwait	1984	36.2	0.6	11.6	3256.9	0.7
Lebanon						
Oman	1986	20.7	1.0	1.9	865.9	0.1
Qatar	1984	792.0	95.0	139.0	36.0	35.0
Saudi Arabia	1986	10396.0	925.0	985.0	187.0	297.0
Syria	1985	169.0	7.0	706.0	4759.0	238.0
United Arab Emirates	1984	3412.0	382.0	484.0	1961.0	127.0
Yemen Arab Republic	1981	45.2	1.0	5.1	608.0	45.0
Yemen PDR						
AFRICA						
Algeria	1985	50.7	230.2	165.0	49783.2	1540.8
Angola	1981	2905.8		215.5	45596.5	3.5
Benin	1982	17988.8	20791.0	1669.7	7403.0	
Botswana						
Burkina Faso	1983	3838.5	3551.1	15356.1	18807.3	258.8
Burundi	1985	11857.0	19.6	158.2	4123.6	407.2
Cameroon	1982	105785.9	2812.4	37085.5	158228.9	1948.6
Cape Verde	1984	185.5	1.2	22.4	6.1	
Central African Rep.	1980	6715.9	496.0	10079.9	301.1	71.9
Chad						
Comoros	1980	1496.0		87.9	1355.2	
Congo	1985	6494.4	593.1	8733.8	22.9	455554.5
Djibouti						
Equatorial Guinea						
Ethiopia	1985	486.5	0.4	133.9	68.6	1.6
Gabon	1983	2348.9	8800.0	79700.0	447484.7	1937.0
Gambia						
Ghana	1982	1193.8	11.6	82.6	189.6	9.2
Guinea						
Guinea-Bissau	1980	1538.0	61.0	1720.0	115.9	45.0
Ivory Coast	1985	787.6	1.9	155.0	118.2	29.3

Continued...

Table cont'd

	Year	0	1	2	3	4
Kenya	1983	7477.5	68.1	1106.3	2631.0	920.8
Lesotho						
Liberia	1984	30.9	7.8	405.7	71.7	6.8
Libya	1981	301.5	10.3	32.3	4592.7	27.3
Madagascar	1986	172999.0	432.9	18997.0	4732.5	2.0
Malawi	1983	120.6	145.6	5.2	0.1	0.5
Maldives	1985	10.6	3.1	0.3	7.4	
Mali	1982	278.0	23.2	445.7	363.3	22.3
Mauritania						
Mauritius	1983	2999.2	23.2	18.6	987.3	157.4
Morocco	1985	5573.2	46.7	6133.6	845.3	5.4
Mozambique	1984	2716.3		564.1	254.5	6.0
Namibia						
Niger	1981	16113.9	4064.7	99486.7	1063.6	1334.8
Nigeria						
Reunion	1986	729.3	45.6	3.6	2.3	57.3
Rwanda	1980	1638.4	510.6	1049.9	2822.4	657.1
Sao Tome e Principe						
Senegal	1981	32578.0	895.1	25597.0	57013.0	6304.6
Seychelles	1985	13.8	14.4	7.6	163.5	7.7
Sierra Leone	1984	99.5	3.3	147.1	5.7	4.5
Somalia	1981	932.9	22.4	18.3	2.0	49.5
South Africa	1984	1177.8	30.6	2433.8	1798.9	37.5
Sudan	1981	72.4	18.7	178.2	13.7	6.8
Swaziland						
Tanzania	1981	2672.1	175.1	1213.9	8.0	16.1
Togo	1981	13003.5	13370.4	33534.2	742.9	
Tunisia	1986	110.9	7.1	42.6	340.7	53.5
Uganda						
Zaire						
Zambia	1982	49.4	1.6	11.0	193.0	11.8
Zimbabwe	1984	167.5	287.6	243.7	16.6	10.9

IMPORTS BY COMMODITY (5-9)

Unit: Percentage of total imports

Year		5	6	7	8	9	Total
LATIN AMERICA							
Argentina	1986	320.4	970.3	494.7	111.5	4.7	7476.6 a
Belize	1984	3.0	2.1	9.5	10.8	1.2	182.0
Bolivia	1985	0.2	144.4		0.1		672.5 a
Brazil	1986	2461.3	1209.8	3835.3	677.0	4.9	15554.6 a
Chile	1986	102.8	1498.5	66.3	30.4	40.0	4225.5 a
Colombia	1985	127.2	278.4	37.9	171.0	55.7	3823.0 a
Costa Rica	1984	60.1	97.2	29.7	42.1	1.7	1212.9 a
Ecuador	1983	284.0	458.0	116.0	122.5	347.5	98175.8
El Salvador	1984	92.2	221.3	24.2	72.5		1813.5
French Guiana	1986	1.2	11.7	13.5	7.4	19.1	258.8
Guatemala	1984	107.5	102.9	11.6	35.0	0.3	1189.5
Guyana							
Mexico	1985	471.4	992.7	2416.4	518.5	3.2	15227.8 c
Nicaragua	1984	178.8	68.5	1.9	73.3	3.2	3885.9
Panama	1984	8.5	13.7	0.6	12.7	2.6	276.0
Paraguay	1986	2565.0	4052.1	62131.7	338.0	97.7	92128.0
Peru	1986	496.4	291.5	738.7	136.4	25.6	2391.2 a
Puerto Rico							
Suriname							
Uruguay	1986	59.3	282.0	25.6	129.2	5.1	1087.5 a
Venezuela	1985	1056.2	6909.0	23520.2	5075.7	182.2	55638.1
CARIBBEAN							
Anguilla							
Antigua	1984	3.6	3.3	14.3	18.0		47.5
Aruba							b
Bahamas	1985	119.6	139.2	199.6	150.5	0.3	3081.1
Barbados	1986	18.9	28.3	248.8	41.8	0.9	552.3
Bermuda	1984	23.1	0.3	8.3	1.6	6.7	40.5

Continued...

Table cont'd

	Year	5	6	7	8	9	Total
British							
Virgin Is	1982	2.5	6.6	19.3	5.0	2.1	1.1
Cayman Islands	1980	0.7	0.3	24.0	0.1	2.1	2.6 a
Cuba	1984	425.2	20.9	2193.1	260.2		5462.0
Dominica	1982	24.6	1.6	4.1	0.5	0.5	66.0
Dominican							
Republic	1984	6.3	25.1	2.8	2.1		735.2 a
Grenada	1982	15.3	0.5	22.5	4.2		50.1
Guadeloupe	1986	23.3	15.4	45.5	19.0	29.4	747.6
Haiti	1981	174.1	78.8	321.7	244.7	13.1	757.5
Honduras	1984	28.9	43.7	2.9	16.0		1491.3
Jamaica	1986	18.6	8.6	19.2	65.5	105.7	597.6 a
Martinique	1986	49.8	70.9	52.2	40.0	73.5	1445.2
Netherlands							
Antilles	1984	52.5	170.8	233.1	191.2		6719.0 b
St Kitts	1983	0.1	0.2	4.1	8.9	0.1	47.1
St Lucia	1981	1.1	16.3	4.0	10.9	0.1	128.2
St Vincent/							
Grenadines	1980		1.1	1.9	2.9		42.9
Trinidad and							
Tobago	1986	766.8	317.7	92.5	38.1	10.7	4962.2
SOUTH AND EAST ASIA							
Bangladesh	1985	47.0	12891.0	292.0	3758.0	337.0	27997.0
Burma	1984	743.0	1207.0	2436.0	268.0	13.0	5207.0
China	1986	6.1	20.6	3.8	17.3	21.0	108.2 c
Fiji	1986	2.2	8.4	0.4	6.4	39.7	312.5
Hong Kong	1986	1502.0	17042.0	33306.0	95783.0	1877.0	276530.0
India	1982	3483.0	26359.0	5793.0	9776.0	176.0	88416.0
Indonesia	1985	210.0	1805.0	98.0	437.0	31.0	18590.0 a
Malaysia	1986	600.0	2596.0	8996.0	1807.0	242.0	35802.0
Nepal	1985	1.0	674.0	38.0	520.0	1.0	2914.7
Pakistan	1986	990.0	21348.0	356.0	7727.0	265.0	56336.0
Papua New							
Guinea	1985	68.0	1.0	12.0	75.0	229.0	1003.0
Philippines	1986	243.0	435.0	433.0	587.0	1308.0	4841.0 a

Continued...

Table cont'd

	Year	5	6	7	8	9	Total
Singapore	1986	2840.0	3633.0	18900.0	4042.0	3126.0	48986.0
South Korea	1986	1068.0	8173.0	11661.0	11094.0	63.0	34715.0 a
Sri Lanka	1984	183.8	1335.9	525.3	7963.4	174.3	37347.0
Taiwan	1986	40.9	306.5	437.8	588.7	0.1	1504.3 c
Thailand	1985	2440.0	35860.0	16977.0	24030.0	3187.0	193366.0
MIDDLE EAST							
Bahrain	1986	1.3	113.7	16.4	2.6	1.7	880.4
Egypt	1983	29.3	447.5	2.6	48.4	1.1	2054.0
Iran							
Iraq							
Jordan	1986	54.5	19.6	1.4	7.3	51.1	256.0
Kuwait	1984	68.4	86.8	126.2	44.3	0.8	3632.4
Lebanon							
Oman	1986	1.7	13.1	59.2	3.9	8.6	976.3
Qatar	1984	246.0	772.0	1493.0	588.0	33.0	4230.0
Saudi Arabia	1986	5621.0	15914.0	24662.0	11342.0	453.0	70780.0
Syria	1985	198.0	326.0	59.0	199.0	4.0	6427.0
United Arab							
Emirates	1984	1426.0	5551.0	8174.0	3794.0	153.0	25464.0
Yemen Arab							
Republic	1981	3.4	13.1	139.6	4.3	4.6	216.6
Yemen PDR							
AFRICA							
Algeria	1985	495.3	182.2	116.8	7.8	156.6	51031.3
Angola	1981		6599.6		1.0	199.6	55521.5
Benin	1982	8322.7	48448.7	34724.7	15434.5	1419.7	156426.6
Botswana							d
Burkina Faso	1983	264.1	1147.3	899.6	222.1		21745.0
Burundi	1985	1967.0	649.3	6577.5	1422.9	547.8	13462.0
Cameroon	1982	4216.8	20520.6	3107.7	3027.5	153.9	326916.5
Cape Verde	1984	0.1	3.4	2.8	0.3		221.8
Central							
African Rep.	1980	2006.3	6119.5	5759.6	16593.0	880.1	24384.0
Chad							

Continued...

327

Table cont'd

	Year	5	6	7	8	9	Total
Comoros	1980	443.1				422.2	2453.1
Congo	1985	59.3	15977.7	907.6	240.4	12.6	488514.6
Djibouti							
Equatorial Guinea							
Ethiopia	1985	4.0	0.7	0.0	1.7	1.4	689.4
Gabon	1983	6718.3	21493.9	3609.5	1711.1	1400.0	752700.0
Gambia							
Ghana	1982	0.1	469.0	0.2	1.9	2.1	2402.0
Guinea							
Guinea-Bissau	1980	12.0	266.0	681.8	68.5		3850.0
Ivory Coast	1985	30.0	52.4	21.5	10.6	11.5	1218.1 c
Kenya	1983	438.5	903.7	216.9	142.3		13044.0
Lesotho							d
Liberia	1984	24.2	50.2	1.2	22.3	3.3	449.1 a
Libya	1981	17.1	576.0	781.4	282.2		4609.0
Madagascar	1986	2714.2	8606.7	3990.5	1636.8	53.4	214165.0
Malawi	1983	1.5	7.5	88.9	1.6	0.5	283.2
Maldives	1985	3.0	12.1	8.5		2.9	47.9 a
Mali	1982	0.3	14.9	242.4	0.2	5.8	767.3
Mauritania							
Mauritius	1983	17.1	151.9	40.7	1164.5	5.6	4396.0
Morocco	1985	4576.9	1859.1	240.3	2456.9	3.1	21740.0
Mozambique	1984	1074.7	45.1	4013.8		482.9	4069.1
Namibia							d
Niger	1981	9591.0	1871.5	617.7	6516.0	1151.1	123589.4
Nigeria							
Reunion	1986	38.7	21.9	45.5	14.1	88.3	901.7
Rwanda	1980	1357.1	7536.3	5723.4	1097.9	2.5	22570.2
Sao Tome e Principe							
Senegal	1981	9166.3	11655.7	6110.3	3059.5	10.1	152389.4
Seychelles	1985	41.4	0.7	7.0	5.2	3.8	198.9
Sierra Leone	1984	21.4	113.0	80.4	14.7	1.9	369.2
Somalia	1981	67.0	205.5	1611.0	77.4	21.8	956.8
South Africa	1984	742.7	4103.9	487.7	177.9	3546.2	25355.0 d

Continued...

Table cont'd

	Year	5	6	7	8	9	Total
Sudan	1981	99.2	2.1	2.4	30.5	3.7	276.4
Swaziland							
Tanzania	1981	32.3	397.6	117.0	43.9	1.0	4680.7
Togo	1981	84.2	7430.2	782.6	391.6	476.9	56572.8
Tunisia	1986	280.8	116.6	74.2	370.7	6.7	1403.7
Uganda							
Zaire							
Zambia	1982	148.9	910.5	320.9	26.9		950.0
Zimbabwe	1984	24.0	419.8	8.4	30.6		1271.1

Notes: a Data reported in million US dollars
b Data for Netherlands Antilles refer to Aruba and Curacao only
c Billion units national currency
d Data for South Africa refer to Southern Africa Customs Union (SACU)
ie Botswana Lesotho Namibia South Africa and Swaziland

SITC codes: 0 Food and live animals
1 Beverages and tobacco
2 Crude materials, excluding fuels
3 Mineral fuels etc
4 Oils and fats
5 Chemicals
6 Basic manufactures
7 Machinery and transport equipment
8 Miscellaneous and manufactured goods
9 Others

EXCHANGE RATES AGAINST THE US DOLLAR 1982-1987

	1982	1983	1984	1985	1986	1987
LATIN AMERICA						
Argentina			0.1	0.1	0.9	2.1
Belize	2.0	2.0	2.0	2.0	2.0	2.0
Bolivia	64.1	231.6	3135.9	0.4	1.9	2.1
Brazil	0.2	0.6	1.8	6.2	13.7	39.2
Chile	50.9	78.8	98.7	161.1	193.0	219.5
Colombia	64.1	78.9	100.8	142.3	194.3	242.6
Costa Rica	37.4	41.1	44.5	50.5	56.0	62.8
Ecuador	30.0	44.1	62.5	69.6	122.8	170.5
El Salvador	2.5	2.5	2.5	2.5	5.0	5.0
French Guiana	6.6	7.6	8.7	9.0	6.9	6.0
Guatemala	1.0	1.0	1.0	1.0	1.9	2.5
Guyana	3.0	3.0	3.8	4.3	4.3	9.8
Mexico	56.4	120.1	167.8	256.9	611.8	1378.2
Nicaragua	10.1	10.1	10.1	26.5	66.5	70.0
Panama	1.0	1.0	1.0	1.0	1.0	1.0
Paraguay	126.0	126.0	201.0	306.7	339.2	550.0
Peru	0.7	1.6	3.5	11.0	13.9	16.8
Puerto Rico	1.0	1.0	1.0	1.0	1.0	1.0
Suriname	1.8	1.8	1.8	1.8	1.8	1.8
Uruguay	13.9	34.5	56.1	101.4	152.0	226.7
Venezuela	4.3	4.3	7.0	7.5	8.1	14.5
CARIBBEAN						
Anguilla						
Antigua	2.7	2.7	2.7	2.7	2.7	2.7
Aruba	1.8	1.8	1.8	1.8	1.8	1.8
Bahamas	1.0	1.0	1.0	1.0	1.0	1.0
Barbados	2.0	2.0	2.0	2.0	2.0	2.0
Bermuda	1.0	1.0	1.0	1.0	1.0	1.0
British Virgin Is	1.0	1.0	1.0	1.0	1.0	1.0
Cayman Islands	0.8	0.8	0.8	0.8	0.8	0.8

Continued...

Table cont'd

	1982	1983	1984	1985	1986	1987
Cuba	0.9	0.9	0.9	0.9	0.8	0.8
Dominica	2.7	2.7	2.7	2.7	2.7	2.7
Dominican Republic	1.0	1.0	1.0	3.1	2.9	3.8
Grenada	2.7	2.7	2.7	2.7	2.7	2.7
Guadeloupe	6.6	7.6	8.7	9.0	6.9	6.0
Haiti	5.0	5.0	5.0	5.0	5.0	5.0
Honduras	2.0	2.0	2.0	2.0	2.0	2.0
Jamaica	1.8	1.9	3.9	5.6	5.5	5.5
Martinique	6.6	7.6	8.7	9.0	6.9	6.0
Netherlands Antilles	1.8	1.8	1.8	1.8	1.8	1.8
St Kitts	2.7	2.7	2.7	2.7	2.7	2.7
St Lucia	2.7	2.7	2.7	2.7	2.7	2.7
St Vincent/ Grenadines	2.7	2.7	2.7	2.7	2.7	2.7
Trinidad and Tobago	2.4	2.4	2.4	2.5	3.6	3.6

SOUTH AND EAST ASIA

	1982	1983	1984	1985	1986	1987
Bangladesh	22.1	24.6	25.4	28.0	30.4	31.0
Burma	7.8	8.0	8.4	8.5	7.3	6.7
China	1.9	2.0	2.3	2.9	3.5	3.7
Fiji	0.9	1.0	1.1	1.2	1.1	1.2
Hong Kong	6.1	7.3	7.8	7.8	7.8	7.8
India	9.5	10.1	11.4	12.4	12.6	13.0
Indonesia	661.4	909.3	1025.9	1110.6	1282.6	1643.8
Malaysia	2.3	2.3	2.3	2.5	2.6	2.5
Nepal	13.2	14.5	16.5	18.2	21.2	21.8
Pakistan	11.8	13.1	14.0	15.9	16.6	17.4
Papua New Guinea	0.7	0.8	0.9	1.0	1.0	0.9
Philippines	8.5	11.1	16.7	18.6	20.4	20.6
Singapore	2.1	2.1	2.1	2.2	2.2	2.1
South Korea	731.1	775.8	806.0	870.0	881.5	822.6
Sri Lanka	20.8	23.5	25.4	27.2	28.0	29.4
Taiwan	39.1	40.1	39.6	39.8	37.8	
Thailand	23.0	23.0	23.6	27.2	26.2	25.7

Continued...

Table cont'd

	1982	1983	1984	1985	1986	1987
MIDDLE EAST						
Bahrain	0.4	0.4	0.4	0.4	0.4	0.4
Egypt	0.7	0.7	0.7	0.7	0.7	0.7
Iran	83.6	86.4	90.0	91.1	78.8	71.5
Iraq	0.3	0.3	0.3	0.3	0.3	0.3
Jordan	0.4	0.4	0.4	0.4	0.3	0.3
Kuwait	0.3	0.3	0.3	0.3	0.3	0.3
Lebanon	4.7	4.5	6.5	16.4	38.4	224.6
Oman	0.3	0.3	0.3	0.3	0.4	0.4
Qatar	3.6	3.6	3.6	3.6	3.6	3.6
Saudi Arabia	3.4	3.5	3.5	3.6	3.7	3.7
Syria	3.9	3.9	3.9	3.9	3.9	11.2
United Arab						
Emirates	3.7	3.7	3.7	3.7	3.7	3.7
Yemen Arab						
Republic	4.6	4.6	5.4	7.4	9.6	10.3
Yemen PDR	0.3	0.3	0.3	0.3	0.3	0.3
AFRICA						
Algeria	4.6	4.8	4.9	5.0	4.7	4.8
Angola	29.9	29.9	29.9	29.9	29.9	29.9
Benin	328.6	381.1	437.0	449.3	346.3	300.5
Botswana	1.0	1.1	1.3	1.9	1.9	1.7
Burkina Faso	328.6	381.1	437.0	449.3	346.3	300.5
Burundi	90.0	93.0	119.7	120.7	114.2	123.6
Cameroon	328.6	381.1	437.0	449.3	346.3	300.5
Cape Verde	63.0	79.9	93.0	85.4	76.6	
Central						
African Rep.	328.6	381.1	437.0	449.3	346.3	300.5
Chad	328.6	381.1	437.0	449.3	346.3	300.5
Comoros	328.6	381.1	437.0	449.3	346.3	300.5
Congo	328.6	381.1	437.0	449.3	346.3	300.5
Djibouti	177.7	177.7	177.7	177.7	177.7	177.7
Equatorial Guinea	219.7	286.9	321.5	449.3	346.3	300.5
Ethiopia	2.1	2.1	2.1	2.1	2.1	2.1
Gabon	328.6	381.0	437.0	449.3	346.3	300.5

Continued...

Table cont'd

	1982	1983	1984	1985	1986	1987
Gambia	2.3	2.6	3.6	3.9	6.8	7.1
Ghana	2.8	3.4	35.3	54.1	89.3	147.1
Guinea	22.4	23.6	25.2	22.5	235.6	
Guinea-Bissau	39.9	84.2	128.6	173.6	239.0	
Ivory Coast	328.6	381.1	437.0	449.3	346.3	300.5
Kenya	10.9	13.3	14.4	16.4	16.2	16.5
Lesotho	1.1	1.1	1.4	2.2	2.3	2.0
Liberia	1.0	1.0	1.0	1.0	1.0	1.0
Libya	0.3	0.3	0.3	0.3	0.3	0.3
Madagascar	349.7	430.5	576.6	662.5	676.3	1069.2
Malawi	1.1	1.2	1.4	1.7	1.9	2.2
Maldives	7.2	7.1	7.1	7.1	7.2	9.2
Mali	328.6	381.1	437.0	449.3	346.3	300.5
Mauritania	51.8	54.8	63.8	77.1	74.4	73.9
Mauritius	10.9	11.7	13.8	15.4	13.5	12.9
Morocco	6.0	7.1	8.8	10.1	9.1	8.4
Mozambique	38.6	41.6	44.0	41.6	40.5	
Namibia	1.1	1.1	1.4	2.2	2.3	2.0
Niger	328.6	381.1	437.0	449.2	346.3	300.5
Nigeria	0.7	0.7	0.8	0.9	1.3	4.0
Reunion	6.5	7.6	8.7	8.9	6.9	6.0
Rwanda	92.8	94.3	100.2	101.3	87.6	79.7
Sao Tome e Principe	41.0	43.2	46.2	41.2	37.0	
Senegal	328.6	381.1	437.0	449.3	346.3	300.5
Seychelles	6.6	6.8	7.1	7.1	6.2	5.6
Sierra Leone	1.2	1.7	2.5	4.7	8.4	30.8
Somalia	10.7	15.8	20.0	39.5	72.0	105.2
South Africa	1.1	1.1	1.4	2.2	2.3	2.0
Sudan	0.9	1.3	1.3	2.3	2.5	2.8
Swaziland	1.1	1.1	1.4	2.2	2.3	2.0
Tanzania	9.3	11.1	15.3	17.5	32.7	64.3
Togo	328.6	381.1	437.0	449.3	346.3	300.5
Tunisia	0.6	0.7	0.8	0.8	0.8	0.8
Uganda	94.1	153.9	3.5	6.7	14.0	42.8

Continued...

Table cont'd

	1982	1983	1984	1985	1986	1987
Zaire	5.7	12.9	36.1	49.9	59.6	112.4
Zambia	0.9	1.3	1.8	2.7	7.3	8.9
Zimbabwe	0.8	1.0	1.2	1.6	1.7	1.7

Notes: a Up to 1984: bolivianos per US $million
b Official rate
c Selling rate
d Up to 1984: Central Bank selling rate. From 1985: Official rate
e End of year exchange rate
f 1987 rate on 30 September
g Official rate up to May 1986
h Principal rate
i Official rate to January 1985 then principal rate
j General internal use of currency suspended 1975 to March 1980
k 1987 rate at end of June
l 1986 rate at end of June
m Kip of Liberation (KL) to 10 December 1979; replaced by Kip (kp) = KL100
n Separate north and south currencies to 3 May 1978 replaced by Dong.
   Dong to 14 September 1985 replaced by New Dong = 10 Dong
o Up to 1980: end of year exchange rate. Bipkwele to 1984 replaced by Franc
p Syli up to 1985 replaced by Guinean Franc. Rate change 6 January 1986
q Mozambique escudo to 16 June 1980 replaced by Metical 1987 rate at end of June

APPENDIX FOUR

PRODUCTION

INDICES OF GENERAL INDUSTRIAL PRODUCTION

Base: 1980 = 100

	1982	1983	1984	1985	1986
LATIN AMERICA					
Argentina	81	90	92	84	94
Belize					
Bolivia	87				
Brazil	90	85	91	99	
Chile					
Colombia	100				
Costa Rica	96				
Ecuador					
El Salvador	81				
French Guiana					
Guatemala	93				
Guyana					
Mexico	107	97	102	107	101
Nicaragua					
Panama					
Paraguay	104	101			
Peru					
Puerto Rico					
Suriname					
Uruguay					
Venezuela					

Continued...

Table cont'd

	1982	1983	1984	1985	1986
CARIBBEAN					
Anguilla					
Antigua					
Aruba					
Bahamas					
Barbados	93	97	100	95	103
Bermuda					
British Virgin Is					
Cayman Islands					
Cuba					
Dominica					
Dominican Republic					
Grenada					
Guadeloupe					
Haiti					
Honduras	100				
Jamaica					
Martinique					
Netherlands Antilles					
St Kitts					
St Lucia					
St Vincent/Grenadines					
Trinidad and Tobago					
SOUTH AND EAST ASIA					
Bangladesh	96	101	105	103	112
Burma					
China	112	124	141	167	
Fiji	109	97	116	103	123
Hong Kong	120	150	145		
India	113	120	131	142	149
Indonesia					
Malaysia	109	122	142	137	151
Nepal					
Pakistan					

Continued...

Table cont'd

	1982	1983	1984	1985	1986
Papua New Guinea					
Philippines	128	142	193	231	261
Singapore					
South Korea	118	137	158	164	195
Sri Lanka					
Taiwan	103	117	132	134	153
Thailand					
MIDDLE EAST					
Bahrain					
Egypt	138	163	169		
Iran					
Iraq					
Jordan	120	126	152	155	157
Kuwait					
Lebanon					
Oman					
Qatar					
Saudi Arabia					
Syria	112	137	139	136	
United Arab Emirates					
Yemen Arab Republic					
Yemen PDR					
AFRICA					
Algeria	125				
Angola					
Benin					
Botswana	105	97	94		
Burkina Faso					
Burundi					
Cameroon					
Cape Verde					
Central African Rep.					
Chad					

Continued...

337

Table cont'd

	1982	1983	1984	1985	1986
Comoros					
Congo					
Djibouti					
Equatorial Guinea					
Ethiopia					
Gabon					
Gambia					
Ghana	75	53			
Guinea					
Guinea-Bissau					
Ivory Coast	97	83	90	106	
Kenya	106	111	115	121	
Lesotho					
Liberia					
Libya					
Madagascar					
Malawi					
Maldives					
Mali					
Mauritania					
Mauritius					
Morocco	108	108	107	108	112
Mozambique					
Namibia					
Niger					
Nigeria	98	87			
Reunion					
Rwanda					
Sao Tome e Principe					
Senegal	113	118	115	134	106
Seychelles	140	159	156		
Sierra Leone					
Somalia					
South Africa	98	102	99	105	108
Sudan					

Continued...

Table cont'd

	1982	1983	1984	1985	1986
Swaziland	88	71			
Tanzania					
Togo					
Tunisia	103	112			
Uganda					
Zaire					
Zambia	100	97	83	92	88
Zimbabwe	105	102	100	109	112

APPENDIX FIVE

CONSUMPTION

TOTAL CONSUMER EXPENDITURE 1982-1986

Unit: Million units of national currencies

	1982	1983	1984	1985	1986
LATIN AMERICA					
Argentina	49	64	473	3655	4200
Belize	388	386	385	404	
Bolivia				248	8084
Brazil	33690	85520	270100	944700	2477457
Chile	932700	1141900	1381700	1785300	2237300
Colombia	1810438	2208216	2722000	3417000	4276000
Costa Rica	56400	76900	99800	119300	141700
Ecuador	262200	369300	520600	712900	927900
El Salvador	6880	7870	9180	11570	15780
French Guiana					
Guatemala	6880	7500	7860	9300	12840
Guyana	876	818	979	1071	1000
Mexico	5780000	10360000	17470000		
Nicaragua	19240	18660	24970	55620	243200
Panama	2310	2480	2880	3080	2930
Paraguay	552000	642000	835000	1066000	1411000
Peru	9560	18220	41000	107010	
Puerto Rico	12900	13800			
Suriname	1094	1250	1002	833	
Uruguay	94080	137800	216300	392500	691900
Venezuela	170182	181273	190632	232200	271900

Continued...

Table cont'd

	1982	1983	1984	1985	1986
CARIBBEAN					
Anguilla					
Antigua	228	261	293		
Aruba					
Bahamas	858				
Barbados	1263	1321	1425	1408	1615
Bermuda					
British					
Virgin Is					
Cayman Islands					
Cuba	8146	8776			
Dominica					
Dominican					
Republic	6000	6300	7802	10240	
Grenada	202	212	216	249	260
Guadeloupe	7037				
Haiti	7190	7870	8680	9470	10510
Honduras	4300	4500	4740	5020	5380
Jamaica	4020	4830	6220	7850	8720
Martinique	7696				
Netherlands					
Antilles					
St Kitts					
St Lucia	244	238			
St Vincent/					
Grenadines	175	187	169	169	
Trinidad and					
Tobago	11100	11570	11020	9330	
SOUTH AND EAST ASIA					
Bangladesh	255700	278200			
Burma	39700	42700	47400	49900	51000
China	474768	516038	576783	700128	838908
Fiji	685	748	794	841	
Hong Kong	111746	130696	149917	162799	193198

Continued...

342

Table cont'd

	1982	1983	1984	1985	1986
India	1137920	1355920	1459620	1635060	1966000
Indonesia	34547693	39853410	44127710	50202868	57008848
Malaysia	33230	36000	39590	40360	37170
Nepal					
Pakistan	266000	294000	340000	396000	423000
Papua New Guinea	1118	1245	1363	1479	1554
Philippines	234486	268188	404699	458929	500050
Singapore	15668	16810	17846	17523	18096
South Korea	33700100	36893300	40298900	43459500	47651500
Sri Lanka	79200	94900	111200	126500	139400
Taiwan	977368	1052627	1144756	1205267	1293716
Thailand	554732	618636	649633	685389	711000
MIDDLE EAST					
Bahrain					
Egypt	12820	16130	19190	22510	26900
Iran	5710	7230	8130	8750	
Iraq					
Jordan	1220	1347	1375	1415	1327
Kuwait	3204	2894	3054	2636	3449
Lebanon					
Oman	795	802	939	1172	
Qatar					
Saudi Arabia	126500	151300	157400	146000	122100
Syria	44990	49690	49120	55155	63521
United Arab Emirates	26800	26700	27200	29900	31000
Yemen Arab Republic	12230	15260	16900	17720	22010
Yemen PDR					

Continued...

Table cont'd

	1982	1983	1984	1985	1986
AFRICA					
Algeria	96600	104300	118300	136200	
Angola					
Benin	388000				
Botswana					
Burkina Faso	321000				
Burundi					
Cameroon	1539000	1716000	2008000		
Cape Verde					
Central African Rep.					
Chad					
Comoros					
Congo					
Djibouti					
Equatorial Guinea					
Ethiopia	7350	8030	7860	8130	9050
Gabon					
Gambia					
Ghana	77620	167100	233000	282800	
Guinea					
Guinea-Bissau					
Ivory Coast	1654500	1769600	1782200	1891700	2004800
Kenya					
Lesotho					
Liberia	620.9	650	621.1	625.6	593.4
Libya	3380				
Madagascar					
Malawi					
Maldives					
Mali	579000				
Mauritania	30730	32210	33180		
Mauritius					
Morocco	61800	64100	74000	81800	91300

Continued...

Table cont'd

	1982	1983	1984	1985	1986
Mozambique					
Namibia					
Niger	483000	523000			
Nigeria	38790	41250	44210	49670	
Reunion					
Rwanda					
Sao Tome e Principe					
Senegal	636000	734000	804000	914000	
Seychelles					
Sierra Leone	1110000	1930000	2813000		
Somalia					
South Africa	44134	50703	58517	65454	77093
Sudan					
Swaziland					
Tanzania					
Togo	195000	202000			
Tunisia	3000	3430	3930	4380	4750
Uganda					
Zaire					
Zambia					
Zimbabwe	3363	3726	4199	4682	5150

345

TRENDS IN CONSUMER PRICES 1982-1987

Percentage annual increase

	1982	1983	1984	1985	1986	1987
LATIN AMERICA						
Argentina	164.8	343.8	626.7	672.1	90.1	131.3
Belize	6.8	5.0	3.7	3.7	1.0	
Bolivia	133.3	269.9	1281.0	11750.0	276.0	15.0
Brazil	97.8	142.1	197.0	226.9	145.2	229.7
Chile	9.9	27.3	19.9	30.7	19.5	19.9
Colombia	24.5	19.8	16.1	24.0	18.9	23.3
Costa Rica	90.1	32.6	12.0	15.1	11.8	16.8
Ecuador	16.3	48.4	31.2	28.0	23.0	29.5
El Salvador	11.7	13.3	11.5	22.3	31.9	
French Guiana						
Guatemala	0.3	4.5	3.4	18.7	36.9	12.3
Guyana	20.2	13.3	25.2	15.0	7.9	
Mexico	58.9	101.8	65.5	57.7	86.2	131.8
Nicaragua	24.8	31.1	35.4	219.5	747.7	
Panama	4.3	2.1	1.6	1.0	-0.1	
Paraguay	6.8	13.4	20.3	25.2	31.7	21.8
Peru	64.4	111.2	110.2	163.4	77.9	85.8
Puerto Rico						
Suriname	7.3	4.4	3.7			
Uruguay	19.0	49.2	55.3	72.2	76.4	63.6
Venezuela	9.6	6.3	12.2	11.4	11.5	28.1
CARIBBEAN						
Anguilla						
Antigua	4.2	2.3	3.9	1.0		
Aruba						
Bahamas	6.0	4.1	3.9	4.6	5.4	
Barbados	10.3	5.3	4.6	3.9	1.3	3.3

Continued...

Table cont'd

	1982	1983	1984	1985	1986	1987
Bermuda						
British Virgin Is						
Cayman Islands						
Cuba						
Dominica	4.5	4.0	2.2	2.1	3.0	
Dominican Republic	7.6	4.8	27.0	37.5	9.7	
Grenada	7.8	6.1	5.6	2.5	0.5	-0.9
Guadeloupe						
Haiti	7.4	10.2	6.4	10.6	3.3	-11.5
Honduras	9.0	8.3	4.7	3.4	4.4	2.5
Jamaica	6.5	11.6	27.8	25.7	15.1	6.7
Martinique						
Netherlands Antilles	6.1	2.8	2.1	0.5	1.3	
St Kitts						
St Lucia	4.6	1.5	1.2	1.3	2.3	
St Vincent/ Grenadines	7.2	5.5	2.7	2.1		
Trinidad and Tobago	11.5	16.7	13.3	7.6	7.7	
SOUTH AND EAST ASIA						
Bangladesh	12.5	9.4	10.5	10.7	11.0	
Burma	5.3	5.7	4.8	6.8	9.2	23.0
China	2.0	2.0	2.7	11.5	6.0	7.3
Fiji	7.0	6.7	5.3	4.4	4.4	
Hong Kong	10.6	9.9	8.5	3.4	3.2	5.3
India	7.9	11.9	8.3	5.6	8.7	8.8
Indonesia	9.5	11.8	10.5	4.7	5.8	9.3
Malaysia	5.8	3.7	3.9	0.3	0.7	1.1
Nepal	11.7	12.4	2.8	8.1	19.0	
Pakistan	5.9	6.2	6.6	5.8	3.7	4.8
Papua New Guinea	5.5	7.9	7.4	3.7	5.5	

Continued...

Table cont'd

	1982	1983	1984	1985	1986	1987
Philippines	10.2	10.0	50.3	23.1	0.8	3.8
Singapore	3.9	1.2	2.6	0.5	-1.4	0.5
South Korea	7.3	3.4	2.3	2.5	2.8	3.0
Sri Lanka	10.8	14.0	16.6	1.5	8.0	7.7
Taiwan	3.0	1.4		-0.2	-0.7	
Thailand	5.3	3.7	0.9	2.4	1.8	2.5
MIDDLE EAST						
Bahrain	8.9	3.0	0.3	-2.6	-2.3	
Egypt	14.8	16.1	17.1	13.3	22.6	19.7
Iran	18.7	19.7	12.5	4.4		
Iraq						
Jordan	7.4	5.0	3.8	3.0		-0.3
Kuwait	7.8	4.7	1.2	1.5	1.0	0.7
Lebanon						
Oman						
Qatar	5.7	2.7	1.1	1.9	1.6	
Saudi Arabia	-0.6	-0.6	-1.2	-3.3	-3.0	
Syria	14.3	6.1	9.2	17.3	36.1	
United Arab Emirates						
Yemen Arab Republic	2.7	5.3	12.8			
Yemen PDR	9.5	11.0				
AFRICA						
Algeria	6.7	7.8	6.3	10.5	12.4	7.5
Angola						
Benin						
Botswana	11.1	10.5	8.6	8.1	10.0	9.8
Burkina Faso	12.0	8.3	4.8	6.9	-2.6	-2.7
Burundi	5.8	8.4	14.4	3.6	1.9	7.3
Cameroon	13.3	16.6	11.4	1.3	3.2	
Cape Verde						

Continued...

Table cont'd

	1982	1983	1984	1985	1986	1987
Central African Rep.	13.0	13.3				
Chad			20.3	5.1	-13.0	
Comoros						
Congo	12.8	7.8	12.7	6.1	2.5	
Djibouti						
Equatorial Guinea					-17.8	
Ethiopia	4.4	0.8	8.4	19.1	-9.8	-2.4
Gabon	16.7	10.4	5.8	7.3	6.3	
Gambia	10.9	10.6	22.1	18.3	56.6	
Ghana	22.3	122.9	39.7	10.3	24.6	
Guinea						
Guinea-Bissau						
Ivory Coast	7.3	5.9	4.3	1.8	6.7	
Kenya	20.4	11.5	10.2	13.0	4.0	5.2
Lesotho						
Liberia	6.0	2.7	1.2	-0.6	3.6	
Libya						
Madagascar	31.8	19.3	9.9	10.6	14.5	15.0
Malawi	9.8	13.5	20.0	10.5	14.0	
Maldives	22.0					
Mali	2.2	9.8				
Mauritania	11.9	1.6				
Mauritius	11.4	5.6	7.4	6.7	1.9	
Morocco	10.5	6.2	12.4	7.7	8.7	2.7
Mozambique						
Namibia						
Niger	11.6	-2.5	8.4	-0.9	-3.2	-6.7
Nigeria	7.7	23.2	39.6	5.5	5.4	
Reunion						
Rwanda	12.6	6.6	5.4	1.7	-1.1	4.1
Sao Tome e Principe						
Senegal	17.4	11.6	11.8	13.0	6.4	-4.3

Continued...

349

Table cont'd

	1982	1983	1984	1985	1986	1987
Seychelles	-0.9	6.1	4.1	0.8	0.3	2.6
Sierra Leone	26.9	68.5	66.6	76.6	80.9	
Somalia	23.6	36.0	91.2	37.8	35.8	
South Africa	14.7	12.3	11.7	16.2	18.6	16.1
Sudan	25.7	30.6	34.1	45.4	26.4	
Swaziland	11.8	11.1	13.0	19.8	11.8	
Tanzania	28.9	27.1	35.3	34.1	32.4	29.9
Togo	11.1	9.4	-3.5	-1.8	4.1	
Tunisia	13.7	8.9	8.4	8.0	5.8	7.2
Uganda						
Zaire	36.2	77.1	52.2	23.8	46.7	90.4
Zambia	12.5	19.6	20.0	37.4	51.6	
Zimbabwe	10.6	23.1	20.2	8.5	14.3	

APPENDIX SIX

INFRASTRUCTURE

BASIC TRANSPORT STATISTICS

Latest available year to 1986

	Railway network (000 km)	Rail passengers (mn p/km)	Rail freight (mn t/km)	Road network (000 km)	Car traffic (mn vehicle/km)
LATIN AMERICA					
Argentina	34.1	12456.0	8760.0	211.4	32095.0
Belize					
Bolivia	3.6	482.0	528.0	41.0	287.4
Brazil	28.1	13797.0	74792.0	1593.7	33320.0
Chile	6.2	1272.0	2484.0	79.1	7018.0
Colombia	2.6	180.0	696.0	106.2	12291.0
Costa Rica	1.0			29.1	
Ecuador	1.0	50.0	14.0	36.2	
El Salvador	0.6	5.0	24.0	12.2	
French Guiana				8.9	
Guatemala	0.8				
Guyana	0.4				
Mexico	20.0	5940.0	45444.0	225.7	
Nicaragua	0.3	60.0	5.0	15.0	
Panama	0.1			8.6	
Paraguay		2.0	30.0	11.3	
Peru	1.9	486.0	1104.0		
Puerto Rico				9.4	
Suriname				9.1	
Uruguay	3.0	339.0	205.0	49.8	2805.0
Venezuela	0.3	12.0	11.0	100.6	37000.0

Continued...

Table cont'd

	Railway network (000 km)	Rail passengers (mn p/km)	Rail freight (mn t/km)	Road network (000 km)	Car traffic (mn vehicle/km)
CARIBBEAN					
Anguilla					
Antigua					
Aruba					
Bahamas					
Barbados					
Bermuda					
British Virgin Is					
Cayman Islands					
Cuba	4.8	2196.0	2160.0		
Dominica					
Dominican Republic				17.8	
Grenada					
Guadeloupe				2.1	
Haiti					
Honduras	0.3			15.4	
Jamaica				16.6	
Martinique				1.8	
Netherlands Antilles					
St Kitts					
St Lucia					
St Vincent/ Grenadines					
Trinidad and Tobago				5.2	
SOUTH AND EAST ASIA					
Bangladesh	2.8	6427.0	801.0		
Burma		3792.0	576.0		
China	52.5	258204.0	874500.0	17.5	
Fiji				4.3	
Hong Kong	0.1	1932.0	72.0		3497.0
India	61.8	250272.0	213432.0	1554.2	

Continued...

Table cont'd

	Railway network (000 km)	Rail passengers (mn p/km)	Rail freight (mn t/km)	Road network (000 km)	Car traffic (mn vehicle/km)
Indonesia	6.4	6768.0	1332.0	219.2	3800.0
Malaysia	2.2	1368.0	1044.0	39.1	
Nepal					
Pakistan	8.8	16848.0	8268.0	103.4	
Papua New Guinea				19.7	
Philippines	1.1	168.0	60.0	162.3	
Singapore				2.6	
South Korea	3.1	23532.0	12660.0	53.7	8288.0
Sri Lanka	1.5	2004.0	216.0	20.7	
Taiwan	1.1				
Thailand	3.7	9264.0	2568.0	83.3	8012.0
MIDDLE EAST					
Bahrain					
Egypt	4.9	14468.0	2303.0	31.6	3600.0
Iran	4.6	5784.0	6762.0	136.4	
Iraq	2.0	1375.0	1065.0	25.3	
Jordan	0.3			5.7	2690.0
Kuwait				3.7	8590.0
Lebanon	0.4			7.0	
Oman					
Qatar					
Saudi Arabia	1.4	87.0	194.0	91.4	
Syria	1.5	900.0	1416.0	28.1	
United Arab Emirates					
Yemen Arab Republic				37.2	1270.0
Yemen PDR					
AFRICA					
Algeria	3.8	1774.0	2750.0	72.1	
Angola				72.3	

Continued...

Table cont'd

	Railway network (000 km)	Rail passengers (mn p/km)	Rail freight (mn t/km)	Road network (000 km)	Car traffic (mn vehicle/km)
Benin	0.6	138.0	177.0	7.4	0.1
Botswana	0.7		1320.0	13.5	
Burkina Faso				11.2	
Burundi				5.1	
Cameroon	1.1	432.0	756.0	52.2	1099.0
Cape Verde					
Central African Rep.				20.3	
Chad					
Comoros					
Congo	3.1	432.0	516.0	8.2	
Djibouti				2.9	
Equatorial Guinea					
Ethiopia	0.8	310.0	131.0	37.9	57.2
Gabon	0.3			7.4	
Gambia				2.4	
Ghana	0.9	380.0	61.0	21.7	
Guinea	0.7				
Guinea-Bissau					
Ivory Coast	1.2	852.0	576.0	53.7	1934.5
Kenya	2.1	1276.0	2246.0	54.6	1957.0
Lesotho				4.3	
Liberia	0.3			5.4	3.0
Libya					
Madagascar	0.9	184.0	145.0	49.7	0.4
Malawi	0.8	108.0	120.0	12.2	
Maldives					
Mali	0.6	156.0	132.0		
Mauritania	0.7			7.3	
Mauritius				1.8	
Morocco	1.8	1932.0	4560.0	57.7	21.0
Mozambique	3.1	387.0	536.0	26.1	
Namibia					

Continued...

Table cont'd

	Railway network (000 km)	Rail passengers (mn p/km)	Rail freight (mn t/km)	Road network (000 km)	Car traffic (mn vehicle/km)
Niger	1.2			19.0	
Nigeria	3.5			108.1	
Reunion					
Rwanda				12.1	283.0
Sao Tome e Principe					
Senegal	1.0	426.0		15.1	248.9
Seychelles				0.3	
Sierra Leone	0.1			7.4	
Somalia				21.3	
South Africa	23.8		90576.0	183.9	40364.0
Sudan	4.8			6.6	
Swaziland	0.3			2.7	
Tanzania	2.6			81.9	
Togo	0.4	79.0	10.0	7.0	246.6
Tunisia	1.5	756.0	1872.0	26.7	3533.0
Uganda	1.3			28.1	198.4
Zaire	4.8			147.0	
Zambia	1.3			37.4	
Zimbabwe	3.4		6576.0	77.9	

CIRCULATION OF VEHICLES 1986

Unit: Thousands

	Passenger cars	Commercial vehicles	Two-wheelers
LATIN AMERICA			
Argentina	3800.0	1425.0	760.0
Belize	3.5	3.6	
Bolivia	50.0	90.0	47.8
Brazil	10000.0	2250.0	1088.9
Chile	500.0	250.0	34.2
Colombia	600.0	300.0	386.0
Costa Rica	85.0	65.0	33.3
Ecuador			12.3
El Salvador	55.0	65.0	41.1
French Guiana	22.0	6.5	15.7
Guatemala	125.0	100.0	
Guyana	30.0	12.5	
Mexico	5200.0	2250.0	420.4
Nicaragua	35.0	30.0	12.4
Panama	140.0	50.0	
Paraguay			
Peru		214.9	
Puerto Rico	1150.0	200.0	12.0
Suriname	32.5	12.5	1.5
Uruguay	200.0	100.0	
Venezuela	1750.0	900.0	500.0
CARIBBEAN			
Anguilla			
Antigua	7.8	2.7	
Aruba			
Bahamas	65.0	13.0	

Continued...

356

Table cont'd

	Passenger cars	Commercial vehicles	Two-wheelers
Barbados	32.9	6.7	
Bermuda	20.0	4.0	
British Virgin Is			
Cayman Islands	8.5	1.3	
Cuba	140.0	160.0	
Dominica	2.5	1.5	
Dominican Republic	105.0	65.0	
Grenada			
Guadeloupe			6.0
Haiti	30.0	15.0	
Honduras	30.0	50.0	6.5
Jamaica	92.8	14.3	4.6
Martinique			17.0
Netherlands Antilles	67.5	14.0	
St Kitts	2.5	1.0	
St Lucia	6.5	4.0	
St Vincent/ Grenadines	4.0	2.0	
Trinidad and Tobago	225.0	75.0	11.0

SOUTH AND EAST ASIA

Bangladesh	50.0	35.0	
Burma	30.0	45.0	
China	250.0	1800.0	
Fiji	33.0	25.0	
Hong Kong	178.4	97.4	17.8
India	1200.0	1000.0	4960.3
Indonesia			5115.9
Malaysia	1100.0	300.0	2404.3

Continued...

Table cont'd

	Passenger cars	Commercial vehicles	Two-wheelers
Nepal			
Pakistan	385.0	280.0	456.0
Papua New Guinea	30.0	55.0	1.9
Philippines	350.0	525.0	288.6
Singapore	240.0	140.0	127.6
South Korea	664.2	645.2	812.3
Sri Lanka	150.0	130.0	161.4
Taiwan	925.0	425.0	
Thailand	550.0	750.0	1841.9
MIDDLE EAST			
Bahrain	94.1	15.5	
Egypt		225.0	263.4
Iran	1600.0	525.0	870.4
Iraq			
Jordan	137.5	62.5	6.5
Kuwait	575.0	205.0	3.9
Lebanon	475.0	55.0	
Oman	110.0	150.0	
Qatar			
Saudi Arabia	1300.0	1400.0	8.3
Syria	100.0	200.0	
United Arab Emirates	225.0	125.0	
Yemen Arab Republic	50.0	75.0	19.6
Yemen PDR	12.0	18.0	
AFRICA			
Algeria	725.0	480.0	
Angola	90.0	50.0	0.3
Benin	17.5	12.0	
Botswana	13.5	25.0	1.5

Continued...

Table cont'd

	Passenger cars	Commercial vehicles	Two-wheelers
Burkina Faso	11.0	14.0	13.4
Burundi	6.5	7.5	
Cameroon	80.0	65.0	57.4
Cape Verde			
Central African Rep.	6.5	6.5	
Chad	7.0	7.0	
Comoros			
Congo	24.0	16.0	
Djibouti	10.0	5.0	
Equatorial Guinea	4.0	3.0	
Ethiopia	43.3	19.0	1.4
Gabon	17.5	17.5	
Gambia			2.0
Ghana	55.0	45.0	
Guinea	12.0	12.0	
Guinea-Bissau	3.0	2.0	
Ivory Coast	160.0	90.0	22.9
Kenya	130.0	130.0	17.9
Lesotho			
Liberia	7.5	2.9	
Libya	400.0	300.0	
Madagascar	55.0	45.0	3.2
Malawi	17.5	17.5	7.5
Maldives			
Mali	15.0	7.5	
Mauritania	8.0	5.0	
Mauritius	30.0	12.0	29.6
Morocco	450.0	200.0	18.5
Mozambique	50.0	20.0	
Namibia			
Niger	17.5	17.5	7.6
Nigeria	700.0	600.0	

Continued...

Table cont'd

	Passenger cars	Commercial vehicles	Two-wheelers
Reunion	125.0	35.0	
Rwanda	12.0	8.0	6.1
Sao Tome e Principe			
Senegal	85.9	26.8	
Seychelles	3.5	1.3	
Sierra Leone	23.2	6.8	
Somalia	5.0	12.5	
South Africa	2998.4	1183.8	333.5
Sudan	45.0	40.0	8.0
Swaziland	15.0	15.0	
Tanzania	45.0	50.0	25.0
Togo	22.5	12.0	1.9
Tunisia	150.0	170.0	12.2
Uganda	30.0	15.0	4.8
Zaire	90.0	85.0	3.3
Zambia	95.0	50.0	
Zimbabwe	175.0	80.0	25.1

BASIC TRANSPORT STATISTICS

Latest available year to 1986

	Railway network (000 km)	Rail passengers (mn p/km)	Rail freight (mn t/km)	Road network (000 km)	Car traffic (mn vehicle/km)
LATIN AMERICA					
Argentina	34.1	12456	8760.0	211.4	32095.0
Belize					
Bolivia	3.6	482	528.0	41.0	287.4
Brazil	28.1	13797	74792.0	1593.7	33320.0
Chile	6.2	1272	2484.0	79.1	7018.0
Colombia	2.6	180	696.0	106.2	12291.0
Costa Rica	1.0		29.1		
Ecuador	1.0	50	14.0	36.2	
El Salvador	0.6	5	24.0	12.2	
French Guiana			8.9		
Guatemala	0.8				
Guyana	0.4				
Mexico	20.0	5940	45444.0	225.7	
Nicaragua	0.3	60	5.0	15.0	
Panama	0.1		8.6		
Paraguay		2	30.0	11.3	
Peru	1.9	486	1104.0		
Puerto Rico			9.4		
Suriname			9.1		
Uruguay	3.0	339	205.0	49.8	2805.0
Venezuela	0.3	12	11.0	100.6	37000.0
CARIBBEAN					
Anguilla					
Antigua					
Aruba					

Continued...

Table cont'd

	Railway network (000 km)	Rail passengers (mn p/km)	Rail freight (mn t/km)	Road network (000 km)	Car traffic (mn vehicle/km)
Bahamas					
Barbados					
Bermuda					
British Virgin Is					
Cayman Islands					
Cuba	4.8	2196	2160.0		
Dominica					
Dominican Republic			17.8		
Grenada					
Guadeloupe			2.1		
Haiti					
Honduras	0.3		15.4		
Jamaica			16.6		
Martinique			1.8		
Netherlands Antilles					
St Kitts					
St Lucia					
St Vincent/ Grenadines					
Trinidad and Tobago			5.2		
SOUTH AND EAST ASIA					
Bangladesh	2.8	6427	801.0		
Burma		3792	576.0		
China	52.5	258204	874500.0	17.5	
Fiji			4.3		
Hong Kong	0.1	1932	72.0		3497.0
India	61.8	250272	213432.0	1554.2	
Indonesia	6.4	6768	1332.0	219.2	3800.0
Malaysia	2.2	1368	1044.0	39.1	
Nepal					
Pakistan	8.8	16848	8268.0	103.4	

Continued...

Table cont'd

	Railway network (000 km)	Rail passengers (mn p/km)	Rail freight (mn t/km)	Road network (000 km)	Car traffic (mn vehicle/km)
Papua New Guinea			19.7		
Philippines	1.1	168	60.0	162.3	
Singapore			2.6		
South Korea	3.1	23532	12660.0	53.7	8288.0
Sri Lanka	1.5	2004	216.0	20.7	
Taiwan	1.1				
Thailand	3.7	9264	2568.0	83.3	8012.0
MIDDLE EAST					
Bahrain					
Egypt	4.9	14468	2303.0	31.6	3600.0
Iran	4.6	5784	6762.0	136.4	
Iraq	2.0	1375	1065.0	25.3	
Jordan	0.3		5.7	2690.0	
Kuwait			3.7	8590.0	
Lebanon	0.4		7.0		
Oman					
Qatar					
Saudi Arabia	1.4	87	194.0	91.4	
Syria	1.5	900	1416.0	28.1	
United Arab Emirates					
Yemen Arab Republic			37.2	1270.0	
Yemen PDR					
AFRICA					
Algeria	3.8	1774	2750.0	72.1	
Angola			72.3		
Benin	0.6	138	177.0	7.4	0.1
Botswana	0.7	1320.0	13.5		
Burkina Faso			11.2		
Burundi			5.1		

Continued...

Table cont'd

	Railway network (000 km)	Rail passengers (mn p/km)	Rail freight (mn t/km)	Road network (000 km)	Car traffic (mn vehicle/km)
Cameroon	1.1	432	756.0	52.2	1099.0
Cape Verde					
Central					
African Rep.			20.3		
Chad					
Comoros					
Congo	3.1	432	516.0	8.2	
Djibouti			2.9		
Equatorial Guinea					
Ethiopia	0.8	310	131.0	37.9	57.2
Gabon	0.3		7.4		
Gambia			2.4		
Ghana	0.9	380	61.0	21.7	
Guinea	0.7				
Guinea-Bissau					
Ivory Coast	1.2	852	576.0	53.7	1934.5
Kenya	2.1	1276	2246.0	54.6	1957.0
Lesotho			4.3		
Liberia	0.3		5.4	3.0	
Libya					
Madagascar	0.9	184	145.0	49.7	0.4
Malawi	0.8	108	120.0	12.2	
Maldives					
Mali	0.6	156	132.0		
Mauritania	0.7		7.3		
Mauritius			1.8		
Morocco	1.8	1932	4560.0	57.7	21.0
Mozambique	3.1	387	536.0	26.1	
Namibia					
Niger	1.2		19.0		
Nigeria	3.5		108.1		
Reunion					
Rwanda			12.1	283.0	

Continued...

Table cont'd

	Railway network (000 km)	Rail passengers (mn p/km)	Rail freight (mn t/km)	Road network (000 km)	Car traffic (mn vehicle/km)
Sao Tome e Principe					
Senegal	1.0	426		15.1	248.9
Seychelles			0.3		
Sierra Leone	0.1		7.4		
Somalia			21.3		
South Africa	23.8	90576.0	183.9	40364.0	
Sudan	4.8		6.6		
Swaziland	0.3		2.7		
Tanzania	2.6		81.9		
Togo	0.4	79	10.0	7.0	246.6
Tunisia	1.5	756	1872.0	26.7	3533.0
Uganda	1.3		28.1	198.4	
Zaire	4.8		147.0		
Zambia	1.3		37.4		
Zimbabwe	3.4	6576.0	77.9		

HEALTH AMENITIES

Latest available year

% of Population with Access to:

	Year	Safe Water	Adequate Sanitary Facilities	Polio* Immunisation 1984	Prenatal Care	Attended Birth	Local Health Care 1982/83	
LATIN AMERICA								
Argentina	1983	67.0	84.0	64.0				
Belize								
Bolivia	1983	43.0	23.0	56.0				
Brazil	1983	75.0	24.0	99.0	75.0	73.0		
Chile	1983	85.0	83.0	86.0	91.0	95.3	94.7	
Colombia	1983	91.0	68.0	60.0	65.0	51.0	87.6	
Costa Rica	1983	88.0	76.0	81.0	54.4	93.0	94.8	
Ecuador	1983	59.0	45.0	36.0	48.7	26.9		
El Salvador	1983	55.0	41.0	44.0	25.5	34.7		f
French Guiana								
Guatemala	1983	51.0	36.0	53.0			59.0	g
Guyana	1983	80.0	90.0	41.0	99.5	92.5	88.8	f
Mexico	1983	74.0	56.0	91.0			50.7	
Nicaragua	1983	56.0	28.0	73.0				
Panama	1983	62.0	66.0	70.0	65.5	83.3		
Paraguay	1983	25.0	84.0	59.0	65.4	21.9		
Peru	1983	52.0	35.0	26.0	46.2	44.2		
Puerto Rico								
Suriname	1983	89.0	100.0	79.0		80.0	100.0	f
Uruguay	1983	83.0	59.0	83.0				
Venezuela	1983	83.0	45.0	59.0		82.1		

Continued...

Table cont'd

	Year	Safe Water	Adequate Sanitary Facil- ities	Polio* Immun- isation 1984	Pre- natal Care	Att- ended Birth	Local Health Care 1982/83	
CARIBBEAN								
Anguilla								
Antigua	1983	95.0	100.0	92.0		82.9	100.0	f
Aruba								
Bahamas	1983	59.0	64.0	62.0	99.0	99.0	100.0	f
Barbados	1983	52.0	100.0	77.0	98.0	98.0	100.0	
Bermuda								
British								
Virgin Is								
Cayman Islands								
Cuba	1982	61.2	31.0	99.0		98.7		
Dominica	1983	77.0	86.0	82.0	96.0	96.0	100.0	f
Dominican								
Republic	1983	62.0	27.0	99.0		98.0		
Grenada	1983	85.0		75.0		81.0		
Guadeloupe								
Haiti	1983	33.0	19.0	12.0	44.8	20.0		
Honduras	1983	69.0	44.0	84.0		50.0		
Jamaica	1983	73.0	90.0	56.0	72.0	89.0		
Martinique								
Netherlands								
Antilles								
St Kitts	1983	75.0	96.0	97.0		96.5	99.0	d,f
St Lucia	1983	70.0	62.0	84.0	95.0	98.0	100.0	f
St Vincent/								
Grenadines	1981	75.0	88.0	90.0	60.0	73.0	80.0	f
Trinidad and								
Tobago	1983	87.0	99.0	66.0	90.0	90.0		
SOUTH AND EAST ASIA								
Bangladesh	1983	40.0	4.0	1.2			45.0	f
Burma	1983	25.0	20.0	1.5	90.9	97.4	44.6	f

Continued...

Table cont'd

	Year	Safe Water	Adequate Sanitary Facil-ities	Polio* Immun-isation 1984	Pre-natal Care	Att-ended Birth	Local Health Care 1982/83	
China								
Fiji	1983	83.3		81.1	97.0	97.6	100.0	
Hong Kong								
India	1983	54.0	8.0	36.9	45.0	32.5	75.0	a
Indonesia	1984	33.0	30.0	6.7	25.8	30.7		b
Malaysia	1983	71.0	75.4	54.6	65.5	82.0		
Nepal	1983	16.0	2.0	5.3	17.0	10.0		
Pakistan	1985	44.0	19.0	44.0	26.0	24.0	64.0	
Papua New Guinea	1983	54.0	50.9	27.4	54.2	33.5	93.0	f
Philippines	1985	64.5	56.5					
Singapore	1983	100.0	85.0	86.0	95.0	99.8	100.0	f
South Korea	1983	85.0		62.4	78.0	65.0	80.0	
Sri Lanka	1983	37.0	66.0	65.4	68.5	86.9	90.0	d f
Taiwan								
Thailand	1983	70.0	45.0	52.7		33.0		
MIDDLE EAST								
Bahrain	1985	100.0	100.0	78.0	85.0	98.0	100.0	
Egypt	1981	90.0	70.0	67.0	40.0	24.0	99.0	d
Iran	1985	71.0	65.0	65.0	11.0		67.0	
Iraq	1985	80.0	69.0	63.0	44.0	60.0	94.0	f
Jordan	1983	97.0	98.0	41.0	58.0	75.0	80.0	
Kuwait	1985	100.0	100.0	91.0	99.0	99.0	100.0	
Lebanon	1985	98.0	75.0	50.0	85.0	45.0	95.0	d
Oman	1983	70.0	60.0	40.0	79.0	60.0	92.0	f
Qatar	1982	95.0	35.0	37.0	95.0	90.0	95.0	d
Saudi Arabia	1983	93.0	86.0	81.0	61.0		90.0	
Syria	1984	71.0	70.0	41.0	21.0	37.0	80.0	d
United Arab Emirates	1985	100.0	86.0	58.0	79.0	96.0		d

Continued...

Table cont'd

	Year	Safe Water	Adequate Sanitary Facilities	Polio* Immunisation 1984	Prenatal Care	Attended Birth	Local Health Care 1982/83	
Yemen, Arab Republic	1983	31.0	12.0	8.0	21.0	12.0	25.0	f
Yemen, PDR	1983	50.0	45.0	7.0	10.0	10.0	75.0	f
AFRICA								
Algeria	1980	77.0	95.0	30.0				
Angola	1983	28.0	17.8	46.0	26.7	14.7		
Benin	1983	14.4	10.2	16.8	27.2	34.3		
Botswana	1984	77.0	36.0	77.0				
Burkina Faso	1984	35.0	8.6	2.0	40.0		70.0	
Burundi	1983	23.4	52.0	6.0	13.6	12.0	45.3	d f
Cameroon	1985	35.9	36.0	6.0				
Cape Verde	1983	31.2	10.4	92.6	96.0	10.0		
Central African Rep.	1980	16.0	19.0	21.0				
Chad	1984	31.0	14.5	1.1				
Comoros	1983	58.1		32.0	69.4	24.0	82.4	d
Congo	1985	50.0	40.0	42.0				
Djibouti	1985	45.0	37.0	20.0	50.0	73.0	37.0	g
Equatorial Guinea	1983	47.0	28.0					
Ethiopia	1984	42.0	5.0	6.0	14.0	58.0	44.0	
Gabon	1983	50.0	50.0	47.5	73.0		80.0	
Gambia	1983	45.0	77.0	70.3	90.0	80.0	90.0	f
Ghana	1983	48.9	26.0		88.0	73.0	64.0	
Guinea	1983	19.8	11.6	44.0			13.0	c,f
Guinea-Bissau	1983	31.0	25.0	14.0			64.0	f
Ivory Coast	1980	20.0	17.1	34.0				
Kenya	1983	27.0	44.4					
Lesotho	1980	37.0	12.4	64.0	40.0	28.0	50.0	f
Liberia	1983	37.3	21.4	22.6	88.0	88.6	35.0	
Libya	1983	90.0	70.0	75.0	76.0	76.0	100.0	

Continued...

369

Table cont'd

	Year	Safe Water	Adequate Sanitary Facil- ities	Polio* Immun- isation 1984	Pre- natal Care	Att- ended Birth	Local Health Care 1982/83	
Madagascar	1983	20.5	8.0	7.0		62.0	65.0	f
Malawi	1984	65.0	55.0	68.0	73.8	58.6	54.0	
Maldives	1983	17.0	15.0	9.0	47.0		97.0	
Mali	1983	6.0	21.2	9.9			20.0	g
Mauritania	1983	37.1	7.0	21.3	58.0	22.6	30.0	
Mauritius	1983	99.0	97.0	88.0	90.0	83.6	100.0	
Morocco	1984	57.0	46.0	44.0				
Mozambique	1983	9.2	10.3	38.0	46.0	28.0	40.0	
Namibia								
Niger	1983	36.5	8.5	5.0	46.5	46.5	48.0	f
Nigeria	1983	36.3	30.0	24.0				
Reunion								
Rwanda	1983	60.0	60.0	26.0				
Sao Tome e Principe	1983	52.0	15.0	28.0	60.0			
Senegal	1983	43.5	87.0	57.0				
Seychelles	1984	95.0	99.0	99.0	99.0	99.0	99.0	
Sierra Leone	1984	24.0	21.0	8.6	30.0	25.0	36.2	
Somalia	1985	33.0	17.0	10.0	2.0	2.0	20.0	
South Africa								
Sudan	1984	40.0	5.0	4.0	20.0	20.0	70.0	
Swaziland	1984	38.0	62.0			50.0		
Tanzania	1983	52.1	78.0	56.0	98.0	74.0	73.0	
Togo	1983	34.8	13.5					
Tunisia	1984	89.0	46.0	61.0	60.0	60.0	91.0	
Uganda	1983	16.0	13.0	2.0			42.0	f

Continued...

Table cont'd

	Year	Safe Water	Adequate Sanitary Facil-ities	Polio* Immun-isation 1984	Pre-natal Care	Att-ended Birth	Local Health Care 1982/83	
Zaire	1983	32.0	10.0	66.0			33.0	f
Zambia	1984	48.0	47.0	44.0	88.0		70.0	
Zimbabwe	1984	52.0	26.0	46.0	89.0	69.0	71.0	

Source: WHO World Health Statistics
Notes: * % of infants vaccinated, 1983/84
   a Immunisation: infants under 24 mths
   b Immunisation: infants under 15 mths
   c Immunisation: measles only
   d All natality statistics 1981 or earlier
   e Local Health Care: urban areas only
   f Local Health Care: data for 1984/85
   g Local Health Care: data for 1981 or earlier

LAND USE AND IRRIGATION 1985

Percentage allocation of land
Of which (%):

	Total area (000 ha)	Land Area	Arable Land	Perm-anent Crops	Perm-anent Pasture	Forest and Wood-land	Other Land	Irri-gated Land
LATIN AMERICA								
Argentina	276689	98.9	9.5	3.5	51.6	21.6	12.7	0.6
Belize	2296	99.3	1.9	0.4	2.1	44.1	50.8	0.1
Bolivia	109858	98.7	3.0	0.1	24.4	50.9	20.3	0.1
Brazil	851197	99.3	7.5	1.4	19.5	66.1	4.8	0.3

Continued...

Table cont'd

	Total area (000 ha)	Land Area	Arable Land	Perm- anent Crops	Perm- anent Pasture	Forest and Wood- land	Other Land	Irri- gated Land
Chile	75695	98.9	7.0	0.3	15.7	20.5	55.4	1.7
Colombia	113891	91.2	3.6	1.4	26.3	43.1	16.8	0.3
Costa Rica	5070	99.9	5.6	6.3	45.0	32.3	10.7	2.2
Ecuador	28356	97.6	5.6	3.3	16.9	43.7	28.0	1.9
El Salvador	2104	98.5	26.9	7.9	29.0	5.2	29.5	5.2
French Guiana	9100	98.0	0.1		0.1	80.2	17.6	
Guatemala	10889	99.6	12.4	4.5	12.3	38.1	32.4	0.7
Guyana	21497	91.6	2.2	0.1	5.7	76.1	7.4	0.6
Mexico	197255	97.5	11.8	0.8	37.8	22.9	24.3	2.5
Nicaragua	13000	91.3	8.4	1.3	39.6	30.2	11.7	0.6
Panama	7708	98.6	5.7	1.7	15.1	52.2	24.0	0.4
Paraguay	40675	97.7	5.1	0.3	38.0	50.0	4.3	0.2
Peru	128522	99.6	2.6	0.2	21.1	54.2	21.4	0.9
Puerto Rico	890	99.6	7.6	6.7	37.4	20.1	27.6	4.4
Suriname	16327	98.9	0.3	0.1	0.2	95.5	2.9	0.3
Uruguay	17622	98.5	7.9	0.3	77.4	3.6	9.4	0.5
Venezuela	91205	96.7	3.4	0.7	19.1	34.7	38.8	0.4
CARIBBEAN								
Anguilla								
Antigua	44	100.0	18.2		9.1	11.4	61.4	
Aruba								
Bahamas	1394	72.2	0.6	0.1	0.1	16.8	54.6	
Barbados	43	100.0	76.7		9.3		14.0	
Bermuda	5	100.0				20.0	80.0	
British Virgin Is	15	100.0	20.0	6.7	33.3	6.7	33.3	
Cayman Islands	26	100.0			7.7	23.1	69.2	
Cuba	11086	100.0	23.1	6.1	23.9	24.6	22.2	7.8
Dominica	75	100.0	9.3	13.3	2.7	41.3	33.3	
Dominican Republic	4873	99.3	23.0	7.2	42.9	12.8	13.4	4.1

Continued...

Table cont'd

	Total area (000 ha)	Land Area	Arable Land	Perm- anent Crops	Perm- anent Pasture	Forest and Wood- land	Other Land	Irri- gated Land
Grenada	34	100.0	14.7	26.5	2.9	8.8	47.1	
Guadeloupe	178	98.9		0.6	14.6	39.9	43.8	1.7
Haiti	2775	99.3	20.0	12.6	17.9	1.9	46.8	2.5
Honduras	11209	99.8	14.1	1.8	30.3	32.7	21.0	0.8
Jamaica	1099	98.5	18.8	5.6	17.7	17.3	39.0	3.1
Martinique	110	96.4	11.8	6.4	20.9	25.5	31.8	5.5
Netherlands Antilles	96	100.0	8.3				91.7	
St Kitts	36	100.0	22.2	16.7	2.8	16.7	41.7	
St Lucia	62	98.4	8.1	19.4	4.8	12.9	53.2	1.6
St Vincent/ Grenadines	34	100.0	38.2	11.8	5.9	41.2	2.9	2.9
Trinidad and Tobago	513.0	100.0	14.0	9.0	2.1	43.9	31.0	4.3

SOUTH AND EAST ASIA

	Total area (000 ha)	Land Area	Arable Land	Perm- anent Crops	Perm- anent Pasture	Forest and Wood- land	Other Land	Irri- gated Land
Bangladesh	14400	93.0	61.6	1.9	4.2	14.9	10.5	14.4
Burma	67655	97.2	14.2	0.7	0.5	47.6	34.2	1.6
China	959696	97.2	10.1	0.4	29.8	14.4	42.5	4.6
Fiji	1827	100.0	8.3	4.8	3.3	64.9	18.7	0.1
Hong Kong	104	95.2	6.7	1.0	1.0	11.5	75.0	2.9
India	328759	90.4	50.3	1.1	3.6	20.4	15.0	12.2
Indonesia	190457	95.1	8.1	2.8	6.2	63.8	14.1	3.7
Malaysia	32975	99.6	3.2	10.1	0.1	60.8	25.5	1.0
Nepal	14080	97.2	16.3	0.2	14.0	16.4	50.2	4.6
Pakistan	79610	96.8	25.2	0.5	6.3	3.8	61.0	19.4
Papua New Guinea	46169	97.8	0.1	0.8	0.2	82.9	13.9	
Philippines	30000	99.4	15.0	11.3	3.9	37.8	31.4	4.8
Singapore	58	98.3	3.4	5.2		5.2	84.5	
South Korea	9848	99.7	20.3	1.5	0.8	66.6	10.6	12.4
Sri Lanka	6561	98.7	16.5	17.1	6.7	36.3	22.1	8.9

Continued...

Table cont'd

	Total area (000 ha)	Land Area	Arable Land	Perm- anent Crops	Perm- anent Pasture	Forest and Wood- land	Other Land	Irri- gated Land
Taiwan								
Thailand	51400	99.6	34.2	3.9	0.6	29.2	31.6	7.0
MIDDLE EAST								
Bahrain	62	100.0	1.6	1.6	6.5		90.3	1.6
Egypt	100145	99.4	2.3	0.2			96.9	2.5
Iran	164800	99.3	8.6	0.4	26.7	10.9	52.6	3.5
Iraq	43492	99.8	12.1	0.5	9.2	4.4	73.7	4.0
Jordan	9774	99.4	3.9	0.4	8.1	0.7	86.4	0.4
Kuwait	1782	100.0	0.2		7.5	0.1	92.2	0.1
Lebanon	1040	98.4	20.2	8.7	1.0	7.7	60.9	8.3
Oman	21246	100.0	0.1	0.2	4.7		95.1	0.2
Qatar	1100	100.0	0.4		4.5		95.1	
Saudi Arabia	214969	100.0	0.5		39.5	0.6	59.4	0.2
Syria	18518	99.4	27.2	3.2	45.0	2.8	21.3	3.5
United Arab Emirates	8360	100.0	0.1	0.1	2.4		97.4	0.1
Yemen Arab Republic	19500	100.0	6.5	0.5	35.9	8.2	49.0	1.3
Yemen PDR	33297	100.0	0.4	0.1	27.2	4.7	67.6	0.2
AFRICA								
Algeria	238174	100.0	2.6	0.2	15.7	1.6	79.9	0.1
Angola	124670	100.0	2.4	0.4	23.3	42.8	31.2	
Benin	11262	98.2	12.3	4.0	3.9	33.0	44.9	0.2
Botswana	58173	97.4	2.3		75.6	1.7	17.8	
Burkina Faso	27420	99.9	9.6		36.5	25.2	28.6	
Burundi	2783	92.2	40.2	7.4	32.7	2.3	9.6	0.2
Cameroon	47544	98.7	12.4	2.2	17.5	52.8	13.9	
Cape Verde	403	100.0	9.4	0.5	6.2	0.2	83.6	0.5
Central African Rep.	62298	100.0	3.0	0.1	4.8	57.5	34.5	

Continued...

Table cont'd

	Total area (000 ha)	Land Area	Arable Land	Perm- anent Crops	Perm- anent Pasture	Forest and Wood- land	Other Land	Irri- gated Land
Chad	128400	98.2	2.3		35.0	11.2	49.6	
Comoros	217	100.0	35.0	9.7	6.9	16.1	32.3	
Congo	34200	99.9	1.9	0.1	29.2	62.2	6.5	
Djibouti	2200	99.9			9.1	0.3	90.5	
Equatorial Guinea	2805	100.0	4.6	3.6	3.7	46.2	41.9	
Ethiopia	122190	90.1	10.3	0.6	37.6	23.8	17.9	0.1
Gabon	26767	96.3	1.1	0.6	17.6	74.7	2.3	
Gambia	1130	88.5	14.6		8.0	16.5	49.5	2.9
Ghana	23854	96.4	4.7	7.1	14.3	35.3	35.0	
Guinea	24586	100.0	6.1	0.3	12.2	41.3	40.1	0.3
Guinea-Bissau	3612	77.9	8.0	0.8	29.9	29.6	9.5	
Ivory Coast	32246	98.6	9.0	3.7	9.3	22.9	53.7	0.2
Kenya	58265	97.7	3.2	0.8	6.4	6.4	80.8	0.1
Lesotho	3035	100.0	9.9		65.9		24.2	
Liberia	11137	86.5	1.1	2.2	2.2	33.8	47.2	
Libya	175954	100.0	1.0	0.2	6.3	0.3	92.3	0.1
Madagascar	58704	99.1	4.3	0.9	57.9	25.7	10.3	1.7
Malawi	11848	79.4	19.8	0.2	15.5	38.1	5.7	0.2
Maldives	30	100.0	10.0		3.3	3.3	83.3	
Mali	124000	98.4	1.4		24.2	7.4	65.4	0.3
Mauritania	103070	100.0	0.3		38.1	14.7	46.9	
Mauritius	186	99.5	53.8	3.8	3.8	31.2	7.0	9.1
Morocco	44655	100.0	15.8	1.0	40.8	11.6	30.8	1.2
Mozambique	80159	97.8	3.6	0.3	54.9	18.8	20.2	0.1
Namibia	82429	99.9	0.8		64.2	22.3	12.5	
Niger	126700	100.0	2.1		8.1	2.8	87.0	
Nigeria	92377	98.6	30.9	2.7	22.7	16.1	26.1	1.4
Reunion	251	99.6	20.3	1.6	4.0	35.1	38.6	2.0
Rwanda	2634	94.7	27.5	10.9	15.9	19.2	21.2	0.6
Sao Tome e Principe	96	100.0	2.1	36.5	1.0		60.4	

Continued...

375

Table cont'd

	Total area (000 ha)	Land Area	Arable Land	Perm- anent Crops	Perm- anent Pasture	Forest and Wood- land	Other Land	Irri- gated Land
Senegal	19619	97.9	26.6		29.1	30.3	11.9	0.9
Seychelles	28	96.4	3.6	17.9		17.9	57.1	
Sierra Leone	7174	99.8	22.8	2.0	30.7	29.1	15.2	0.2
Somalia	63766	98.4	1.6		45.2	15.1	36.4	0.3
South Africa	122104	100.0	10.1	0.7	66.6	3.7	18.9	0.9
Sudan	250581	94.8	4.7		22.3	21.6	46.2	0.7
Swaziland	1736	99.1	10.1	0.2	62.8	6.0	19.9	3.6
Tanzania	94509	93.8	4.4	1.1	37.0	45.1	6.1	0.1
Togo	5679	95.8	23.9	1.2	3.5	25.5	41.6	
Tunisia	16361	95.0	19.9	7.5	16.0	2.9	48.8	1.3
Uganda	23604	84.6	20.8	7.2	21.2	24.6	10.8	0.1
Zaire	234541	96.7	2.6	0.3	3.9	75.0	14.9	
Zambia	75261	98.4	6.9		46.5	39.1	6.0	
Zimbabwe	39058	99.0	6.8	0.2	12.4	61.0	18.6	0.4

INDEX